The Difficult Divorce

THE DIFFICULT DIVORCE

Therapy for Children
and Families

MARLA BETH ISAACS
BRAULIO MONTALVO
DAVID ABELSOHN

Basic Books, Inc., Publishers   New York

Library of Congress Cataloging-in-Publication Data

Isaacs, Marla Beth.
    The difficult divorce.

    Bibliography: p. 289.
    Includes index.
    1. Divorce therapy.   2. Family psychotherapy.
I. Montalvo, Braulio.   II. Abelsohn, David.   III. Title.
RC488.6.I83   1986   616.89′156   85–73888
ISBN   0–465–01656–1

To Our Parents

IN THE FIRST YEAR of the reign of King Julief, two thousand married couples were separated, by the magistrates, with their own consent. The emperor was so indignant, on learning these particulars, that he abolished the privilege of divorce. In the course of the following year, the number of marriages in Agra was less than before by three thousand; the number of adulteries was greater by seven thousand; three hundred women were burned alive for poisoning their husbands; seventy-five men were burned for the murder of their wives; and the quantity of furniture broken and destroyed, in the interior of private families, amounted to the value of three millions of rupees. The emperor reestablished the privilege of divorce.

NILES' REGISTER
XXVIII (June 11, 1825), 229

Contents

Preface and Acknowledgments

THE WORK that culminated in this book began in 1978, when a small group of clinicians interested in therapy with divorcing families met informally to discuss our cases. Community interest in our work grew with our own efforts to find more effective ways of helping families who were separating. This led, one year later, to a far more ambitious endeavor, the Families of Divorce Project. We were very fortunate to receive the generous support and funding of the Pew Memorial Trust, without which our work could not have taken place. This foundation shared our vision of a specialized treatment, training, and research center and enabled us to grapple with the dilemmas confronting separating families.

Since late in 1984, our research has been supported by a grant from the National Institute of Mental Health (grant number MH37925–02).

What characterized the project throughout was the sharing and collaboration with each other and with other team members. As we struggled with families, working alone, it was always a welcome relief to receive the collective wisdom of colleagues behind the one-way mirror. As we worked together in this way and made videotapes for group scrutiny, we slowly developed concepts and a way of working. Simultaneously we were gathering our research data and trying to make sense of the numbers.

The Jarret family case, discussed in chapter 8, "Arresting Abdication Dynamics," is a revised version of D. Abelsohn, "Dealing with the Abdication Dynamic in the Post Divorce Family: A Context for Adolescent Crisis," *Family Process* 22(1983). Chapter 10, "Assisting with Blending," is a revised version of M. Isaacs, "Facilitating Restructuring and Relinkage: Issues in Divorce Therapy," in *Therapy with Remarriage Families*, ed. L. Messinger (The Family Therapy Collections, An Aspen Publication, Rockville, Md., and London, 1982). And the drawings by children in chapter 11 are from M. Isaacs and I. Levin, "Who's in My Family? A Longitudinal Study of Drawings of Children of Divorce," *Journal of Divorce* 7(Summer 1984) (copyright 1984 by The Haworth Press, Inc.). They are reprinted with permission.

We owe deep thanks to many people who assisted in the preparation of the book that has come out of the project. Jo Ann Miller, our editor at Basic Books, shepherded the book from the start and waited patiently for us to finish. In editing our manuscript, Nina Gunzenhauser transformed it with her clarity of thinking. George Leon, our senior research associate, carefully critiqued the manuscript. His contribution to the research and to the shaping of our final chapter is gratefully acknowledged. We thank Mary Eno and Virginia Simons for their contribution in the important early stages of the project. Pat Tapman, our administrative assistant, gave us valuable technical assistance on the manuscript. Harry Aponte's early administrative support at the Philadelphia Child Guidance Clinic was important to the development of the total project. Our legal colleagues—Rochelle Coth Weissbarth, Christine Polk Ruth, Elaine Smith, and Judge Edward Rosenberg—taught us to respect the legal intricacies of divorce work. Finally, we would especially like to thank the families with whom we worked directly and who taught us so much.

MARLA BETH ISAACS
BRAULIO MONTALVO
DAVID ABELSOHN

I would like to thank several people. Judith Wallerstein first interested me in children of divorce and gave generously of her ideas and experience when I was setting up our divorce project. Mary Eno has been a friend throughout and an important source of support. I would like to express a special note of appreciation to my family: my husband, Larry Hirschhorn, for his help in the final stage of the manuscript, but more importantly for his always being there for me, and my two children, Aaron and Daniel, for pulling me away from my work and teaching me things about children that no one else could.

MARLA BETH ISAACS

The Difficult Divorce

All names, locations, and other identifying
characteristics of the individuals
portrayed in this book have been changed.

1

Introduction: Premises and Assumptions

Divorce poses radical demands. Couples who divorce must re-organize their relationships during and after the separation. They must find intimacy in other settings while remaining involved, whether intensely or peripherally, with their children. They must cope with an array of feelings such as loss, anger, guilt, and relief. They must maintain or recover their self-confidence, including confidence in their ability to handle the needs of the children without the help of the former partner and in the more elusive capacity to endure the inevitable mistakes that occur while the family reorganizes. Both the couple and the children must rapidly change their relationships to their own as well as their shared social networks. Allegiances to members within those networks must be shifted and new coalitions with legal experts and other outsiders entered into. The family must often adapt to a radical shift in its socioeconomic position. One or both parents, more often the mother, may have a marked drop in income and change in life style.

While these changes deeply affect the stress levels of both adults and children, many families cope with them successfully. Most divorcing parents buffer their children from the impact of adult conflict and the disruptions of family life; others, however, do not. It is these divorces that we term difficult and that concern us in this book.

Within the difficult divorce there are adults who cannot control their disputes and frequently recruit the children into taking sides. There are those who lose confidence in their ability to carry out the tasks of parenting and those who abdicate their caretaking responsibilities. In some divorces we run into all of these problems. This book addresses ways of working with the difficult divorce.

Working with the Difficult Divorce

As the case studies in this volume will demonstrate, the difficult divorce is not a single phenomenon. It manifests itself in numerous ways. Whatever its manifestation, however, the following four simple principles or guidelines have become the basis of our work.

1. Therapy must focus on both of the parents' efforts toward reorganizing their relationships with each other and with their children.
2. The well-being of the children must be a priority.
3. Therapy must deal with the realities of divorce and therefore work with subsystems within the family.
4. Hostile parents can be brought together for therapeutic work if the encounter is controlled.

A great deal of our focus is on the common stresses that arise: lapses in parental responsibility, uncontrolled disputes, and recruitment of the children into taking sides. In warring couples our work involves trying to prevent a protracted conflict.

A Reorganizationally Focused Therapy

Although the family's postseparation level of adjustment in large part reflects its preseparation history, what counts most in the long run is the family's ability to negotiate the many radical changes necessitated by a divorce and its ability to reorganize in ways that safeguard the development of its members. Part of the work of the family entails mourning the losses brought about by divorce. In full perspective, however, it is the family's efforts to grapple with fundamental changes that determine the outcome.

We place special emphasis on problem solving—parent with parent, and parent with child—that allows family members to struggle face to face with each other during the process of reorganizing the unit. We view the immediate family (mother, father, and their children) as the unit of direct intervention, but we include in our conceptualization of the problem the effects of the broader social network, including grandparents, friends, and lawyers.

One aspect of therapy with families undergoing separation and divorce that is often overlooked is the obvious need for both parents to participate. In most cases one parent—usually the custodial parent—is concerned about the children and calls a therapist. The other parent may be considered irrelevant in the treatment or may be unwanted. For example, the mother who calls in the first or second year of the separation complaining that her child is misbehaving in school may be unaware that the divorcing process is figuring centrally in the child's life. The therapist may make the same mistake if the complaint is not expressly divorce-related.

It is the therapist's job early on, often in the initial phone call, to begin to shape events so that ultimately the noncustodial parent, most often the father, is included in the therapy process. In every case study we present, the therapy included both the mother and the father, yet in at least half of the families the custodial parent did not at first want to include her former husband. How we first involve the father in divorce therapy varies from family to family. He may come with his children, alone, or even with his wife if it is a first session for the family. But we have found that when we are unable to work with both parents, our task is immeasurably more difficult.

Children as a Priority

When separating adults are in individual therapy, their children's needs may be overlooked. It is not uncommon for the therapist to stay with the material brought up by the adult patient, who may be focused on his or her own needs, and fail to inquire independently or sufficiently about how the children are doing. In contrast, our priority is the children. This does not mean that we are neglecting the needs of the parents; rather, we have found that parents' postseparation adjustment is enhanced when they are successful with their children. We work on helping the parent retain or recover competence. We also work heavily on amplifying certain processes of feedback from the children to the parents, in an effort to enhance the parents' awareness of what aspects of the separation are particularly difficult for their children.

This approach is not only a tactical imperative. Our research teaches us that children may be less likely than their parents to bounce back from the stress of separation. We believe that the family is not a community of equals and that the children are indeed more vulnerable than the adults in the family hierarchy.

Thus our primary treatment goal is for both parents to continue to be responsible for their children, despite the upheaval in their own lives. Toward this end, we help the couple develop their relationship as *parents*, as opposed to their relationship as *spouses*. It is not easy for people to preserve their parenting relationship while dissolving their relationship as husband and wife. Those who succeed demonstrate a workable capacity to control their disagreement. These couples, even when divorcing, are able to figure out how far to use with each other their skills of demanding, overlooking, and forgiving. In the process they preserve their continuity as a problem-solving unit.

The Need for Subsystem Therapy

We work on the assumption that the practical demands of the dividing family must be obeyed. While some therapies insist upon having the entire family present at every session, we believe that such an approach negates the boundary-making efforts of those who are separating. It also denies that their hostility and aggression curtail some of what they can do together. By treating them as a divided unit, the therapy conforms to the reality of the family. This approach does not preclude seeing them together at times, to show that in some ways they also remain one family, one unit. For example, we might begin by seeing the husband and wife separately, then meet with each parent and the children; with the children as a closed sibling unit; with both parents; and, if necessary, with the whole family.

By definition, divorce breaks up the old family and creates new subgroups. Our therapy therefore emphasizes composition and pays careful attention to identifying which subgroups must be worked with and why. The unit has to maintain some subsystems, shed others, and develop new ones. In working with subsystems, we follow two elementary principles: we support those that will help the family fulfill its functions, and we attempt to limit the influence of antagonistic groupings.

The Controlled Encounter

To work with the antagonists in the parental subsystem, we proceed with what we call the "controlled encounter." Warring couples are brought face to face in a planned, structured manner. The reason for divorce impasse is frequently that people, in trying to become victors over each other, miscalculate the impact that their actions, intentions, and expressed feelings have on their spouses. For example, when a couple is trying to resolve an issue of visitation, the husband may ask for far more than he wants because he is certain that his wife will never give him as much as he really wants. She in turn interprets his asking for so much as his wanting everything. She sees him as greedy, out to take advantage of her, just as she felt he did in the marriage. She therefore resolves to give him very little, which confirms her husband's belief that she will be unreasonable and that he had better grab whatever he can get. The impasse persists. Thus at the heart of the "difficult divorce" there may be a miscalculation in human problem solving during the tortuous quest for parity. We have found, moreover, that for each family certain topics, such as money or visitation, are likely to stimulate miscalculation. These are the "hot" topics.

In the controlled encounter, we work to minimize miscalculation. We pay careful attention to which topic is to be discussed, what limits should be set on the discussion, and when we should prevent premature dismissal and hasty resolutions. In general we slow the parents down. Although we do value the loose, carefree moment, the spontaneous exchange without any problem-solving purpose, our decided preference is to tame volatility and support reason. We help parents visualize and anticipate the consequences of their behavior. We ask them to imagine vividly the consequences of an inappropriate separation—to consider the expense, the aggravation, the embroilment with lawyers, and most important, the impact on the children.

The Plan of the Book

This book describes different ways in which families fail to traverse the divorce experience, as well as ways in which therapists can help dividing families. Chapters 2 and 3 deal with preseparation problems that occur when spouses become self-made prisoners in the same house, each antagonistic yet unwilling to be the one who leaves. At some point the adults cannot contain their stress, which spills over on the children. We discuss two such families in stagnant preseparation crises, a phenomenon seen more and more frequently by mental health services. The adults are constantly warring, the children are symptomatic, and the atmosphere in the home is extraordinarily tense.

Chapters 4 and 5 deal with the dilemma posed by the couple, often long-separated, that continues to fight to the point where each spouse is financially and emotionally drained. We describe ways of lessening the destructive chronic elements of this process by bringing unsolved conflicts to the surface and tackling them. The emphasis is on preventing the psychosocial consequences of an uninterrupted escalating fight. Efforts are made to organize the interaction and control the encounter between the participants, in order to facilitate negotiation and problem solving of topics that had been neglected or that typically had led to further fighting. The therapy employs mediation skills and assumes that, regardless of what unconscious forces drive the couple, some capacity for judgment and affective control is available.

Chapter 6 explores further how therapists attempt to cool down the possibility of explosive violence by shifting the balance of aggression between the couple. The emphasis is on how potential violence, not always obvious, presents to therapists and how to work to defuse a dangerous situation. It shows how children can activate or draw help from the outside for competent problem solving when it is not available within their overstressed family. Though children often react symptomatically to the parental conflict, the focus here is on the processes between the parents underlying the variety of symptoms that seem to originate exclusively within the child. This includes psychosomatic symptoms and thoughts of running away.

Chapter 7 deals with ways of helping youngsters support each other during extreme escalations in the crisis of parental separation. Reactions to the parental conflict—depression and physical aggression toward the parent—are discussed. Identifying saddened or angered youngsters is seen as a first step toward the more significant task of influencing the reorganizational dynamics that follow the protracted process of separation. In this chapter, work with older adolescent and young adult siblings is presented. By virtue of their age, personality development, and sibling-group affiliation, they are able to respond actively to the parents, giving controlled feedback of their own. We see how the therapist can work to change sibling relationships to maximize the support that brothers and sisters can give each other in the midst of their parents' separation.

Chapter 8 looks directly at how the therapist helps reverse the processes of abdication of parental responsibility, often seen in separating families with troubled adolescents. When adults compete to be not in charge, the therapist works to restore the locus of essential nurturance and control in the parents. The therapist supports the parents' efforts to have youngsters meet age-appropriate responsibilities, and seeks to prevent untoward reactions such as truancy, school failure, drug abuse, suicidal ideation, pregnancy, and abortion.

Chapter 9 deals with the dilemmas of the expert witness confronted with the critical task of fashioning a custody evaluation. We call for a new kind of custody evaluation, moving beyond the inadequate question of who is the better parent to an exploration of the potential for change in the total family situation. A family-based evaluation actively using the dimension of time is presented. The family's flexibility is tested through measured requests for change in key areas. How the evaluation report is fashioned and how the expert witness handles the broader context of the court appearance and concomitant pressure from lawyers is the focus.

At some point in many divorces, one if not both of the parents may become involved in a new relationship and consider remarrying. It is that parent's hope that the children will accept and like the new partner, and in some families acceptance occurs rather quickly. In others, however, the children's linkage to the new partner is thwarted from the start. Chapter 10 describes problems in the blending process and ways in which both parts of the family—the mother and the father—can be worked with to promote the formation of new boundaries to facilitate blending.

The clinically derived perspective in this book draws support from the quantitative findings of our longitudinal study, which follows structural shifts and emotional fluctuations in 103 separating families. The final chapter presents some of our results as families are followed from the first through the third year of separation. We present general trends in adjustment and focus on the postseparation relationship between the parents, on visitation arrangements, and on the role of grandparents. We also report our findings, derived from the analysis of children's family drawings over time, on how the divorce experience alters the child's understanding of the family structure.

The aim of this book is to highlight the predictable yet critical ways in which couples typically fail to navigate the divorcing process, and to describe a therapy for helping families trapped in the typical situations of the difficult divorce. This is a therapy that openly emphasizes how parents, despite the trauma they face, can manage to protect their children and pragmatically negotiate with each other in the children's interest. That is, it is a therapy that assumes that most families retain, in some changed form, their primary socializing and protective functions, and that they can maintain those functions despite the demands of unit reorganization.

For colleagues in the mental health field we present a subsystems-oriented and reorganizationally focused manner of working with separating families. For those in the social sciences and education we present more material on how a major problem in our society is dealt with on the level of the family, and how the broader social system—therapists, lawyers, and the courts—is brought in to help families resolve what they cannot resolve themselves. Our legal colleagues—lawyers and judges—can learn something of the other side from our case studies, that is, some of the effects of legal intervention on children as well as on adults. And for those people who are themselves grappling with divorce we offer the experience of our families, from whom they can perhaps learn of the pitfalls to avoid for themselves and their children.

2

Managing Preseparation Crises

MOST separating couples go through a relatively prolonged stage in which they go back and forth in deciding whether or not to make the break with each other. Eventually the decision is made, however, and they separate physically and begin the business of reorganizing as a separated family. But some couples get stuck in the making and unmaking of the decision, or in agreeing not to make the decision, hoping that time alone will change their circumstances. The obstacles entail more than separation anxiety. There are thorny issues pertaining to anticipated consequences and attempts to control them. Worries about finances, custody, and visitation are not simply internal psychological events. They represent real concerns that require responsible decision making, yet they occur while the participants may still be working at changing the other's mind, or even at taking revenge, instead of resolving differences.

With such couples, the most critical determination is whether a separation is inevitable or whether reconciliation is a realistic possibility. One couple, who insisted that they indeed wanted to divorce, appeared together at their first interview behaving unlike the typical preseparated family. They positioned themselves very close to each other instead of at opposite ends of the waiting room, and engaged in what looked like friendly dialogue, if not a muted courtship. What the couple's behavior makes clear is that the therapist cannot take at face value what one or the other says on the phone. An accurate assessment often cannot be made until after a meeting with the participants.

Some couples who do not ultimately want to separate will nonetheless find their way to a divorce service. However, a service such as ours that is clearly advertised in the community as a specialized divorce service, not a marriage counseling service, encourages self-selection. Before meeting the therapist, the participants must decide for themselves what they want to do with their relationship. When they call, we ask explicitly if this could be a trial separation and what the chances are of reconciliation, clearly conveying that we consider divorce a momentous decision.

A well-identified divorce service also brings in couples who might otherwise feel threatened by the possibility of reconciliation. For example, one woman who had left her grieving husband called the service because she was concerned about her children. When she was told that her husband would need to participate as well, her major concern was that he would take this initiative to mean that she was ready to consider returning to him. We reassured her that ours was not a marriage counseling service. She gave her husband a brochure that spelled out our objectives. These reassurances alleviated her fear and allowed the process to continue. There will always be couples with whom the wish and determination to separate is not mutual. The clinician's first sign of the skew in the relationship characterizing many deadlocked couples is often that one wants in and the other wants out. Such couples have to work on this issue of separation when they first face the therapist.

This chapter presents an example of a couple deadlocked in the pre-separation stage and illustrates some of the means employed by the therapist to facilitate appropriate problem solving.* To get that process started, we do not deal with issues in a specific order: first property, then finances, and then the children. We are more interested in motivating the parents to problem solve, and we adhere to no particular order, although care of the children usually has to be a priority.

To make the care of the children a priority, we do not hesitate to play upon either the underlying or the exposed guilt of most divorcing parents. We accomplish part of the effective therapy of divorce not only by working with their wish to engage in reparatory and buffering behavior in regard to their children but by heightening and utilizing guilt constructively, modulating it and channeling it into effective avenues of expression. This therapy is possible because it speaks to the couple's deepest underlying wishes to be responsible parents. It prizes dealing with such concrete divorce-specific issues as visitation arrangements, and it clarifies the confusing interplay

* Virginia Simons was the therapist for this family.

between the adults as separating spouses and as continuing parents. Differentiating these roles, which is not always naturally or quickly accomplished, constitutes one of the main ways of bringing relief from frustration and stress to those involved in the divorce process.

A classic situation of the deadlocked divorce is the couple who does not physically separate. Although at least one participant (and often both) has ostensibly decided to separate and divorce, the two remain together in the same house, creating stress for both themselves and their children. In many of these families the potential for violence, particularly spouse abuse, is high, and it is not unusual for the police to be called in on a fairly regular basis. Some mothers assign to the children, or to one particular child, the job of phoning the police. In other families, the adults make the call for outside help, in front of the watchful eyes of the children. Whether the role is assigned or chosen, the children in these families attempt to protect and make peace between their parents. If, under pressure, the children take sides, the sibling subsystem is split in half. One of the most tense situations is when the children are unable to take sides, unable to abandon any one parent and feeling they are displeasing both. Caught in such an arrangement, one six-year-old finally took sides by reaching for a butcher knife and trying to stab his father. Only then did his parents understand that the situation had gotten out of hand.

The initial therapy with these families is crisis intervention. The participants come to therapy in a chaotic, disorganized state. The tension for everyone is almost at the breaking point, yet the participants cannot detach from each other. Because the situation is so dangerous, therapy must be intense, aiming at quick resolution of the ostensible crisis. Through careful structuring, work that might ordinarily take a few months can be collapsed into just two or three weeks. A focus on the children's plight and the pain of the adults can heighten stress and provoke a controlled separation. In this way of working, more talking is never an acceptable substitute for decisive action. If the therapy is successful, the couple separates soon after.

A Workable Beginning

With couples of this type, the therapy generally begins with a phone call from one parent who is concerned about the welfare of the children. Invariably, this parent wants to come in with the children and does not want the spouse to participate. All sorts of excuses will arise: "We *are* separated;

we just live in the same house." "He's not interested in the children and wouldn't come." "We can't be in the same room together."

With families who have already effected a physical separation, it is appropriate to have only one spouse present at the first meeting, thus respecting and emphasizing the boundaries that have been erected. With families who are still living in the same house, however, this move would be a tactical error. Although they may refuse to come in together, insisting that they are "separated" (often more vehemently than physically separated couples do), the therapist must not accept this family myth, which it is the job of therapy to explode. In order for such couples to separate, they must begin to see that they have not separated. Thus if the parents are living together, the therapist insists that the entire family come to the first session. In order to ensure the participation of both parents from the outset, the therapist has the option of informing the parent who makes the initial call that an appointment can be scheduled only after the therapist has heard from the other spouse. If necessary, the parents are reassured that they will not be in the same room together without the children for more than ten minutes. Should one parent fear either that a joint session will turn into marital work or that initiating therapy will be interpreted by the spouse as representing a desire to get back together, the therapist emphatically dispels this notion and makes it clear that the focus will be on the children.

Before agreeing to appear at the interview, parents may want to speak to their lawyers or may want their lawyers to speak with the therapist. By emphasizing that the focus will be on how the children are doing and by offering a time-limited interaction with the spouse, the therapist makes it possible to initiate joint work in a "safe" environment. The incentive is the ostensible wish of most parents to care for their children's needs during the process of separating.

Setting the Stage

To meet the needs of families in the process of reorganizing, a boundary-conscious therapy is employed—that is, one in which the therapist capitalizes on changing the composition of the unit in the room. The therapist might meet with the entire family briefly, see the spouses together and separately, and see the children with their parents and by themselves. This emphasis on shifting composition gives the therapist more ground on which to maneuver while heightening the therapist's leverage.

The first step is to talk to both parents together, working within whatever time limit was promised on the telephone. The therapist asks each parent in turn how he or she views the children's situation, starting with the parent who did not initiate the therapy. This step develops hunches about the extent to which the parents are observing the children competently or are engaged in distorting or editing what they see. In very young children, warning signals include excessive dependency, regression, and changes in eating and sleeping habits; with adolescents, more attention is paid to upholding and breaking rules, school behavior and performance, and relationships with peers. This focus reassures the parents that therapy will center on the concern that brought them in for help, while also outlining for them the areas in which they as parents need to be vigilant.

No attempt is made to get the parents to talk to each other—in fact, this is generally discouraged because the participants are on such unfriendly terms. The couple is thereby reassured that, unlike past dialogues, this joint endeavor will not permit runaway hostilities. At this stage, all communication is through the therapist, who keeps careful track of time. If additional time is needed, the therapist negotiates a new contract before going on, even recontracting at three-minute intervals, if necessary. With this format, each parent feels more in control of the time spent with the adversary. Having a handle on the duration of stress, they feel safer.

Each parent is then seen separately, after which the family is brought together for a short time. Meeting with the entire family allows the therapist to observe the parents' behavior with the children and the way the children position themselves around the parents. Do they go quickly to one parent? Are preferences displayed? Is there a pecking order among them? The children are then seen without the parents; the purpose is to learn more about their problems and to assess their coping strategies. The time spent alone with the children provides the therapist with the most important leverage in moving the parents toward change. At the close of the session, the therapist discusses with the couple what he or she has learned or not learned about the children and their problems.

No therapy, of course, can always follow a prescribed order. In the case described later in this chapter, the children were initially too uncomfortable to leave their mother and meet alone with the therapist. Rather than forcing the issue, the therapist decided to wait until the second session to get the leverage needed from meeting alone with the children.

From a clinical standpoint, families in preseparation crises are usually of two types: those in which primarily the children are symptomatic and the adults are without conspicuous emotional disturbance; and those with more pervasive problems, in which the children are symptomatic and one or both of the adults are disturbed. In the latter, the boundaries between the adults and children are grossly inadequate. In addition, the parents are more apt to pull in their own parents in complicated ways.

These two kinds of families are similar in form and must focus on similar issues in therapy, but they necessitate different approaches. Each couple has to figure out how to deal with certain contemporary contingencies— how to utilize their parental power to take care of the children responsibly; how to become especially protective of their children during the prolonged transition period; and how to give priority to their children's needs, rather than to their own fighting and ongoing adversarial relationship. What remain constant for the therapist are the demands of crisis management: breaking the stalemate of an overstrained couple living together yet separate, while in the process the children are stressed immeasurably. The objective is not only to remove obstacles but to push the process along and facilitate a responsible separation. We encourage therapist contact with the lawyers at the start, in order to clarify the purpose of the therapy, but our overall thrust is for the adults to deal with their lawyers without the therapist interfering with that initiative.

Two case histories will be used to illustrate the two types of preseparation families and some ways of dealing with the phenomena they present. The family described in this chapter, the Allens, represents the first type. This rather resourceful middle-class couple, well into the process of divorce, had been living apart for months when the husband moved back into the house shortly before a court hearing on support, claiming he could no longer afford to pay rent elsewhere. In the next chapter we present the Franks, who illustrate the second preseparation family type. They faced a situation similar to the Allens', but the father appeared to have a very frail personality organization, and exchanges between him and his wife were full of confusing communications. This family was lower working class, on the verge of having to go on welfare.

Work with the first family, the Allens, involved two sessions, each lasting an hour and a half; the second session was held two weeks after the first. They illustrate four generic issues of diagnosis and treatment with preseparated families: the predicament of the children, the lawyers' part in keeping the couple together, the therapist's effect on the couple's dealings with their lawyers, and finally, the use of differentiated and confrontational feedback as a therapeutic tool to break the stalemate.

Initial Contact

Mr. and Mrs. Allen were both in their second marriages. They had two daughters, Carlotta (age five) and Deborah (age seven). Both parents wanted to divorce. Mr. Allen had left the house and lived elsewhere for three months. Shortly before a court hearing on support, he had moved back in, on the advice of his lawyer. At the time of the initial interview he had been back in the home for five months. It was Mrs. Allen who called the clinic.

The therapist told Mrs. Allen that if she and her husband were still living together, her husband would need to come in also. Mr. Allen was not interested in therapy, and it involved three conversations between him and the director of the project, two calls between him and the therapist, and a call from his lawyer to get him to come in. Still he had to be assured by the director of the project that the therapist would limit the time he would have to spend alone with his wife. This back and forth preparation is commonplace and necessary.

Interviews begin with the signing of a document in which the parents agree that no material that emerges in the work with the therapist will be used against each other later in court. This agreement encourages them to commit themselves to a different kind of endeavor; they do not have to look good and they are not there to gather ammunition against each other. It also encourages confidentiality for both spouses and makes clear that the therapist is not meant to be employed for the benefit of one parent over the other.

The transcript that follows begins with the signing. Mr. Allen voices confusion about why he and his wife are there. Note how quickly they move to attack one another:

Mr. Allen: Let me tell you why I'm confused. We are *not* divorced and we're not even separated. We're living in the same house with the children. I'm not aware that at this time the children have any particular problems. So I'm confused about what is to be accomplished at this stage. I could understand it more if we were already divorced or separated.

Although the couple is well along in the divorce proceedings, the husband is genuinely confused as to why he has been asked to come to therapy at this point.

Mrs. Allen (*exasperated*):   But we *are* living a separated life. Just because you sleep there at night, Henry, does not mean we are carrying on a normal family situation!

In less than thirty seconds, the parents are at each other. The therapist *must* take control.

(*Mr. Allen dismisses his wife with a gesture of his hand and looks away from her. In turn, she looks away in disgust.*)

Focusing on the Children: Different Perceptions

Such rapid escalation of spousal conflict is common with these families and is why the therapy requires the previously discussed ground rules. Notice that during the period of uncontrolled hostility the spouses focus on defending themselves or attacking the other. When this happens, the needs of the children are lost. So enveloping and repetitive are these processes that the therapist must firmly, and if necessary forcefully, reorganize the system of exchange, refocusing the discussion on the needs of the children. This is done by asking very specific questions about how the children are handling the situation. The therapist wants first a bona fide check on the children and then some assessment of the different perceptions of each parent. These are obtained from the parents' reports and from direct observation. In the process, the therapist tries to avoid seeing the children merely as projections of conflicts elsewhere in the family.

In order to engage the parent who was more reluctant to be there and to dispel the idea that the therapist has taken sides with the initiator, the therapist starts with the reluctant parent. Mr. Allen's statements confirmed that the separation and divorce would probably be emotionally upsetting to all. He felt that his wife was trying to keep the children away from him, but expected that this would get straightened out once a legal agreement spelled out his access to them. He did not, however, report seeing any anxiousness or nervousness in the children, who he said "talked rather easily and freely about the situation."

Mrs. Allen presented a very different picture: "You mention divorce to them and they cry. They just cry." She reported that when she told the children they were coming to the session because Mom and Dad would be getting a divorce, the children said they didn't want to talk about it.

In relating this, the mother herself grew tearful. The therapist allowed her to express her feelings but did not dwell on them. Instead, she returned to the basic task of exploring the parents' observations of the children's reactions to the imminent divorce. She asked about the children's sleeping and eating habits and inquired whether they were clinging to their parents or to each other or exhibiting other signs of distress. The parents acknowledged that they had observed clinging behavior, and the therapist investigated whether this behavior was present before the period of heightened tension and whether it was more pronounced with one parent or the other. She was particularly interested in the parents' differing perceptions of the problem, which helped her grasp the dynamics of the couple's relationship and their relationships with the children.

Mrs. Allen reported that after her husband filed for joint custody, Carlotta said she didn't want to live with her father and for days afterward clung tenaciously to her mother. The therapist checked with Mr. Allen to see if he had noticed this; he had not. The mother also reported that although neither child had trouble sleeping, they both had nightmares.

At this point the therapist had learned from both parents of each child's reactions to the strain accompanying the imminent divorce, but she didn't yet know how the siblings were operating as a subsystem—for example, whether they were protecting or undermining each other. To check on this, the therapist asked whether Carlotta was also clinging to her older sister. The mother confirmed that Carlotta had been closer to Deborah lately and that she hugged and kissed her and told her how much she loved her. The father had also noticed this but believed that Carlotta had always done so because "she's a very loving child." The mother noted that Carlotta, who was usually talkative and outgoing, had been very quiet, and that Deborah had been unable to keep her mind on her schoolwork and had been daydreaming a lot. "There's something wrong with me," Deborah had told her mother with distress, "because I can't think."

Respecting Agreed Limits: Recontracting for More Time

Ten minutes have now passed, and the therapist, wishing to continue a little longer and seeing that the participants are doing fairly well, breaks into the conversation and explicitly negotiates their consent to spend extra time with each other:

Mrs. Allen: Carlotta has been closer to Deborah. She hugs and kisses her a lot more often and tells her how much she loves her. I noticed that.

Therapist (*interrupting the flow*):   I want
to respect the time limit. The ten minutes
is up, but I would like to try to get a little
bit more information on the children. Can
we go about five more minutes?

(*Both parents look at each other and nod in agreement, signaling to the therapist
that they can handle being together longer. Being able to grant permission
increases the feeling that they too control aspects of this uncomfortable situation
and can hold violence in check.*)

   Through the parents' reports, the therapist was assembling a picture of
the children before actually seeing them. She wondered whether the father
was minimizing the children's problems or whether it was a point of
strength that he did not see the children as vulnerable or pathological. The
therapist was also trying to discern to what extent the parents' personal
distress colored their views of the children and the extent to which they
perceived their children's needs as separate from their own personal and
adversarial needs. One hallmark of a "successful" divorce is the parents'
ability to see the children objectively during the process of separating.
When a couple loses sight of the children's independent reality, the divorce
process is not going well.

   Mr. Allen feared that his wife was trying to block his access to the children. He felt unprotected without a legal guarantee of time with them. He
had not noticed that the children were undergoing any stress with the
situation at home, but Mrs. Allen was very concerned about the children
and did see signs of stress. At this time, the couple had no apparent ability
to cooperate. Even in a highly structured and contained interview, the
therapist observed that they were quick to take any opportunity to snipe
at each other.

Reasons for the Stalemate

After the parents shared their observations about the children, each parent
was seen separately to discuss his or her own plight. The therapist began
with the father:

Therapist: I just wanted to spend a few
minutes talking to you about why the
situation is the way it is and what your
plans are.

Mr. Allen: A little over a year ago, she moved out of the bedroom and stopped being a wife altogether. She stopped cooking and having anything to do with me and stopped talking to me. She was harassing me constantly, trying to get me out of the house, and the kids had been a part of this kind of thing for over a year already. I finally had enough, and that's when I moved out, last April. Toward the end of July I moved back in because she got such a heavy support order against me that I couldn't afford to stay outside and pay the bills. I *had* to move back in.

The father in fact moved back just prior to a scheduled court hearing on support.

Therapist: You're hoping to renegotiate the support payments?

Mr. Allen (*emphatically*): Since the day I moved back in, I have been trying to get her to negotiate, and she won't.

Therapist: So when do you plan to live in separate houses?

Mr. Allen: Not until we get divorced or come to a settlement beforehand. If she will negotiate in good faith and come to some separation agreement, I'll move out the next day.

Therapist (*dismayed*): What if the divorce is not for six months?

The therapist is trying to create a sense of urgency about time.

Mr. Allen: It *won't* be for at least six months, according to my lawyer, because she contested the divorce. She said she's going to drag it out as long as possible and make it cost me as much as possible, so it's going to be at least six months.

Therapist (*speaking slowly, voicing increasing concern*): There's a real danger here.

The attempt is to make Mr. Allen feel that the therapist understands his situation but that she can be firm, out of concern for the children. He is very angry at his wife and holds her responsible for sabotaging their negotiations. He feels that he has no choice but to stay in the house until they reach an agreement about the support payments. His belief that the children are not suffering is obviously useful to him, making it easier for him to adhere to his position.

Working for a Higher-Level Coalition

Although the therapist sympathizes with Mr. Allen, she proceeds to refocus her concern from *his* plight to that of the children. The whole orientation thus far is one of containment and structure as the therapist emphasizes the cognitive problem-solving capacities of the parents. As she proposes the following ground rules, the father nods quietly in agreement.

Therapist: I understand the jam you're in, but I want you to know that my stance is going to be different. After I talk to your wife and after I talk to the children, I'll tell you what I think is going to be best for the children, and what kind of toll this is really taking on them. I know that in the long run you also, as a father, take their best welfare into consideration. *Their* future is what we have to consider—the next ten, twenty, thirty years of their lives, and your relationship with them. So I wanted you to know that I'm not going to have a lot of sympathy for the jam you're in. Up to a point I will, but when it comes to the kids, I'm going to tell you what I think. Okay?

The message seems to convey to the parent, "I read your deepest wishes—that I put your children first."

Mr. Allen (*nods*): Sure.

The "Sure," accompanied by the appropriate attitudinal and nonverbal gestures, communicates consent for the therapist to proceed with a forceful, direct style.

The therapist obtains leverage by assuring the parent that he or she is on the side of the children. This assurance implies a fundamental principle organizing the therapy: that the therapist is forming a higher-level coalition with the mother or father, who is not just a wounded spouse but a parent concerned with the children. The couple we cannot help in this format is that couple who cannot sense that we are with them when we are attacking them about the children.

Mr. Allen was relieved to find that the therapist did not attempt to repair his marriage. At the same time the therapist's statements prepared him for later surprises that her forceful feedback might bring. The central message from the therapist was: "I will not indulge your defenses. I have your permission to talk straight." This is important in all therapy but particularly important in divorce work, where people come in a vulnerable state, conveying that they are already too far down and do not want to be kicked further. The therapist cannot assume consent. He or she must get their consent to—in a way—kick them further.

We see some of this defensive posture in the individual session with Mrs. Allen, as the therapist identifies some of her pressing concerns. The mother presents herself as someone who *cannot* support herself and her children, and the therapist explores this most fundamental obstacle which the woman declares is keeping her in the house. Notice how persuasively the mother tries to have the therapist validate this perception:

Mrs. Allen: I *cannot* support me and the children, I just can't do it. If I could, I would not still be in the house. I would have been gone a long time ago. When Henry left, he decided he would pay me $550 a month. My monthly expenses are a minimum of $1,700 a month. I was not able to earn enough money to pay the difference. The month he left I had a ten-year-old car that fell apart. I mean, everything happened!

These obstacles and others that she lists, such as her lack of job skills and feelings of helplessness, are experienced cumulatively with despair, lumped together into one insurmountable mass, pressuring her from every side: "I mean, *everything* happened!" The therapist must display an honest measure of appreciation and commiseration concerning these obstacles because they truly represent the situation of many women undergoing divorce. The honest, attentive commiseration enhances the opportunity for the therapist to be listened to and eventually dispels whatever defensive embellishment may be made of the realistic financial situation.

The Lawyer-Client Relationship

Often, couples who have decided to separate discuss their problems as though no one else were involved in their situation. They believe they control the relationships with such outsiders as lawyers, in-laws, and the therapist. This belief, however, is usually incorrect. The key feature of the couple in the modern family is that it delegates functions that were once internal—not so much to parents and in-laws, but to outside experts such as lawyers. Lawyers, as well as relatives, must be viewed as crucial partic-ipants, especially in terms of their influence on the couple's behavior. While attempting to develop leverage with people who are themselves vying for power, the therapist should never overlook the power exerted by attorneys. In fact, most emergency work with divorcing people entails monitoring the influence of the other expert, the lawyer, without engaging in detrimental competition.

Some might argue that the therapist should never become involved with legal matters. No one wants to be accused of violating the jurisdiction of other significant participants, particularly those with whom one will need to be in indirect but implicit collaboration for the benefit of clients. Yet if the therapist is to see the whole picture, he or she must understand the potential for noncollaborative interplays among the couple, the therapist, and the lawyers. With some couples, the stalemate will not break unless the parents modify their relationship with their lawyers.

In the approach taken here, the therapist generally does not deal directly with lawyers; instead, he or she encourages the parents to reshape their relationship with their attorneys and to evaluate critically the advice that is being offered. This indirect approach helps the parents long after the therapist's involvement with the family has ceased. The objective is to encourage people to make their own responsible decisions. The point is not to allow anyone to get away with the claim "My lawyer made me do it," while at the same time acting as though the lawyer is working under his or her direction.

In working with divorce crises where lawyers are involved, an inevitable task is that of clarifying the boundary blurring that occurs between lawyer and client. Respecting Mrs. Allen's feeling of being overwhelmed, the ther-apist grounds her by asking about any plans she might have to go to work, narrowing and concretizing further what the mother thinks is holding her back.

Mrs. Allen: My lawyer told me *not* to go to work. I could go tomorrow and get a job. I was offered a *good* job a week ago,

The interviewing now shifts the mother's reasons for lack of movement due

so I called my lawyer. I would like to work, it would be better for me.
Therapist: The lawyer is telling you no. Why?
Mrs. Allen: Because it looks like I have *nothing* this way. When it comes to going to court, I have no money.

to intrapersonal issues—that is, her lack of skills and feelings of helplessness—to the actual person who is restraining her. The problem has moved from self to the interpersonal arena.

It would be very easy for the therapist to take this claim at face value and conclude that the woman simply has the wrong lawyer. However, the task is to see whether the situation stems more from the parent's dependency and/or machinations, or from the lawyer's control over the situation. This should not be judged quickly. It may indeed be that the woman was advised not to go to work before the court hearing, or it may be that she has unwittingly maneuvered to make her lawyer enslave her. Observe how the therapist tries to find out:

Therapist: I understand Henry was out of the house for a while. What's keeping him there now?
Mrs. Allen: My understanding of his reason for returning, as I see it. . . . Well, there's *nothing* between us, absolutely nothing. I told him before he moved in that there would be nothing. I asked him to stay away and give me time to think.

She is sliding away from responding to the therapist's question about what is keeping her husband in the house. She does not want to address that issue because it pertains to her refusal to negotiate effectively with him.

Therapist: So what's keeping him there?

The therapist persists.

Mrs. Allen: I don't know. I guess he doesn't want to pay what the court ordered him to pay if he stayed away.
Therapist: So the financial part of it is what's keeping him there?
Mrs. Allen: Actually, I would settle for less, and I told my lawyer that.

What seems to be at work here is his lawyer's influence. Even though the father wanted to stay away, the lawyer may have advised him to return for financial reasons. If he seems to be able to pay rent in two places, the court will conclude that he has more financial resources than he actually does, and he will be at a disadvantage in future financial settlements.

Mrs. Allen has now admitted that she would settle for less. The therapist has to figure out the extent to which Mrs. Allen is participating without a sense of her own rights, being influenced without a clear position of her own. To find out more, the therapist continues her probe:

Therapist: And what did your lawyer say about your settling for less?
Mrs. Allen: "No, you won't, shut up, and go back and stay where you are." I cannot tell you how many hours I spend with my lawyer in his office discussing this or that or my concern for the children.

Mrs. Allen reports that her lawyer has told her to stay in the house, but psychologically she experiences the mandate as telling her to stay in the situation, to continue to withstand stress for herself and her children.

Indeed, it appeared as though Mrs. Allen had displaced responsibility onto the lawyer. She was calling him constantly, and he was giving her extra time. He was almost becoming her confidant or therapist. Maybe the lawyer also felt harassed, pulled into areas that were not his domain. At one point he said to her with exasperation, "Tanya, I didn't marry him! What do you want from me?" It is not difficult to imagine the impact of a client such as this on a lawyer.

The therapist has to consider the adult's special vulnerability and need for guidance in the midst of the divorce process, and the possibility for an intense lawyer-client relationship to develop. Lawyers enter the scene in the middle of a highly emotionally charged atmosphere. Their communications are perceived in a special way, so it is simplistic to think that their advice will pertain only to legal matters.

To get Mrs. Allen to question further her attachment to her lawyer and his advice, the therapist worked to intensify her concern for her children. In the transcript that follows, the therapist helps her fantasize the worst outcome for the children as she thinks about what is in store for them during the court processes:

Mrs. Allen: Courts do not recognize the emotional effect on a child.

Therapist: That's what your lawyer tells you?

Mrs. Allen: He says they absolutely do not recognize it. Tell them that the kids have been beaten, tell them that there's no food in the house, that means something. But tell them the emotional part of it, they don't hear it. It does exist and it's very important.

Therapist (*with conviction*): You're absolutely right.

Mrs. Allen (*becoming agitated*): What they're going through is part of them, and it's either going to make them good people or bad people.

Therapist: And the aftermath of this could be incredible. . . . What I want to know is, how bad does it have to get for the kids before you tell your lawyer to jam it, or whatever you need to tell him? If the courts are anything like the courts I know, it could be a year or eighteen months before any of this gets settled.

By confirming the mother strongly in her viewpoint, the therapist enters into a coalition with her and leads her to consider: if the court won't, who will? This heightens her emotionalism, and a renewed sense of urgency develops in the mother. The choice of language "to jam it" conveys a very assertive demarcation of boundaries.

Mrs. Allen: If it were a year from now, I think my kids would be permanently damaged; *I* would be permanently damaged!

The therapist is realistic and if anything underestimates how long the case could drag on in the courts. Her description, nonetheless, highlights those aspects of the uncontrollable context that are likely to elicit from the mother an increasing sense of indignation and decisiveness.

The immediate goal of mobilizing constructive anger has been reached. The woman is now sufficiently upset about the children's predicament that the therapist can press on, as she did with the father, with the idea that she's not about to have a great deal of sympathy for the parent and will put the children's welfare first. Of course, this move shifts the responsibility from the lawyer's shoulders to the woman's own. The move is ultimately syntonic, fitting with what the parent "wants." The responsibility is returned to where it belongs, with the parents instead of the outsider.

The therapist must now decide on which side of the couple-system she must concentrate in order to precipitate change. Couples are not symmetrical or perfectly equilibrated systems. They come skewed. Change is more likely to come about in this case through the mother. The father, in apparent complementarity to his wife, allocates to her the capacity to see the pain of the children, while he tends to deny it. The difficult decision for the therapist is to figure out where the fixed system is most likely to break, and who is more likely to get out of the stagnant cycle first.

Mrs. Allen, who was already aware of her children's distress but not using it to change, has now become worked up enough to consider separation as imminent. After dealing with the therapist, she finds her lawyer's advice of "holding firm" in negotiations with her husband more difficult to follow, once she becomes convinced that the harm to the children is reaching critical dimensions. What was a difficult situation becomes amplified into a crisis situation, and movement is made possible.

The Evaluation of the Children in the Family

With the parents ready to reconsider the situation of the children, the next step is to observe the children with the parents systematically. As an aid to diagnosis, the therapist summons time-tested notions of how children manifest distress in symbolic play, expressing the conflict within the family.

Two scared little girls entered the room and sat flanking their mother. Deborah, the elder, would not leave her mother's side, confirming for the therapist that she was indeed a child under special stress. She told her mother that she would not be comfortable seeing the therapist alone, even for a few minutes. Five-year-old Carlotta could hardly sit still and talked in a manic, pressured way. The therapist wondered whether she would learn anything more about the child than her frenetic behavior at this time, and whether it would be worth stressing her further in a first meeting. She then noticed that the little girl had taken the mother and father hand puppets, put one inside the other, and then set them side by side in the empty chair between her parents. It was as if by this gesture she was attempting to close the space between her parents. Climbing next onto her father's lap, she first cuddled with him and hugged him, but only moments later she started to hit him, perhaps revealing her inability to integrate opposites—to love her father while her mother was hating him.

The therapist not only looked at what was happening in the room but inquired about the everyday life of the children. They talked about a confusing change of bedrooms which made the confusing changes in relationships more concrete for the children.

Deborah: We have three rooms. There's one big room that my mom and my dad *used* to share, but now, since they aren't really getting along, my dad has Carlotta's room and so Carlotta and my mom share a room. But now I've been sleeping in her room, because she locks the door while she's asleep so my dad can't get in, and they do that all the time . . . (*her voice trails off, depressed*).

The girl is logically presenting that her dad doesn't get in. The intonation makes clear that she's not depressed for herself alone but for her dad also, who is locked out.

Therapist: So you sleep in Carlotta's room, and Carlotta sleeps with your mom?
Deborah: No, I have my own room that I've always had, but I sleep with my mom now.

In addition to all the other upheaval in the house, the children no longer have the stability of their own space, and bedtime has become another arena for the tug-of-war between the parents.

Highlighting the Children's Needs

The format that most families expect to go through is to bring the children to the therapist in order to receive guidance on how to handle them. They expect the therapist to meet with the children and return to the parents with expert feedback. In the case of the Allens, the therapist had not met alone with the youngsters and was not yet ready to give the expected extensive feedback when she again met with the parents as a couple. But she had observed the children's distress and was ready to use it to induce larger organizational changes. What she had learned from the children became a lever with which to budge the couple from their intransigent "can't split" position.

The older girl had been reluctant to leave the room, to leave her mother, and the therapist pointed this out as a sign of her distress. It provided the opportunity to convey to the parents that the children would need more than the usual automatic gestures of support during the experience of separation. This message helped distract the parents from their own pain and confusion, and focus them on constructive activity that would actually help themselves as well as the children. The children's successful traversing of the experience would then become a marker, a set of sign posts to the parents that would tell them they they were doing what was needed. The therapist wondered out loud if perhaps the children did not want things to be brought up in the session because they were protecting their parents. She advised them simply to figure out, as parents, ways of protecting their children and began to talk with them about possible ways of doing so.

At this point, to highlight and normalize her message, a consultant who had been observing the session joined the therapist. The expansion of the group in this way suggests to the parents that they have extra resources for dealing with their problems. Throughout the discussion that follows, the parents' separation is made incidental but contingent on the business of preparing the children. The more the parents feel that they can prepare their children effectively, the easier it should be for them to separate. The emphasis during feedback-giving is deliberately kept on the surface, on the innocent and straightforward task of giving information about the youngsters. The more fundamental organizational features, specifically bringing the split parents together to protect the children, is left implicit.

Consultant (*introduces himself*):   How are you? (*They shake hands.*) It's nice to meet you. I thought I would just come in for a minute. I want to tell you that many parents have been in your boat. You're not alone in this world.

Mrs. Allen: I realize that.

Consultant: This situation has been traversed by *many* couples. The situation with the room is one that will give a bit

The consultant, after normalizing their situation by conveying that many couples experience it, begins to focus on the children. He picks the more of a prop to Deborah, if you think about when to give her access and you guys agree at least that she will have, that it will not be indispensable that you lock her out. Because . . .

issue of changing bedrooms and where the elder girl sleeps. Though Deborah's words had not indicated for certain that she was locked out, her tone and inflection of urgency and depression had impressed the consultant.

Mrs. Allen (*emphatically*): I *don't* lock her out. If the door is locked, she is in there. I do not lock her out, *ever.*
Consultant: It's interesting how Deborah framed what she said about the bedroom. She framed it as if in a sense she was locked out.
Mrs. Allen: Oh, did she?
Consultant: Yes, and it may be more, that she's talking about what happens psychologically, that she feels locked out.
Mrs. Allen: That's right. I understand that.

By answering this statement of the mother's, the consultant subtly moves from the external to the child's internal life. In the process, the mother's sense of being the *only* expert on what's happening is eroded and she becomes convinced that she had better accept some outside guidance.

Consultant: As long as you know that, your radar can get fine-tuned on where you can give the support. (*He begins to talk slowly, quietly, almost hypnotically.*) There will be routines that only you two would know about, everything from favorite breakfasts to favorite toys, to little things that are favorite activities. I would increase all that—anything that you know, from the deep knowledge you have of these children, that will tend to make them feel a little bit more secure and sturdy; and that's what parents do.

These practical bits of information are intended to buffer the stress of their transition to becoming more responsible parents. The message is that as long as they are embarking on this journey, the road will be smoother if they take care of the children. The specific suggestions give the sense that there is much the parents can do. They help to counter the parents'

And in a way, that recipe is always concocted by the family. You know your children. From what we know by now of couples who move through and do a pretty good job—and I think you people will—you can expect that while you're doing this you'll find the other, more painful aspects of the split easier to manage. You know, to the extent that you feel, "Boy, we have stood by the kids," you have done well. So that it will pay if you get finicky, careful, really observant about what the children respond to with a sense of safety.

feeling that they are incompetent or empty and have little to offer their children. The emphasis is on having them credit themselves and call on their inventiveness. The incidental aside, "and I think you people will," reassures them in a way that makes the directive irresistible.

Emphasizing *we*, the consultant creates a vivid image of a triumphant parental couple.

The consultant's gentle and hypnotic tone helps to lower the parents' defenses, allowing them to receive the message that there is a way of equipping themselves despite the strain of splitting. The harsher message, that the basic situation must change, also manages to imply that the situation itself is to blame, and not them. The situation is dissociated as a separate force from the actors that helped to shape it.

Consultant (*speeding up his pace*): You know we cannot pull miracles.
Mrs. Allen: I understand.
Consultant: If you're in a situation where there is chronic tension, concern for the routines and for how you can support the children will *help*, but that's all. We don't have magic wands in that sense at all, and we want to be candid with you. (*The pace slackens and the tone becomes hypnotic.*) But there are things you can do. There are favorite breakfasts and nighttime routines, favorite stories, favorite little outings, things that Deborah likes to do when she's with you, the comic books that she likes, toys. There are favorite TV programs.

This approach works by bringing a sense of realistic proportion to the nature of the task, helping the parents avoid being overwhelmed. It also discourages any sense of mystification and defensiveness toward the therapist. To make the message more palatable, and to seed the parents' unconscious with it, the consultant quickly returns to the quieter, more irresistible style in which he talks about how

Mrs. Allen (*interrupting*):   I could sit down and watch her favorite TV show with her, but I hate TV and always argue with her about it. . . .

Consultant: There'll be some stretching that you have to do.

Mrs. Allen: So I'll sit down and watch that horrible TV show. (*She laughs.*)

Consultant: It'll prove useful to you; these will be your tools in helping them through. There's also the more difficult task (*his voice gets louder and he turns to the therapist*), which I don't know if we have a chance to cover today, but they're going to have to talk to the kids about the coming split and what it means. Otherwise, from what we know already, the fantasies will brew that maybe they won't see one of you any more. (*The consultant looks in turn at each parent.*) That maybe . . .

Mrs. Allen (*interrupting with excitement*):   I know they have that fantasy. I can tell they have that.

Consultant (*looking intently at each*):   But that fantasy can yield to reason. It can yield to reassurance that you'll never lose Daddy, never lose Mother.

Mrs. Allen: I've tried to talk to them about it.

Therapist: You can also help their fantasy of being abandoned by showing them that, as parents, you will give them what they need, you will protect them.

Consultant: What happens when you talk to them about the divorce?

Mrs. Allen: They cry, and then I cry.

parents *can* help the children in little ways. The sequence weaves in and out between the two messages: that the parents are rich in ways to help the children, and that the living situation must change. By attending to one, they cannot help but take in the other. This interspersing and linking together of different messages facilitates the process of problem solving toward a constructive goal.

The consultant heightens the parents' attention by drifting away from them, now addressing the therapist. This is a message about a task for which he hopes to discourage a refusal. By not addressing the couple on this issue, yet maintaining their attention on it, he slips through their defenses.

The emphasis is on the word "never." The father's fear that a concerted effort was in place to keep the children away from him was simultaneously countered with this move.

Mr. Allen: When I talk to them, they don't cry at all.

The parents are about to polarize into two opposing and depressed camps and enter into head-on conflict.

Consultant (*to the father*):   They don't cry, that's fine. (*To the mother:*) You are a crier, a competent crier, you know.
(*Mrs. Allen laughs.*)

The consultant intercedes to defuse the conflict, by accepting the two polarized realities. He acknowledges each, the husband's and the wife's, but goes on to concentrate on Mrs. Allen, who is on the verge of tears as she thinks about her children and is about to give in to her depression. Giving in to her depression would allow her to escape her duty as a parent "legitimately"; therefore the consultant does not indulge her affect, attempting instead to reverse it through humor.

Consultant: That's fine. You've got to take this in style. You're a crier, you get a subscription to Kleenex and you do your job (*gets up to leave*). Listen, I think you're doing what you can, but I hope you also get the negatives in your therapist's message, because we have learned thus far from working with families that we can't skirt around this one. We may not be of great value to you, if some of the other things don't somehow stabilize. But I have no doubt that you can do a lot to support the children throughout. (*The consultant leaves the room.*)

The atmosphere is lightened with the comment about "a subscription to Kleenex," and he continues to push for their competency as parents.
The "other things" refers to their marital impasse.

Therapist: What I would like to do is

The overall message here

schedule something in two weeks, because this has been going on a long time, and you need to do your work and one week is too soon. You need a couple of weeks. is that coming to the sessions and just talking is not sufficient. The parents are expected to accomplish something between themselves and thereby effect changes with respect to the children.

The session restored Mrs. Allen's confidence in her ability to cope. She began the session feeling that as a "good" mother she could not tell her children about the impending separation. She ended the session feeling that she has to prepare her children and that she and her husband have many ways in which to support them. Mr. Allen goes along hesitantly. He displays a "wait and see" attitude but shows obvious concern for the plight of the children. Each parent feels that the therapists have sympathy for his or her discrete situation but that the separation must take place and must be handled responsibly.

Checking for Hardening and Polarization

Although this is not always the case, work with this family was accomplished in two sessions. The therapist entered the second session with the idea of checking to see what changes had been made, and if necessary to re-escalate the crisis. A pattern similar to that of the first meeting was followed. Each parent was seen individually, the children were seen together, and the therapist ended by giving feedback to both parents. Now that each parent was more comfortable with the therapist, she was able to be more aggressive with them, without worrying that they might leave precipitously. The children were now comfortable enough to be seen without their parents, thus enabling the therapist to construct a convincing statement to the parents about why they had to break the stalemate before it damaged them or the children. Everyone had to understand the situation as a race against detrimental processes that would continue to take an increasing toll unless interrupted.

The therapist first evaluated whether there had been any shift in the Allens' positions or in their ways of buffering the children against stress during the intervening two weeks. The therapist was interested in finding out, for example, if the father was now able to see that his children were under stress, and if the parents had made any changes vis-à-vis their attorneys.

The therapist must routinely check for a hardening and retrenchment of positions. In this case, she began with the father, the more resistant of the pair, and learned that he had solidified his previous viewpoint even further. He insisted that the children were doing fine and continued to complain to the therapist about all the money his wife was taking.

This hardening is usually due to a talk with the lawyer between sessions and to defensiveness and resistance toward the therapist. From the husband's perspective, the therapist had sided more with the wife. However, it is precisely this hardening that the therapist can utilize to facilitate change. The hardening increases the distance between husband and wife, renders their situation more intolerable, and makes the break between them more likely. A no-lose situation is created. If the initial therapeutic attempt does not work as it is ostensibly intended—to convince both parents that they must separate for the sake of the children—it works by further entrenching and polarizing them into vehemently held positions from which they must eventually seek an escape. At this stage, the therapist must characterize all movement as not enough, in order to increase the possibility of change. In this case, the therapist relates to this stage by telling the spouses they are frozen in dead center, without intimating that they are hardening and perhaps about to change.

After checking for hardening and retrenchment in the husband, the therapist now does the same with the wife. Mrs. Allen has definitely been affected by the previous session. She has become more aware of how the children feel and how nervous they are. To calm them down, she has tried to show less worry and has been reading to them more. The last session's message about the need to talk to the girls about the separation reached her: after the last session, she took the girls to a restaurant and told them that she and their father would be separating.

The basic situation remains unchanged, however; the couple has made no plans and no moves toward separation. It becomes clear that it will be necessary to push them in that direction as a primary therapeutic task. After reassuring Mrs. Allen that she is doing what she can to support her children, the therapist returns to tease out the basic issue: the prolonging of the tense living situation for the parents and their children. Will the mother present the same reasons for remaining in the house, or has there been a shift in the way she presents her lawyer's advice?

Mrs. Allen (*defensively*): As I told you before, the only reason I stayed in the house is that my lawyer said, "Shut up and stay there."

Therapist: Uh huh, but your lawyer doesn't live there.

Mrs. Allen: Well, that's what I told him.

Therapist (*slowly and doubtingly*): Yes, yes.

This confrontation, a reminder of the mother's painful reality, in microcosm portends the therapeutics to come. Mrs. Allen is not taking responsibility for her actions. Her "as I told you before" attempts to steer the therapist away from this topic, declaring the issue closed and putting exclusive blame on her lawyer for the situation. The therapist's obviously sarcastic retort begins the process of eroding the mother's defensive position.

Reorganizing the Boundaries Between Lawyer and Client

What happens next is a long therapeutic struggle aimed at altering the relationship between the mother and her lawyer. The reorganization of boundaries entails grappling actively with the person whose relations with the lawyer seem to be most responsible for preventing change. This can seldom be done by having the person reconsider the tie to the legal profession. The experience, when effective, involves an actual affective tug-of-war between the therapist, the client, and the lawyer. Initially, Mrs. Allen took no responsibility for her actions, repeating her lawyer's advice to "hang in there." She presented herself as totally helpless and her husband as totally unrealistic. For example, although he had agreed to pay for child care, he had chosen a day care center that made no provision for transporting the children from their school; if she were working, she would not be able to pick the children up. In the following transcript, when the therapist tries to be useful and offer straightforward suggestions, Mrs. Allen escalates her attempts to prove her own incompetence and lack of resourcefulness.

Therapist: I can understand why your lawyer feels that you're poor and pitiful and helpless, and that you're not ever going to be able to make it out in the world without all of Henry's money. You had a job, but you're coming to him with stories about how helpless you are. I can see why he would say you have to stay in the house. Poor you (*mockingly*). You know you can't make it. You can't make it unless you . . .

A powerful reversal of a cornerstone idea is now employed. The lawyer is made a victim of Mrs. Allen—specifically of her helpless act—and not, as Mrs. Allen would have it, the other way around. This shift of figure and ground is unexpected and catches her off guard, permitting her to see the situation anew. The whole exchange has her ally, the therapist, "leading" her, and facilitates cognitive reorganization on Mrs. Allen's part.

Mrs. Allen (*interrupting angrily*): No, I can't, not unless I have money. I can't, unless I have money for things . . .

Therapist (*interrupting just as angrily*): I can see, then, why the lawyer says what he does. What will happen is that Henry will stay, and you'll have to dig in your heels and figure out how you're going to survive and how the kids are going to survive, and you know what the ramifications of all this can be. But if you're willing to change that, and you're willing to go in and tell your lawyer that you're strong and one way or another you're going to find a way and you're going to make it work, and you'll check every resource possible . . .

Mrs. Allen (*firmly*): I can't do that.

Mrs. Allen, responding to the therapist's intensity, fights hard to defend her position as helpless. The therapist herself continues to fight back hard, not capitulating to Mrs. Allen's self-perception as helpless. The therapist continues to point out how one can affect the kind of advice received from a lawyer. Matching Mrs. Allen's intensity with her own, the therapist works actively at disengaging her from the unhelpful coalition with her lawyer.

Therapist: Then I don't think you have a choice.

The head-on approach is not working. The therapist

Mrs. Allen: I really can't. I have no money, absolutely no family to back me up, none. I can't go out and get a job. I can't do it.

begins to change her style, which will make it more difficult for Mrs. Allen to continue to fight so intensely with the therapist.

Mrs. Allen escalates the tug-of-war by summoning her strongest defenses. She rattles off new evidence of her helplessness, testing the therapist's resolve.

Therapist: I hear you, but I'm not going to be sympathetic to you, because I've seen women who have been living a single life for years and years, and they do it. They figure out a way. They check every resource possible. They go to all kinds of lengths, you know.

The therapist, who had been her friend, is no longer buying any more excuses.

Mrs. Allen: I did the same thing.

Therapist: But then you're stuck.

Mrs. Allen: I am stuck.

Therapist: So maybe you *are* doing all you can do for the kids. But you're going to have to think of how much of whatever money you do get from him may have to go into therapy for them once all this is over.

Mrs. Allen: I don't feel that's my responsibility.

Therapist: Well, if you're going to get all of Henry's money, then I think you need to think about that.

Mrs. Allen: Well, I don't want all his money. I have repeatedly told him that I don't want all his money. I really don't!

Since Mrs. Allen calls for an impasse and is about to defeat the therapist, the therapist summons a special offensive, speaking to Mrs. Allen's darker side. This offensive guilt trips the mother on two counts—trying to take all of her husband's money (a motive she was always careful to deny), and neglecting the inevitability of the children's pain, which initially she went out of the way to appear sensitive about.

Therapist: I'm not sure that's so. If you feel, honestly feel, that you are as helpless as you make out to be, then your lawyer's going to fight for everything that he can get from Henry.

By working from the imputation that Mrs. Allen has her own greedy motivations, the therapist manages to move her.

In this same hour, Mrs. Allen went through different phases in reacting to the therapist's pressure for change. After her initial resistance, she explored different alternatives, ranging from irresponsibly leaving the children to taking a job as a waitress, and earning enough money to leave with the children within a few weeks. In response to the therapist's efforts, she was beginning to move from her previous position.

Checking the Children

The therapist next proceeds to check the children's reactions. If a couple is very tense and we find that the children are fine, then we assume that the parents are adequately defending the children from their own anxiety. In the kind of situation we are examining with the Allens, however, it is very unusual for the children to be doing fine.

Generally, in meeting alone with the children, the therapist sets up a casual and friendly atmosphere that is receptive to indirect messages coming from the children's play and from their casual remarks. The therapist is particularly careful not to arouse any feeling that the children are betraying or "telling on" their parents. Much of the atmosphere is set by helping both parents convey to the children that talking with this adult is safe.

In meeting alone with the Allen children, the therapist learned that each parent had been upsetting the children. Deborah, the elder child, was loyal to both parents and asked the therapist not to tell her mother *or* her father. With great difficulty, yet with clear relief, she admitted that her father kept pumping her, asking whether her mother had been drinking. Her mother had warned Deborah that if he asked her anything that she didn't know how to answer, she should say, "I don't know." Carlotta chimed in saying that the same thing kept happening to her, and that her mother kept complaining about their father not giving enough money. When the therapist asked the children whether the parents' fighting made them worry, Deborah talked about their dog, who ran upstairs and hid whenever their parents started yelling. Later, more openly, she admitted the fighting always scared her.

This kind of outpouring of information from the children is not unusual. Children in this especially stressful situation hope that the adult whom the parents are consulting will help their parents by taking charge. In extreme cases it is common for the children to wish for, or assign to the therapist, magical powers to unify the parents and stop the fighting.

Reinforcing the children's coping skills often entails asking for their active ideas for dealing with the parents' frightening arguments. Here, the older girl is helped to form a manner of coping and to discover the limits of her power:

Deborah (*tentatively*):   It might be a little hard to do. Like keep my mom and dad always away from each other. If my mom says one word to my dad, then you know that they're going to fight. So if my mom is in the same room as my dad, if we separate them, they'll probably stay away from each other.

The therapist very gently responded that much of that was the parents' job, but conveyed by her sheltering stance that she had heard their plea to her to do something. She let them know that she was there to help their parents and differentiated for the children what properly belonged in the adult sphere, letting them know that it was not *their* job to separate their parents. She questioned them further, though, about what they might do to make the fighting easier to tolerate. Deborah suggested that when her parents were in the same room together, she and her sister could go outside or upstairs, away from the fighting. The therapist supported this suggestion, which offered the children a momentary means of escape from an upside-down hierarchy. To help them identify warning signs that a fight was coming on, the therapist asked if they knew *when* to expect trouble. If primed to respond to a set of signals, the children could at least get out of the way. Finally, she checked the children's understanding of what was happening to their parents and what was likely to happen to them. They understood that their parents were planning to get a divorce, but they knew no particulars, including when and how they would get to see each of their parents.

Feedback Regarding the Children as Leverage for Change

A fundamental tool in dealing with the difficult divorce is to provide the parents with feedback on the children so that the opportunity for family modification can be established. In one family, the therapist may develop leverage by emphasizing the effect of parental hostility on the children. In another, the therapist may talk about the consequences of the present sleeping arrangement.

After talking alone with the Allen children, the therapist met with the parents. The meeting will be recounted in detail, to show how the manner in which the feedback is given—a long, hammering monologue—heightens the emotional intensity. Through an emotion-filled confrontation, the therapist escalates the stress so that the split will become a viable option, an appropriate means of escape. The power of the therapist in creating intensity derives from what she has accurately observed and her ability to convey it with authority and urgency.

After a set of initial exchanges recruiting the parents' attention and preparing them for harsh input, the therapist accelerates the pace. A flood of observations is given, one right after the other; there is no cognitive resting place for the parent. Now that for a fleeting moment they are receptive, the therapist packs it all in, and the impact is cumulative. This technique fails if it in any way spares the parents, by giving observations piecemeal and permitting the parents to defend themselves from each bit of information. The overall implosive effect is necessary because of the family's skill in dodging change. But the ultimate power of the feedback lies not only in the manner of delivering it but in how it is integrated with the parents' own discovery of known truths that have been denied.

Therapist: I do have some things that I want to tell you both, and I need a solemn promise, from both of you, that none of what I have to tell you will land on the kids. These are issues that you need to know about as parents, and you will deal with them as parents, and there will be no repercussions on the children, at all! Can you do that?

The whole tone is authoritative, summoning the parents to order and to the development of a contract that will firm up the protective boundaries between them and the children. The intensity is in direct proportion to the parents' avoidance. The therapist says they *must* address these issues, because they have said they would not.

Mr. Allen: Sure.

Therapist: And you, Tanya?

Mrs. Allen: I can do that.

Therapist: Okay. Now first of all, there are signs that the children are distressed, very bold signs, and I don't know how in the world, Henry, you can miss them! One thing that happens is that they get caught in traffic control—which of you are going where, when, and they don't know which of you they can be with. Okay? If they're with you (*in a tone of open alarm and indignation, looking at the father*), does Mom know, and is it really okay, and is she okay? It's a complete set-up for your kids. The other thing is that Deborah in particular does have some times when she doesn't feel good down deep inside. I don't know how long she's felt this, but she does, and you two are going to have to figure out some way for her to start feeling better about herself. I'm not sure how you're going to do that, but you need to get moving on it.

The therapist makes no effort to be neutral. She does not just address the parents as a symmetrical pair. She capitalizes on the skew between them, which in this case is that the father is harder to handle and more resistant to recognizing the children's pain. Thus she hits harder at him. There is no attempt to be indirect. The therapist is addressing the toxic triangular arrangement in which children commonly find themselves in a difficult divorce. She highlights the coordination issue—the conflict involved in obtaining permission from one parent without having willing consent from the other—and singles out especially the internal pain and the injury to self-esteem in their older daughter. Just listing the problem announces the area of need while carefully disqualifying the therapist as someone who can either give the answer or foster dependence. "You two are going to have to figure out. . . . I'm not sure how you're going to do that."

Okay, the children also are getting very mixed up and confused about who's telling them the truth and who's not. One of you tells them one thing, and the other tells them another thing. They love you both but the confusion is going to take its toll.

The list continues. It now focuses on the youngsters' confusion under the charge of two disputing adults who constantly pose contradictory demands for the children.

It must stop! Don't tell them anything if it's at all contradictory. The other thing that's going on is that they don't know what's happening next week, they don't know what's happening next month, they don't know which end's up. And for the kids to stay in limbo like that is obviously not good. Not at all! They know generally, vaguely, that you two are going to get a divorce. They don't know anything about when. They don't know what's going to happen to their toys, to their rooms, to their house, or to the two of you. Okay? Something else is going on that is just as important. The children are feeling like umpires, as if you two are the children and they are the grown-ups. For example, Deborah said that you two can't be in the same room together without fighting, and she wondered if there was some way she and Carlotta could separate you. The children need you two to get moving and separate rather than stay together. (*Slowly now*) You came here because you wanted me to tell you what the kids need, and that's about as clear as I can get! The children are very protective and loyal to the two of you, and I hope that you keep

The "it" in "It must stop" makes the impossible and stressful situation more concrete.

For the therapeutic process, it is important to see that this conclusion is presented as an inescapable result of having witnessed the plight of the children and the parents' failure to what I'm telling you in confidence. And I would like to say that I'm glad that you signed those papers about not going to court, because if you did go to court, and you, Henry, could not recognize these signs, then you'd be missing something with your kids.

change the situation. The therapist clearly sees the constant hierarchical reversal as an extraordinary development, a far-gone situation. She conveys: if this is the way you stay together, by burdening your children into being parents and umpires, then they are better off if you separate. The directive is: if you stay together, it has to be without sacrificing the children in this fashion.

Mr. Allen: Nothing you told me here was missed.

Therapist (*looking at the father intently*): Earlier in this session you said that there was nothing unusual going on. But there is! There are true signs of distress that you must address. (*Looking at them both*) I will tell you that as parents you *must* address this problem.

This is a moment of confrontation, when the therapist finally holds the father accountable for what he had "not seen" and wanted not to address. He had seen the signs but defensively had not given them the weight they deserved. Now that the signs have been detailed and the therapist's intensity and conviction have reached new heights of specificity, he finally recognizes that he has seen them all.

Mr. Allen (*respectfully*): I agree.

Therapist: You two have my hands tied. There's nothing else I can do except to tell you what I see going on with your kids and to warn you as parents that things have to change. You need to get your negotiations out of deadlock. You have clear signs before you that the children are

The therapist transfers responsibility from her to the parents. She does this by dramatically blaming them for her impotence as a helper. This continues the process of having being emotionally damaged, and I hope you have a strong support network to handle your guilt if you don't do something soon! I'm talking about your getting something settled tomorrow, the next day, the end of this week. You don't wait two weeks. You do it now! them reclaim responsibility, which began during the first session with, "If the courts won't, who will?" She is now saying, "I won't, so who will?" This amounts to the successive removal of props and throws the parents back on their own resources.

This confrontation with reality took about five minutes and was obviously painful for the parents. The confrontation was tolerated in spite of the pain because the parents really wanted to know what was going on with the children and, despite conduct to the contrary, they also wanted to protect them from the consequences of the separation. The mother, visibly shaken, asked the therapist for a recap. In complying with her request, the therapist delivered an additional strong message and more detailed feedback on both children:

Therapist: Deborah is not feeling good. Carlotta's not feeling good either, but she's a little better protected because she's the youngest, and somehow she knows how to get more affection for herself.
Mrs. Allen: Yeah, that's true.
Therapist: Deborah hurts more, and she reacts by going off and being alone. She needs to be alone some, but sometimes you do need to get her busy doing things with people. She's hurting, and she's more alone in her hurt than Carlotta. Okay? The other thing is that I feel like my hands are tied. I ask what kinds of resources are there, what kinds of ways can you move. And you say you can't. If that's the case, there's nothing else I can do. My advice to you is to go to whomever or wherever you need to get out of this deadlock, and by tomorrow, or the end of the week, see that something has changed. It's up to you two

to get moving, and as for the question of
how or where or why, you need to come
up with the answers yourselves. Maybe
you both need to sit down with your
lawyers and give them a long lecture about
the fact that *you're* hiring *them,* and that
you're going to figure out a way to
negotiate and get off dead center. Then do
it. Things *must* change. And whatever you
can do to change the situation at home,
start *today,* when you leave here. Okay?
That's all. (*The therapist now slows her
pace.*) So we'll see what happens, and you
can let me hear in two or three weeks
what kind of work you've done, or I may
not hear from you again. It's up to you.
(*She rises and goes to the door.*)

This procedure puts pressure on the therapist to be a careful diagnostician
and to come up with observations that will have an impact on the parents.
It is most effective when the observations are about things that the parents
have indeed seen and minimized. One advantage of this way of working
is that it treats the participants as people who have some capacity left to
disentangle from their maladaptive arrangements. Some authorities question the value of telling parents things they already know in part, since
people do not always change in response to information they receive. But
more than telling is involved. What is decisive is that after heightening
tension and outlining the issues that must be addressed, the therapist is
quickly released from the process, exiting in such a way as to leave with
them the responsibility for change.

The therapist did not set up another appointment with this family, further
developing the therapeutic tension. The session ended with the mother
asking for the therapist's phone number, but no guarantee was offered to
her or to her husband that there would be any additional sessions. To set
up another appointment would have been a tactical error, diluting the
central message that talk is no substitute for action. By telling the couple
that she might not hear from them again, she kept their anxiety alive as
she led them to the threshold of responsibility.

Conclusion

Three weeks after this session, Mrs. Allen convinced her lawyer that she could make do with less of her husband's money. She got a loan, a job, and an apartment, and left with the children. In just two long sessions, the therapist helped the couple break a stalemate of nearly a year and a half.

It would be natural to expect that a couple so angry and stalemated would almost by definition have trouble completing the postseparation tasks without harming the children. Yet, clinically, this is not necessarily the case. Living apart in the same house is so unnatural that the tension inherent in that situation turns out to be more dangerous to the children than separation or the events that tend to follow separation. Couples helped out of this situation generally find great relief and discover ways to be more helpful to their children during the postseparation period. They find they have regained some of their individual resources, which were tied up while they were trapped and close to violence in the same house. Mrs. Allen allowed her husband full access to the children and even protected his relationship with them. Deborah told her mother that she was relieved to be "away from all that fighting," and both parents were able to make progress in their own lives, even though they had not resolved their most fundamental differences.

After the mother and children moved, the father began to fulfill all the criteria for good parenting. This father, who had been sacrificing his children because of the adversarial relationship between himself and his wife, now became so considerate of the children that he delayed introducing them to his new girlfriend until he had a strong relationship with her. He also decided not to impair the children's relationships with the grandparents on his wife's side and saw to it that the children continued to get together with his in-laws. This proved decisive in promoting flexible boundaries and family harmony. The grandparents felt that they had not stood in the way of their daughter's escaping an unhappy marriage and that the divorce had not brought them the misery of losing their grandchildren. (His own parents, too old and far away, never became a consideration in the adjustment.)

His concern extended beyond the immediate social network. He wanted to have a relationship with his children's teachers as well, and decided to live nearby to give his children easy access to him. In every area in which we can assess good parenting, the father displayed behavior that was impressive and beneficial. The therapist had seen no potential for any of this when the father was in the standstill, tension-filled situation of living in the same house with someone whom he hated and who hated him.

The therapist had also tended to see little potential for the mother to stress the children unduly, yet we learned at the follow-up interview seven months later that the mother, unlike the father, had introduced the youngsters to her new partner prematurely and in a not altogether sensitive manner. This had created some temporary distress, particularly in the older girl, who was reluctant to accompany the two of them to church because it used to be a sacrosanct domain of the father's. With some minimal direction from the therapist, who fine-tuned and paced the process, the mother resolved this issue.

Follow-up to therapy follows a basic format to determine whether the family has met most of the criteria for adequate adjustment. The therapist checks: (1) whether the children and the adults have settled down into healthy patterns of behavior and whether the adults' resources for parenting are emerging now that stress is reduced; (2) how the parents are managing to communicate with each other about inescapable issues of logistics concerning the children; (3) whether the parents have structured visitation so that the children have comfortable access to the visiting parent; and (4) whether in-laws are acting to promote family harmony by respecting boundaries rather than forming intrusive, warring clans. In the follow-up interview with the Allens, both adults were pleased with their respective accomplishments in finding new partners and in maintaining sensible arrangements for dealing with each other, and the children were symptom-free.

3

Managing Extreme
Preseparation Crises

WHILE two families may present what appears on the surface to be the same difficult stagnant preseparation, the participants may in fact have very different coping resources and levels of disturbance. In the previous chapter, we described a family in which the parents were relatively free of overt personality problems. In this chapter, we describe a second type of family, in which one of the parents is extremely disturbed.

The Franks had two young children, five-year-old Sam and eight-year-old Jenny. The father had been out of the home for five weeks and returned, uninvited, one month before our initial meeting. While no actual violence had occurred, the threat of violence overshadowed the family.

As with the previous family, the atmosphere in the house was tension-ridden. There was bedroom shuffling, in which the children lost their space and were locked inside the mother's bedroom with her. Moreover, the daughter in this family felt that she had to remain in the bedroom with her mother, in case the mother needed her to call the police for protection against the father. The therapist became concerned about the extent of the father's problems in controlling his impulses. There had been incidents at night in which the father had come dashing into the bedroom when the door was unlocked, and had violently plucked his son from the mother's bed. The father gave the appearance of being out of control and on the verge of decompensation.

In this family it was the father who originally called the Families of Divorce Project requesting an appointment. He complained that his wife was turning his children against him, and that she had told the children that he was not their real father and that he was having an affair. At first his wife was not interested in participating, but she agreed to come in after her lawyer became involved.

Mrs. Frank felt that her husband had been harassing her, and her lawyer threatened to file an injunction to keep him away from her and force him to leave the house. This injunction was never in fact filed, but Mr. Frank looked upon it as something his wife was trying to do to legally keep him away from his children. The children were very frightened and confused. Neither could concentrate in school, and both reported that they were always thinking about what was going on at home.

A major difference between the Allen and Frank families had to do with socioeconomic status. The Allens were an upper-middle-class family in which the father had a stable and rewarding career. The Frank family was lower class, about to have to go on welfare. The father worked two jobs, fearing imminent joblessness, while struggling openly with anxiety.

Despite the differences between the two families the therapist employed a similar format, shifting the composition of the group within the session and working with the different subgroups. The manifest emphasis was on the children's suffering and on ways of using feedback on the children to motivate change in the parents' situation. The therapist also evaluated how each participant was utilizing their lawyers' services. In contrast to the Allen family, the therapist had to help Mr. Frank get involved with a lawyer in a serious, formal way. He had used a lawyer only sporadically and in a way that did not allow him to feel he had an ally. The mother did feel her lawyer was an ally. The mother's lawyer did not seem to be obstructing the process of separation as did the Allens' lawyers.

Also unlike the Allens, the family in this emergency divorce case was one in which not only the children but the two adult participants were displaying signs of extreme distress. Fear was rampant. The mother feared her husband's violence, and the children feared that the police might take away their father if he became violent or that they would be taken away by him. The father was afraid he would lose his children, and his extreme anxiety was interfering with his cognitive functioning. His speech was pressured; he frequently hesitated, and his thoughts were scattered. He was unable to be consistently coherent or to stay on one topic. He looked despondent, was erratic in taking care of himself physically, and despaired about being alone. His fear that his son would be taken from him initially appeared to be unfounded. The wife appeared to want her husband to have access to the youngsters and could not understand why he was so worried about losing his son. As the case unfolded, however, it became clear that the father's fears were justified. There were insinuations from the mother, including the threatened injunction, that she might try to keep the children away from him. The children's fear of being alone with him could easily be traced back to his wife's anxiety.

Deviousness and concealment characterized the communication between husband and wife in this family. The therapist repeatedly had to work on calming the father, who frequently cried and had difficulty keeping to the topic in the sessions. More than in the Allens' case, the crisis therapy required that the therapist (1) take charge generally, because the people were too scattered and disorganized to do sensible problem solving; (2) modulate and control the mood and tension level; (3) maintain the participants' focus; and (4) provide hope.

Mr. Frank feared that his wife was so powerful that she could take away the children—who were all he felt he had—and leave him heartbroken and bankrupt. To help him reorganize quickly, a separate session was held in which the therapist emphasized the importance of his getting the right kind of lawyer, one who would offer steady protection by being unequivocally on his side.

Focusing on the Children

As was the case with the Allens, the therapist needed to understand fully the plight of the children, both to get ideas for how the parents could improve the situation and to use the information as a tool for motivating the parents to change. In the Frank family the children were deeply stressed and were immediately able to share their concerns with the therapist. In the time the therapist spent alone with them in the first session, they talked of their fears and worries:

Therapist: What do you know about why your parents brought you here today? Let's start with the oldest.
Jenny: To help us out.
Therapist: Do you know why they want to help you out?
Jenny: So I don't get worried.

Therapist: What have you been worried about?

Jenny (*hesitantly*):   In case my dad hits my mom. That's what I'm really scared of.

Therapist: That's what you're most worried about. Do you think about it a lot?

Jenny: Yeah.

Therapist: How often have you seen that happen?

The fear of imminent violence is the overriding emotion. The two children cope differently. The girl denies and tends to minimize to protect the image of her parents.

Jenny: He never did it before.

Sam (*interrupting*):   No, Mom was on the phone and he . . .

Jenny (*annoyed*):   He just threw a bag at her, that's all.

Therapist: But you get scared, though. So he never did hit her, but you get worried.

Her efforts at denial are thwarted by her brother's insistence on a violent reality. She tries to control her sibling's perception in what looks like the futile position of a parental child.

The children then told the therapist about the time their father came rushing into their mother's bedroom, where the children shared their mother's bed, grabbed Sam, and took him from the room. To get a less one-sided picture, the therapist asked them what their *mother* did that scared them. The girl replied quickly that she was afraid her mother might call the police to come and get her father. Both children described what it was like when their mother and father fought. The therapist then tried to assess the extent to which the children were able to get out of the middle when the parents fought:

Therapist: When they're fighting, do you stay in the room or do you try to get out of the room?

Jenny: My mom tells Sam to go take a bath or go read something.

Therapist (*to Jenny*):   And what does she say to you?

Jenny: She says, "Jenny, take Sam upstairs, and when he falls asleep, come down." See, she wants me with her just in case he hits her. Then I can go run and call the police.

This parental child not only has to take care of her brother, she has to take care of her mother as well. She is keenly aware

Therapist: That's a pretty big job. How old are you?

Jenny: Eight, going to be nine.

Therapist: That's a pretty big job for a nine-year-old.

Jenny (*slowly*): I really don't want to call the police on my dad.

Therapist: I don't blame you at all. You haven't had to do that yet, have you?

Jenny: No.

Therapist: It sounds like that might make it hard for you to concentrate in school.

of the situation and will take the opportunity to recruit the therapist to help free her from this disloyalty to her father. The job of bodyguard does not bother her as much as having to betray her father.

Sam interrupted to tell the therapist that he had trouble paying attention and that his teacher often had to tell him four or five times to do something. Both children admitted to being worried about their parents even during recess. Each child was torn between the parents and each was used by them. The girl was asked to stand watch for her mother at all times, and sometimes when the father needed comforting he took the boy into bed with him, using him as a security blanket. The situation had affected not only the children's performance at school but their playtime with peers. The dilemma had different effects on the two children. The girl was in a hyperagitated state. The plight of the boy was not as apparent until the second session, although in the first session he had demonstrated his special concern for instances of aggression between the parents.

Since the girl slept with her mother at night, it would have been easy to confuse her symptoms of clinging with plain regression and a search for her own security. But she revealed that her outstanding purpose was to be there in case her father became violent and she had to call the police. By insisting that the children sleep with her and calling Jenny downstairs in the middle of arguments with her spouse, the mother was giving the child the clear message that she must at all costs be available to her as a bodyguard.

In an extremely tense preseparation situation, a child may not dare relinquish the role of bodyguard even when very ill. This happened in the Frank family. After a couple of sessions, the therapist learned that Jenny had been ill with a fever, and her mother, who was working, had tried to take the children to stay with her own mother, as she had always done when the children were ill. This time Jenny refused. She raced out of the grandmother's house in pursuit of her mother. She was not afraid of being abandoned but rather afraid for her mother's safety. She worried that her mother would not be able to cope with her father if her mother returned home alone. It took the mother hours to convince her daughter that she, the mother, was indeed all right and would not be harmed by the father.

Feedback Regarding the Children

As with the Allens, the therapist's procedure was to give immediate feedback to the parents on what she had learned about the children. In this case the therapist gathered this information in the first session, so was able to give the feedback then. She began by reminding the parents that the children were seen because they, the parents, had requested it. The therapist acknowledged their competence in the things they were doing right and prepared them for the specific observations on their youngsters' reactions, which she presented with special intensity:

Therapist (*to both parents*): I didn't spend more time with your children today because their troubles are very evident and I wanted to have time to get back to you. Let me start by congratulating you; your children both love each of you dearly. But you've given them jobs that a five-year-old and an eight-year-old have no business having. (*Turning to the mother:*) Your daughter is not your bodyguard. (*To both parents:*) The children are not there to protect each of you. They can't concentrate in school, they can't stop thinking about Mommy and Daddy even at recess. I'm not talking about one of your children, but about *both* of your children! They're scared when you even look at each other, they're scared about the police being called, they're scared about just about everything having to do with your relationship. You have *got* to begin this week to get them out of the middle. You're not going to be able to do it *all* in one week, though.
Mr. Frank: I understand.

(Mrs. Frank nods her head quietly.)

Therapist (*firmly*):   But you'd better start now, because this can't go on. You might not work out what is going to happen to the two of you immediately, but your children have to start getting out of the middle. You have very, very good children who love you dearly. They care about you immensely, and they won't give up their jobs so quickly, so if you tell them, "I'm not going to employ you anymore," or "You don't have to protect me," you're going to find that they won't listen right away. (*To the mother:*) They are going to want to get in bed with you, they're going to want to hover around you and make sure you're okay, and your job for the next week is to convince them that you do not need their protection—that you won't fall apart without them. It won't be easy. (*To both parents:*) I want to see you next week, but I want to see you only on one condition, and that's that the two of you can begin in here to listen to each other. You have a week to think about whether you are able to do that. (*To the father:*) I don't want to see you again if you are going to think that she doesn't mean what she says in here and won't do what she says she will. (*To the mother:*) And the same goes for you. If you're not willing to listen to what he says and to what he says he will do, then I can't help you at all.

The therapist is declaring the children's protective function to be an active one, against which the parents will have to struggle. The important consideration in the formulation is that the children are defined as independent actors involved in "wanting" to rescue them.

The therapist tailors the feedback to address the specific way of interacting that characterizes the stalemate for this couple. She has observed that they don't listen to each other and that they are actively engaged in disqualifying each other. Of course, they are hungry for help for the children and are told that such help is contingent on restraint on their part. The therapist ends the session without permitting the parents to

discuss her observations,
so that the message will
not be diluted.

Reasons for the Stalemate

The nature of the stalemate here was different from that of our first family's stalemate. Unlike the Allens, who had tense but clear positions, this couple seemed incapable of establishing clear positions or receiving straightforward communication. The conversational circuits were routinely overloaded and communication became distorted, not allowing them to resolve anything. Although the husband appeared far more scared, confused, and out of touch with reality than did his wife, close analysis uncovered her part in sustaining his disorganization.

The husband was trying to detach himself from his wife while simultaneously hoping and trying to keep her. He regarded his effort to hold onto her as reasonable, even though the wife had made a clear decision to divorce. Their conversation revealed why the husband persisted in his hope for a reconciliation:

Mrs. Frank: I've been waiting for this appointment to come up. I felt that maybe he and I should have gone into marriage counseling before we put the children into this.

Therapist: Do you see any hope in your relationship?

Mr. Frank (*interrupting*): I've been married eleven years and we have it difficult, but still, I don't want my freedom. She wants her freedom.

Mrs. Frank: I don't want my freedom. I just can't live with you anymore, I can't put up with things. I think it will harm the children if we stay together.

The therapist was thoroughly confused by this interaction. Was the wife talking about marriage counseling because she wanted a reconciliation? When asked, she insisted that she definitely wanted a divorce and that she only mentioned marriage counseling because she thought a counselor could convince her husband that there was no future for the two of them.

For a fleeting moment, the therapist experienced the confusion in which the husband lived. The wife was unable to talk clearly to him. She had trouble taking a consistent position with him and making clear that she wanted a divorce. When she tried to do so, he would answer by becoming scattered, fearful, and incoherent, in such a way as to let her know, "Straight talk doesn't get through to me." The only way she could prevent him from becoming totally disorganized was to imply, "You can still have a piece of me, you can still have me around." It was as if she could move further away from him only by throwing consolation prizes at him, one of them being the possibility that she would get back together with him, if he allowed her this or that concession.

A cycle had started in which the husband became further confused and wondered whether there was a chance of reconciliation. Then his wife would indicate that she did not understand why he kept coming after her as if there were some hope, when she was trying to move away and get him out of her life. The husband naturally became exasperated at these confusing messages from her: "I love you, I don't love you; I'm leaving you, I'm not leaving you." At the same time, he had no awareness of how his odd and scared behavior was reciprocally organizing his wife's ambivalence. Eventually, as the man appeared crazier and crazier, the woman's response was more consistently, "I have to leave this crazy man." But she was still offering mixed messages. The more she tried to break away, the less the husband believed that she meant what she said, and the more he pursued her.

When one perceives the cycle from the standpoint of the husband's power, what is impressive is how his helplessness and confusion, once unleashed, compelled her to offer compromises, which in turn glued her more solidly into the cycle. As the wife's behavior became more openly and consciously deceptive in her efforts to placate him, he became more reactive and out of control.

Eroding the Stalemate: Shifting the Balance of Security

By the end of the second session, the wife's behavior had changed. While in the previous session she had seemed afraid to disagree openly with her husband, in the second session she managed to talk to him openly and clearly. Among many factors facilitating her change was the fact that her husband looked stronger, more put together, and better able to handle problems. He had gotten a lawyer and also had the support of the therapist, and he was now feeling protected; he was more coherent and less likely to become disorganized. Because of these changes, the wife felt freer to confront him in a less ambivalent way with the possibility of her leaving.

In the first session, one of the main objectives had been to lower the husband's anxiety level; the wife was asked to reassure him that she was not going to prevent him from seeing the children. But in meeting alone with the wife, the therapist had urged her to be assertive when the time seemed right. By the end of the second session, the time did seem right, and the wife was prepared both to talk straight and to reassure her husband.

The therapist's intervention facilitated this change in a number of ways. In meeting alone with her, the therapist asked the wife directly whether she thought her husband would fall apart. Such a question can be taken in two different ways: (1) The wife may feel that if the therapist is asking that question she is well aware of the possibility of its happening. The wife believes that if the husband falls apart, the therapist can handle it. (2) Conversely, the wife may feel that by asking that question the therapist is indicating that she does not think the husband will fall apart, that he is stronger than his wife has given him credit for. In either case, the intervention takes away the wife's excuse that she cannot act because he will fall apart.

The therapist talked to the wife directly about how she had been communicating with her husband. The therapist emphasized to her that none of her excessive pain, her enormous distress, or her justified complaints had been used in a constructive and pointed way to change her relationship with her husband. In her despair and her fear, she had been sounding like a wife who was staying, not one who was divorcing. She was uttering false reassurances and blurring the idea that she wished to terminate the relationship. About the only thing her husband could read between the lines accurately was that she might leave and take the children with her. While alone with the wife at the end of the second session, the therapist worked at unscrambling and reordering the messages and at giving her guidelines for relating to her husband differently. The assumption was that clear messages from her would stabilize her husband, whereas her confusing messages had further disorganized him.

Therapist: Do you understand what it is that you have to do in the next week?
Mrs. Frank: No.

Therapist: Okay, let me say it again. I want you to listen very carefully. A lot hinges on this, okay? You have to talk like a divorcing woman. No marriage counseling mentioned! *Nothing* that will give him any hope. You have to talk as if you mean it, to your lawyer and to him, when it has to do with his access to the children—that you want him to remain their father and that you can't imagine it being any other way. And you have to try to protect those children. Okay?

Checking for Hardening and Polarization

Parents in the divorce crisis situation can feel so totally defenseless that they may have the impulse to snatch a child away before the child is snatched from them. In this context, going for full custody is a desperate move that can lead to further escalation and polarization; the other parent retrenches, demanding full custody while fearing kidnapping.

In the second session with the Franks, the father signaled a hardening of his position, dropping cryptic remarks about a state where fathers were more often given custody. The implication was that he planned to run off with one of his children, and in talking alone with the therapist he admitted that he had decided to fight to get custody of his son. The basic diagnostic question was whether the father's intention of seeking custody was arrived at thoughtfully. To what extent did it have to do with the children's well-being, and to what extent was it an attempt to prevail over his wife? It was clear to the therapist that what he really wanted, aside from getting his wife back, was liberal access to his young children. He often stated that his wife was a good mother, and in fact he wanted her to give up her part-time job so she could have more time with the children. It was his fear of having the children removed that caused him to try to use custody vindic-tively against his wife. Whenever the issue of custody is used in this way, the therapist does best to help the parents examine—relentlessly and crit-ically—the decision to seek custody, siding with the best interests of the children, unafraid to wind up supporting one parent.

Fighting for custody receded as a major issue for the Franks, but the separation stalemate continued. When a stalemate continues and the therapist is defeated, the defeat can usually be turned to therapeutic profit. The therapist throws in the towel, letting both parents know that it is now up to them to find a solution. The power of the stalemate quickly becomes evident to the participants themselves.

Having lost the expert after an obviously grueling try on her part, Mr. Frank initiated a very open, frank dialogue with his wife, in which she reassured him that if she got custody he would have access to the children. In this dialogue, Mrs. Frank confronted her husband directly with everything she previously had been unable to say. Eye to eye, pointing her finger at him, she looked assertive and no longer afraid that he would fall apart. At times she encountered his usual defense of jumping from one topic to another. When faced with this tactic, the wife stopped the conversation and said, "Wait a moment. Did you get it? Is that clear?" Only when she got a clear-cut acknowledgment that there *was* understanding and closure would she accept a shift of topics. This was a very impressive moment. It displayed how well the woman knew her husband and how this knowledge had not been used constructively until then.

The following truce-seeking dialogue took place after the therapist left the room:

Mr. Frank (*to therapist as they are leaving the session*):   Could I talk to my wife for a second?
Therapist: Sure, we're finished, and the room is free for ten minutes. The video may still be running.

(*The couple goes back into the room.*)

Mr. Frank: Can we talk? Every time we're talking the kids are always there. It's the first time we're by ourselves in a long time, right?
Mrs. Frank: Uh huh.

The structuring of the interaction without the children's protective interference is crucial. The children have always been there because they were bodyguarding and because the parents felt they could talk only with the children there.

Mr. Frank: Want to have a truce?
Mrs. Frank (*suspiciously*):   What do you mean, a truce?

Mr. Frank: I know now our marriage is shot, okay? I realize that now (*sad and nostalgically*). I know you don't love me anymore. I loved you, Doris.

Mrs. Frank: I loved you, too.

The mourning process is about to begin but is quickly interrupted by the husband, who fears that he might be carried away by overwhelming emotions and thus lose sight of his task.

Mr. Frank (*abruptly*):   Okay, it's over.

Mrs. Frank: It's over. I loved you too much, and I told you that.

Mr. Frank: Until the divorce comes, let's be friends, okay, because if we're enemies to each other. . . .

Mrs. Frank: I tried to be nice, but you would sit there and harass me, stay in the kitchen, follow me around and harass me. How could I be friendly with you when you were doing these things to me? I accepted that you moved back in, fine. What was I going to do about it? But I didn't need you harassing me.

Mr. Frank: Is that why you got the court order?

Mrs. Frank: What do you think? You came knocking on the bedroom door, threatening me.

Mr. Frank (*emphatically*):   I didn't threaten you!

Mrs. Frank: Yes, you did! Yes, you did! You can't remember.

Mr. Frank: All I said was that I was going to turn you in.

Mrs. Frank: No, you didn't . . . not that night. You were looking for papers and I didn't know what papers you were talking about.

Mr. Frank: My mail.

Mrs. Frank: No, you weren't. Your mail was coming to the house then. You were

He returns to a more task-oriented tone.

On his returning right after an escape attempt, the wife feels increasingly harassed and tense.

In a rupturing marriage there are so many grievances and unsettled accounts that a runaway fight can start at any moment.

An old pattern in the relationship, in which she acted as his portable memory, like the reminding mother, now fosters trouble. He was looking for bills or something. You don't even remember.

Mr. Frank: Oh, the bank statements.

Mrs. Frank: You were looking for papers and I didn't even know what you were talking about and you started in on me.

Mr. Frank (*beseechingly*): All right, from now on.

Mrs. Frank: And you harassed me.

Mr. Frank (*angrily*): And you harassed me.

Mrs. Frank: I didn't say anything, but when you started I had to defend myself. Didn't I?

Mr. Frank: Okay, okay. We'll have a truce until we get a divorce. If we're enemies, then I'm going to get everything I can and you're going to get everything you can.

Mrs. Frank: I'm not looking at it like that.

Mr. Frank: Well, that's what it's going to come down to. You told me that you want the house, you want me to pay the mortgage, you want me to do this and that.

Mrs. Frank: I'll live there with the children.

Mr. Frank: Huh?

Mrs. Frank: I'll live there with the children.

Mr. Frank: But it doesn't work that way.

Mrs. Frank: This is not for us to decide. You say what you want and I'll say what I want . . . because we're going to end up arguing and I'm not going to argue anymore.

angry because he couldn't find his papers and he felt entitled to her help. She was supposed to be available and to anticipate his needs.

The husband's "I'm going to get everything I can" is straight from the therapist, from their private preparatory session. While he finds it difficult to maintain the task-oriented process, he works to get back on track. This entails restraining himself from bringing up any material that might make them slip into being struggling adversaries again.

They are struggling with what they can decide and what they must leave to a higher authority. They begin to use the appeal to a higher authority as a way to control their fighting.

In the next segment, the wife tries to break down her husband's very frightening belief system, which is rooted in actual experiences in his peer network—family and friends in the surrounding community who had indeed been fleeced by their wives during their own divorces. According to the husband, these men had been "taken to the cleaners," and they had convinced him that this inevitably would happen to him. The wife understands this very well, and when trying to break her husband's negative trance-like stance she tells him, "Don't listen to your brother, don't listen to all these men who have been taken to the cleaners. We're other people." She also draws on their mutual memories of happier years, saying, "How can you not trust me? We lived together for so long." Elevating the discussion above petty quarreling, she uses her best resources, resources the therapist had not realized she had:

Mrs. Frank: I know Bill. I know what
they said to you.

(*Mr. Frank laughs.*)

Mrs. Frank: If you can't trust me after all
these years, divorce or no divorce, that's
the problem with you, because I told you
everything, every little thing we did that
day. We went here. I spent this and I spent
that. I was honest with you, and I think
that's what ruined it. I'm not Lotty and
Pete and I'm not Dan and neither are you
and I'm not their friend Mike and the
other guy who was taken to the cleaners or
the other guy. We're different people! Do
we have money? We don't have any
money, and I'm not going to take you for
everything you have. What do you have?
Nothing. All we have is the house, that's
all we have. That's all we own. I'm not out
for money. I'm not out for nothing. Do
you understand what I'm saying?
Mr. Frank: I understand right now. Let's
have a truce, okay?
Mrs. Frank: Besides that, do you   She does not let him
understand what I'm saying about those   change the subject until he
people . . . like your brother Stanley? Our   acknowledges that he has
circumstances aren't like that, because   heard her.
whatever comes of this, I am hoping I will
get the children, but until the papers are

drawn up properly we won't know. Your
brother just took off. He didn't care about
the children.

When reassuring her husband about the children, the wife kept meeting
his eyes and saying, "You can have them on weekends, you can have them
mornings, in the middle of the week. . . ." Through the repetition of this
point, she in effect countered his negative mindset by trying to persuade
him to get his head together and think for himself. One could almost hear
the man's sigh of relief as he came to believe her.

The wife's efforts were in line with the therapist's instructions of just a
few minutes earlier. By reassuring her husband that she would never steal
the children from him, she allowed the productive process to continue:

Mr. Frank: What about my kids?
Mrs. Frank: When you'll see them and
all?
Mr. Frank: What days will I see the kids?
Mrs. Frank: During the week . . .
Sundays, Saturdays too, if you want.
Mr. Frank: The reason I got scared was
that you weren't bringing the kids home
when you said you would.
Mrs. Frank: You mean the time I was
going over to my mother's. Come on, Mac,
you know me better than that. And the
kids called you that afternoon, too.
Mr. Frank: Yeah, late.
Mrs. Frank: No, they didn't. They called
on Thursday. It was 6:30. I'm not them.
I'm not those people. You have to
remember that we're not them—not only
me, but you, too.

She must keep repeating
that they are different
from the people who have
been talking to him, or he
snaps back to his previous
way of thinking. As he
offers a truce, she accepts
on the condition that he
stops harassing her. The
process of hard
negotiation can begin
because she is clear on
what they want as
concessions—he ostensibly

a truce, and she the immediate cessation of harassment.

Mr. Frank: For now, let's have a truce about arguing in front of them.

Mrs. Frank: All I'm asking is that you stop harassing me like you've been doing. That wasn't right. It wasn't fair.

Mr. Frank: Look at us. Look at us, Doris. I'm ready for the mental hospital, and you're one step behind me. I can't sleep at night. I can't even work.

He is changing the subject. He is saying, "We are in a desperate state. We're ready for the mental hospital."

Mrs. Frank: How do you think I feel when I'm over there [at the day care center] with those children? My mind has to be on those children, they're my responsibility. How do you think I feel? Then I think of my kids someday having to go to something like that. That's why I'm thankful I have this little job, so that they can be with me.

Mr. Frank: From now on, if I'm home and ask for them, can I have them?

Mrs. Frank: If you have them home at the right time when I get home for dinner. We have activities going on over there . . . each day they do something and Sam loves this because there's another little boy there his age and there's Jim and there's. . . .

She accepts the truce and reassures him, but clearly gives the conditions, which he needs in order to control his behavior. He will know now when it is appropriate for him to ask for the children and when his wife is likely to refuse. These conditions and limits will prevent him from personalizing a refusal and from seeing it as yet another arbitrary instance of keeping the children from him. Even then, the tendency will be for him to see her as

Mr. Frank: He says he loves to be with me, too!

Mrs. Frank: Yeah, I know that, but there are activities going on and I would like him to be there, involved with the activities. When they have the special arts and crafts, he loves that. I'm not stopping them from seeing you.

Mr. Frank: You sounded like you were.

Mrs. Frank (*jumping back at him, as if caught in the act*): What did you do to me? Okay? Think about the things you did to me. How you followed me around the house, okay? How you . . . think of what you did to me, okay? I didn't ask Jenny what you talked about or what's going on. I didn't ask her questions, I didn't. I know *you* did. You had to, because of what she said to me. You had to, okay? Because what she asked me had to come from you, because she never would have thought. . . .

preventing him from seeing his children, as in his remark, "You sounded like you were." It takes very little to threaten him. The mother's position here is reasonably organized around respect for the children's needs, yet he feels it is another attempt to block him. The wife is not without guilt, because in the past she has kept the children from him out of spite. Thus she flares up and counterattacks. Notice that she uses his pumping the children as her point of attack, an area where he too is guilty. Now they are really sparring.

Mr. Frank: Are you going to stay at your mother's this Saturday?

Mrs. Frank: Saturday we're going to have a lawn sale, so we're going to be there Saturday.

Mr. Frank: Are you coming home Saturday night?

The wife's counterattack mixes with the effects of his preparation session with the therapist. He decides not to respond to her, instead ending the fight. His main concern is knowing where the kids are so he can get to see them.

Mrs. Frank: Yeah, but we're going up there all day, all right?

Mr. Frank: Are you working the dinner Saturday night at school?

Mrs. Frank: Yeah. Let's go. I have a job to go back to. We can sit and talk again.

(*They walk out.*)

The couple's dialogue displayed some tangible accomplishments. They were able to talk to each other for the first time in a relatively clear way; they engaged in honest problem solving about the husband's wish to have access to the children; and the wife communicated her demand not to be harassed.

Their pattern of pulling surprises, even after some minor accomplishments, is typical of the difficult separation process. The noble effort on the wife's part to reassure her husband, and on his part to attempt a truce, had useful but short-lived results. By the end of the third session, the pattern of agitation and confusion had reasserted itself. Through her lawyer, the wife was again threatening her husband with an injunction, this time for mental harassment. The husband was being encouraged by his lawyer to fight for custody of both children as the only way to win custody of his son. And while the couple had agreed that they wanted to sell their house and split the profits, they were making no moves toward either that or the separation.

The therapist faced these developments by declaring defeat. She ended the session, telling the couple not to come back unless they were willing to do certain things: straighten things out with their lawyers, settle on a custody arrangement that would protect their children, and agree on a date for selling the house.

One week later, the therapist received a call from the mother, who was about to make another provocative and confusing move. She had decided to move out with the children and only later let her husband know where she had gone. In an extended phone conversation, the therapist struggled to persuade the mother to act differently. Had she pulled that surprise, her husband's notion that the children were being taken from him would have been confirmed, and inevitably would have led to a counterattack. The therapist warned the mother that if she moved first and two days later sent an explanatory letter, she would really be provoking her husband into an explosive reaction. The man owned a gun and had already left bullets in ashtrays for the children to find, in a kind of "unconscious" intimidating communication. It appeared that the wife was constructing a scenario in which the husband would act crazy and violent, so that when the time came for legal decisions, she could present herself to the authorities as the appropriate custodial parent.

To head off this turn of events, the therapist further recommended that Mrs. Frank write letters to her husband and her lawyer, saying that she was moving to her mother's house but that her husband should not think for a minute that she was planning to keep the children from him. The therapist even suggested that the husband was sufficiently rational that he might help her move.

Postseparation Work

The success or failure in adapting to divorce in a three-generational family can be displayed in the grandparents' manner of welcome and way of supporting the second generation during their return home from a failed marriage. In the healthy three-generational family, the welcome tends to be temporary and incomplete, not encouraging a permanent stay. Mrs. Frank's parents welcomed her into their home and offered her a sense of security and protection (she talked as though she had three bodyguards—her mother, her father, and her brother). Still, her parents were sending her some clear messages that she could not stay there permanently. Her father, for example, was recuperating from an illness and was not pleased to have the children running up and down the stairs.

With the separation, the children's fears of being kidnapped increased. In attempting to control the fears, the therapist held sessions with the eager, possessive father (the one feared) and the children. In these sessions, the father reassured his children that when he took them back to his house, they did not need to fear that he would keep them forever. But the therapist needed to work on the way the wife was fueling the fire by signaling the children that their father's house was a special place of danger. The therapist sought both to calm the wife's fears and to encourage her to help the husband act in a less crazy and frightening fashion. The wife was applauded for anything she did that reassured her husband that the children would not be taken away from him. Together, the therapist and the wife thought of numerous ways in which the wife could tell her husband that she wanted him to have access to the children. Mrs. Frank was reminded again and again that it was to her advantage that the children be more comfortable with their father.

The therapist also tried to ensure that there were boundaries between what the children could and could not hear. The children knew that the relationship between their parents was a volatile one and that their parents were doing all sorts of odd things behind each other's backs, so they pursued their mother and father when the two were talking. Eavesdropping, they managed to overhear bits of incomplete and scary information. For example, the mother had not told them directly that their father would kidnap them, but they overheard her talking to him about this on the phone. The therapist stressed the importance of the mother not allowing herself to be overheard by the children when discussing certain topics.

The Allens' preseparation problems, discussed in the previous chapter, were resolved without excessive involvement from their social network. Their respective clans remained in the background, avoided making open, explicit coalitions during the couple's tug-of-war, and did not embroil themselves overprotectively with the children. With the Franks, however, this was not the case. Here, the families actively took sides, fanning the fire between the husband and the wife. When all else had been tried, the therapist asked the members of both sides of the family to join in a session. This move is reserved for couples whose problems are so enmeshed with the social network, particularly with their parents, that it becomes important to bring the others in. In these families, the pair cannot avoid the effects on their own relationship of their relatives, in-laws, lawyers, and friends. In such cases, what happens between the couple and members of their social network can be so intertwined with their own doings that clarification of boundaries between them must receive the highest priority.

We do not assume, however, that a rift between the couple must inevitably be reflected in rifts at other levels of the family's hierarchy. Generally we find that a three-generational system can actually have fairly innocuous and noncoalitionary participation from in-laws, even when at its center is a seriously conflicted couple. Thus we prefer to operate as if the troubled couple is not necessarily caught in divisive patterns that reflect the divisiveness between the two sets of in-laws—that is that the couple's relationship is not necessarily isomorphic to a positive or negative relationship with the spouses' social networks. A collaborative and friendly set of grandparents who reach out to each other and to the couple can be found. An overemphasis on hierarchical isomorphism can lead the therapist to ignore the importance of the permeability of the boundaries through which the network is constituted.

The session with the Frank families, however, revealed that the warring clans were very involved. They immediately went at each other's throats, yelling accusations. The marital couple sat quietly as their respective families battled it out. The wife's mother accused her son-in-law of being an alcoholic and of not bringing the children back on time after visitation. The husband's father accused his daughter-in-law of having undermined the children's relationship with their father even during the marriage. The antagonisms went back a long way, and in working with the two excited groups the therapist was able to achieve little in the way of resolution, except that the battle lines were drawn even tighter, clarifying for the couple the boundaries of the two systems that were indeed involved in pathologic overlap.

There are those who would argue that if this session with the whole network had been held much earlier, the resolution would have come sooner and the therapy would have been briefer. We think differently. Our idea of the proper timing for such an approach is generally conservative. We prefer that the couple have a chance to try on their own and stretch their own resources before involving relatives in therapy sessions. The aim is to have the couple first recognize their ability or inability to defend themselves against their relatives' "help." If this is to happen, the reorganizational effort should, if possible, not violate or circumvent the husband's and wife's attempts, however beleaguered, to stand on their own two feet as a relatively self-sufficient subsystem. Though it is true that divorce entails the split between the two larger systems, first and foremost the split involves two people.

In spite of—or maybe because of—this opportune proliferation and diffusion of the war, which spreads from the couple into the clans and locks in there, the Franks soon afterward appeared to be in far better shape. After the separation, the husband continued to improve his self-presentation. Within two weeks after the separation, he came to the follow-up appointment speaking with complete clarity and looking as though he had begun to take care of himself physically. He despaired less about being alone and in fact found a men's organization through which he had made friends—this time not his brother or neighborhood pals, who could not commiserate with him without agitating him about the problems he was having with his children. Though he was hardly free from the influence of his family, his new friendships enabled him to gain some perspective on the advice he was getting from his brother and the rest of his family. He was still worried that his wife would sabotage his relationship with the children, but he was not obsessed with this and was adhering to the visitation schedule. In addition he was open to finding ways of countering the children's fears of being kidnapped.

The wife, while still highly suspicious of her husband, had not cut the children off from him. Though under stress herself, at the follow-up interview she appeared physically healthy for the first time since treatment had begun. She reported that Jennifer's teacher had remarked that for the first time in weeks the child seemed much less tense.

Conclusion

We have seen how two families dealt with the difficult decision of separating while in some ways wanting to stay together. We have looked at how participants in the deadlocked preseparation situation used lawyers, how their own personal resources came into play, and to what extent they penalized the children. In the family discussed in the previous chapter, further stagnation was averted, and additional rounds of tension and physical violence were eliminated. In the family discussed in this chapter, the possibility of the crisis turning into serious violence was curtailed. Given the husband's anger at his wife, his feeling of total helplessness, and the presence of a gun, it is easy to imagine that in an impulsive moment, perhaps after drinking too much, he might have used this weapon. The therapy offered a reliable arena for sober problem solving and self-restraint, permitting each partner to stand up against the other and against the larger forces of their social network. New boundaries were established. They moved as a couple past the crisis stage to a difficult but livable postseparation situation.

4

Warring Couples: Sporadic and Scared Fighters

COUPLES can get so entrenched in combat positions that even well after they physically separate, often years after, they have not truly split. Their fighting acts as the glue. The husband and wife set out to engage in productive dialogue that will allow them to separate, but find themselves drawn into automatic escalations of fighting. These couples generally find their way to the helping professions when their children become sufficiently symptomatic to come to the attention of higher authorities in the school, or when their own pain and that of the children impel a judge to mandate an immediate referral.

Therapy with such couples involves a built-in dilemma. In facilitating concession making between two people, we may be misjudging the bargaining power of each partner. For example, a wife may appear to have presented her needs and defended her rights adequately, when actually she has been too yielding, sacrificing her best interests in exchange for an immediate agreement and a release from the tense situation. It is not unusual for a therapist to find that the person who looks weak is actually controlling the person who looks tough, or that they take turns being weak and tough. We therefore compensate by being skeptical of agreements, not buying an agreement and holding the couple to live up to it without first making sure that they both feel that their best interests are being served. If we are wrong in assessing negotiations and accept an inequitable settlement, we help freeze a bad situation that in the long run proves to be no settlement at all. If one partner has second thoughts, the emotional turmoil, sabotage, and detouring of conflict through the children may begin anew.

Therapists often assume that both partners in a warring couple have equal bargaining power and an equal capacity to survive the split. But this underlying assumption of justice and symmetry can become a pitfall. It is precisely our freedom to *not* be neutral, to be skeptical of pseudoresolutions, that allows us to be therapeutic with conflicting couples.

After repeated bouts of combat, couples differentiate into at least two clinical types: those who tend to avoid direct contact with each other, and those who engage in frequent above-board fighting. In both types, the partners make unilateral moves and communicate with each other through the children, specifically through unshared decisions about the youngsters and concomitant or subsequent battles about visitation.

The first type can be characterized as sporadic and scared fighters. Their behavior can be understood developmentally as a cycle: the couple becomes heated up over unresolved issues and, after long periods of repeated clashes, understandably choose to avoid each other. They have fought and failed, and they decide not to fight. They avoid direct communication with each other for fear of igniting the unproductive, escalating type of fighting to which they have grown accustomed, but they have periodic collisions. They are held together in a tense and unsatisfactory status quo from which they perceive any effort toward increased communication as carrying the threat of more futile fighting.

The second type can be characterized as frequent and direct fighters. Rather than colliding sporadically and then going into hiding, and working on each other only indirectly through the children, they seem to thrive on the very process of chronic frontal fighting.

When dealing with both types, the therapist is usually working with an easily overheated situation. To make constructive dialogue possible again, the therapist must do more than just bring the couple together in the hope that on their own they will find some new manner of negotiating. If the two are simply encouraged to enact their feelings, there will be either fast short circuits or runaway fights with "blood on the walls." The result will be more hurt feelings, for some a silent intention to avoid each other forever, and a conviction that no outside expert can help them. To deal with such a situation, we employ variations on an elementary four-stage procedure which consists of individual preparation of each participant, the encounter, evaluation of the encounter, and new attempts at dialogue. The therapy is centered on the couple as the heart of the family. Parents and children are brought together when necessary, to coordinate and test changes, but the basic work is with the couple.

In the family presented in this chapter, the sporadic fighting is ostensibly propelled by identifiable unilateral decisions, particularly decisions concerning the children's schooling. Here, the utilization of the procedure is almost straightforward. In the next chapter, a family of the second type is presented. Their conflict is characterized by constant squirmishes, particularly around visitation, that obscure the issues and make it more difficult to identify the one who is making the decisions. In that case, more elaborate and forceful techniques had to be summoned to dislodge the couple from their entrenched fighting positions.

Stage One: Someone in Your Corner

The first step is for the therapist to secure the trust of each participant. To interrupt the cycle of clashes and avoidance, the therapist works from the part to the whole. Each participant is dealt with separately until both are ready for interaction with each other. The purpose of this stage is to ensure that each person feels he or she has an advocate in the therapist, trusts the therapist, and has given thought to the themes they want discussed when they meet as spouses. The therapist's job in these individual sessions is, in fact, largely to anticipate themes through which the participants can begin to talk. The themes chosen should be likely to lead to some productive dialogue and must therefore emerge from pressing issues.

The Trezano couple had been separated for eight months when the mother decided on her own that it would be to everybody's advantage if the two teen-age children went to a boarding school in a different part of the state. Their home was in a poor and dangerous neighborhood, and her low income made the children eligible for enrollment in a state-funded boarding school that had an excellent academic reputation. Removing the youngsters from their immediate surroundings meant, of course, interfering with the father's visitation. Clearly, the mother was proposing a big change not only for the youngsters but also for herself and her husband. She did not want to bring up the matter with her husband, however, and was about to take unilateral action.

Mrs. Trezano's decision perpetuated a pattern of conflict avoidance that

promised to produce a severe collision. The Trezanos had entered a prolonged period of brittle avoidance after rounds of explosive physical fights.
These fights ended and the avoidance began after Mr. Trezano called the
police on an enraged Mrs. Trezano, who had raided and ransacked his
apartment, looking for her husband's girlfriend. Their frail and bitter peace
was having obvious consequences. One child was in psychosomatic distress,
presenting with severe stomach pains that had no organic origin, and the
other child was full of escape fantasies, while Mr. and Mrs. Trezano lived
in constant fear of facing each other. Mrs. Trezano was preoccupied with
fears that she was being followed and spied on.

Mrs. Trezano initiated treatment. To motivate Mrs. Trezano to bring up
with her husband the subject of the youngsters going upstate, the therapist
calmly stressed that it would be in her own best interest to include him in
the decision. There were several reasons for advocating the husband's involvement. For one, if the boarding school officials learned that the mother
had sent the children without her husband's consent, they would be likely
to have doubts about the nature of the parental agreement behind the
choice of school. The youngsters, moreover, knowing that both parents
were not behind the decision, could exploit the disagreement if they did
not like the school. It might be easier for the children to get themselves
expelled, defeating the mother's and perhaps fulfilling the father's expectation that the children would support him because he had been left out
of the decision.

The process of preparing each participant before the couple enters a
controlled encounter involves more than motivating the participants and
finding a likely theme around which to promote dialogue. It also involves
working on fear reduction while developing readiness for confrontation.
To press Mrs. Trezano beyond her unwillingness to discuss the issue with
her husband, the therapist dealt with her fears. Her overwhelming fear
was that she might cave in to him and he would be successful in controlling
her. She felt vulnerable with him and feared being exploited. Throughout,
the emphasis was on upholding her defenses, on how she must change
strictly on the rational merits of the situation and not because she might
be yielding to her husband. In the following segment, Mrs. Trezano stead-
fastly resists the idea of a joint meeting with her husband. The therapist
has suggested that it would be better for the youngsters and the school if
Mr. Trezano was in on the decision.

Mrs. Trezano (*interrupting*):   He does
know! He doesn't like the idea.
Therapist: Oh, you two have spoken?

Mrs. Trezano (*shaking her head*): No. The children spoke to him.

Therapist (*interrupting firmly*): No. This is a parental affair. (*Therapist sweeps his hand back and forth.*)

By sweeping his hand back and forth between her chair and the one where the husband would be seated, the therapist visually conveys his strong bias toward creating a new pathway direct from her to him and not through the children.

Mrs. Trezano: Look, I will do for the children whatever is necessary. But there are a lot of things that he and I are not going to agree on, did not agree on when we were together, and will not agree on. And now that I have the ability I will do whatever I think is best, disregarding totally how he feels about it.

Therapist (*calmly*): Well, I think that you will. That's true. But he needs to be able to ask some questions about the boarding school.

The mother is reassured in this way that she is not about to be compelled to do as the therapist says, that she is entitled to disagree. Her boundaries and defenses are respected before she is asked to attend to her husband. As she "disregards totally" the husband's feelings, the therapist regards him by saying, "He needs to be able to. . . ."

Mrs. Trezano: Well, he'll have his opportunity to talk to the person in charge there, I'm sure. I do believe they will contact him. I gave them his address.

Therapist: Dina, you're playing this so defensive and scared.

Mrs. Trezano (*loudly*): I'm not scared and not defensive. I'm adamant.

Therapist: Hang on. Excuse me. (*He pauses, then says quickly, sympathetically:*) Let me say, this is not a useful way of thinking about it and not a decent way for the kids, who get caught in the middle.

The therapist resists and pleads with her, "Let go of the defenses for a moment."

Mrs. Trezano (*arguing and interrupting*): But it's a lot better than it has been. It . . .
Therapist (*interrupting*): Hang on. You don't have to convince me of that. I know that.
Mrs. Trezano: So you can't expect me to go from one extreme to the other (*she moves her hands from wide apart to intertwined*) just like that.
Therapist: What extreme are you talking about? I'm not saying you guys have to be friendly.
Mrs. Trezano (*interrupting the therapist*): The extreme of total noncommunication. No cooperation at all. To just smooth as pie, talking, blah, blah, blah.
Therapist: I'm not talking about that at all. I'm talking about having a meeting together. Maybe having a fifteen-minute session, or a ten-minute session, where he can ask you some simple things about the school. Where is it? What is it? And that's it. If it gets too unpleasant, I don't want to sit here, I don't want to put you through it, we stop.

The therapist must forcefully defend himself from being put in the position of expecting an impossible leap. He transforms what the mother thinks is an extreme expectation, that she be friendly, into a simple task—a ten- or fifteen-minute meeting. The comment dispels her fear that she will be forced to be friendly in a discontinuous leap. Sensing her anxiety, the therapist makes the request manageable and flexible. Indeed he lessens the time requirement from fifteen to ten, and later to five minutes, around "simple questions." In the end she is given total control over the ultimate decision to stop. This is not a ploy. Had she not been ready, the therapist would have proceeded as if employing a desensitizing hierarchy of stimuli and retreated to what was manageable.

Mrs. Trezano (*interrupting*): It is unpleasant, the very thought of it.
Therapist: Of course.
Mrs. Trezano: I'm not ready for it, not now, maybe later. And let me tell you. . . .

(*She changes the subject completely.*)

Therapist: Hang on. Would it really be that tough for you?

Mrs. Trezano: Yes, it would.

Therapist: Are you sure, or is this something that you could have built up in your head?

Mrs. Trezano: Yes, I avoid my husband, period. The phone. . . .

Therapist: Why would it be so tough?

Mrs. Trezano: Because there is still a lot of anger.

Therapist: Of course, I would not expect otherwise.

Mrs. Trezano: And now I'm not ready. I want the severance of the marriage, and then I can deal with him as a separate person.

Therapist: Am I misreading you?

Mrs. Trezano: What?

Therapist: Do I think you're stronger than you really are?

Mrs. Trezano (*momentarily confused*): I don't know. I don't know how strong I really am.

Therapist: Well, you're saying you're not strong.

From now on, the quality most demanded of the therapist is flexibility and tenacity. He sticks by his task as she tries to shake him off.

The question here puzzles her, because it appeals to her official presentation of self. When scared she usually presents bravado and strength, then thinks that people have been pushing her to appear stronger than she feels.

Mrs. Trezano: I'm avoiding unpleasantness.

Therapist: Yes, coming together with an ex is never fun, but couples do it all the time for five, ten minutes.

She denies that she is not brave. The therapist's comment normalizes and renders commonplace the dreaded task.

Mrs. Trezano: We will eventually.

This is a first yield.

Therapist (*sarcastically*): Eventually, in three or five years, when for the kids, who are in the middle now, it's too late. . . .

The procrastination and postponement manipulations are

Mrs. Trezano (*softening, calming*):   Hey, I can do it. I *can* do anything.
Therapist (*quickly, supportively*):   I think you can too.

addressed through sarcasm. She is particularly vulnerable to this move, because she must constantly and defensively prove she is strong. Perceiving the shift, the therapist supports her.

Mrs. Trezano: I just don't prefer to do certain things. And I don't *have* to, I don't.
Therapist (*interrupting*):   Let me come in on that. You don't *have* to do it. (*Softly:*) You don't have to do anything. I honestly think, having got to know you very well and the kids well, and Frank a little bit, that it would be very useful. If the school knew you and he were not talking, there might be a problem. For you and him to talk won't be any big deal. I'll keep tight control of it and would suggest with you that we have some sort of a signal that if it's not going well. . . .
Mrs. Trezano: I'll get up and go and smoke me a cigarette. . . . (*Prolonged pause.*) Okay, we can give it a try. I mean this is really not my thing. I'd prefer not to be bothered by it. But I'll do it.
Therapist: I'll tell you, I think the kids would appreciate it a lot.
Mrs. Trezano: Mmm. Maybe they will.

The wife must be supported very specifically around the notion that she *is* a free agent. She is not being forced; she is choosing. The therapist would of course lose all leverage if he insisted, "You have to." The therapist offers support, making clear that he will monitor any possibilities of excessive conflict.

A good preparation entails getting both the parents and the therapist ready for the encounter. In view of the mother's anxiety, the therapist suggests a simulation, so that she can bring out her worst fantasies about the forthcoming encounter and so that the therapist can be equipped to deal with them. The therapist, knowing the father's priority, plays out precisely the father's concern:

Therapist: Listen, just for rehearsal's sake, let me pretend I'm him.

The benevolent friend (i.e., the therapist) is

Mrs. Trezano: Okay, and I can be no one else but me.
(*They both laugh, releasing tension.*)
Therapist: And let's go through some things, and you must help me, some things he might want to ask or say.
Mrs. Trezano: Okay.
Therapist: The first is, hey, what about this boarding school thing? I've heard it from the kids. What's it about?
Mrs. Trezano: Okay, I heard. . . .

transformed into the adversarial husband. She is allowed to become no one else but "rigid me," thereby maintaining control while helping the "husband."

In the next session alone with the father, the therapist helped him face his wife without excessive fear. The father needed to be similarly reassured that the therapist would keep negotiations centered on prearranged themes and would be in control of the discussion.

Stage Two: Trying It Out

The work of the participants when they are brought together is Stage Two. The therapist approaches this stage in full awareness that if the participants could have resolved their conflicts simply by getting together and fighting, they would have done so by now. Naturally some fighting will occur, and the therapist, acting as advocate and/or referee, will have to intervene. When doing so, the therapist attempts to deflect or redefine the attack, to modulate its intensity instead of forcing the couple to enact their deepest conflicts with each other. Often the therapist becomes the momentary advocate of the participant most under duress, the one most likely to flee or explode out of fear that the other will be implacable and will prevail. For example, in Stage Two with the Trezanos, the wife, feeling very depressed and vulnerable, accused her husband of wanting only to curtail her autonomy. The therapist, seeing that this attack could short-circuit the transaction, reacted and inserted himself between them.

When the participants are involved in patterns of intimidation and subordination, the general principle is for the therapist to feel free to side with one of them and, if necessary, work directly as an advocate for that person. In the past it has been customary to refrain from forming coalitions, in the belief that this fosters patterns of dependence on the therapist that cripples the participant in later conflicts with the former spouse. In our experience with fiery, conflictual couples, however, it is often the only way to proceed. The therapist must be ready to stand up for one person until that person can muster the appropriate attitude and strength to deal directly with the former spouse.

The therapist establishes an even-handed and fair image so that he or she will have the freedom to stay longer on one side, in order to promote therapeutic tension and new developments. The therapist may intercept and handle a devastating communication from one spouse to the other, allowing the shielded spouse time to muster the resolve to take on later conflicts directly. The therapist must be ready to step in and to become the butt of one participant's anger, to buffer the impact of an overwhelming assault on the weaker one.

Of course, this way of working can misfire if the therapist simply steps in, takes over for a spouse who cannot handle an assault, and then leaves that spouse in the same emotional shape as at the beginning of the inter-action. The therapist must know when to step out as well as when to step in, and in stepping out must be sure to leave the shielded spouse feeling stronger and more confident. In the extended segments that follow, the Trezanos have a conflict-filled moment early in their encounter, and the therapist quickly steps in.

Mr. Trezano (*urgently, almost pleading*):
All I want to know is, in the future, that's all, when things come up concerning the kids as far as their health is concerned and education, overall welfare, would it be possible that I be informed, because you see . . .

Mrs. Trezano (*interrupting*): But you've already said you have confidence in me concerning those things.	This comment is forcefully and snappily made, jolting the husband.
Mr. Trezano: But the point is I'm being left out (*he indicates with his hands being pushed aside*). Tell me what is happening?	He is becoming increasingly defensive.
Mrs. Trezano (*intimidatingly*): But that's between you and the children. I'm not going to consult you. That's a statement.	She reverts to favoring a triangular pathway: he has to get to her through the children.
Therapist (*calmly*): No, Dina. Hang on. No. The two of you are sort of agreeing.	To prevent the husband's retreat, the therapist offers

Frank is simply saying (*he slowly leans forward to engage the mother more intensively, excluding the father*) that for important issues around the kids . . .
Mr. Trezano (*interrupting*):   That's all.

Therapist: He would like to be informed. And you, too, said that for important issues around the kids you'd like to discuss it with Frank. You said that's important.
Mrs. Trezano (*turning to the therapist*): Hold on. I see absolutely no reason to talk with Frank about the children because the children can communicate to you (*she points aggressively at her husband*) whatever is necessary.
Therapist (*interrupting and indicating with his hands for the mother to talk to him, not to her husband*):   No. If I can correct you on that.
Mrs. Trezano: I don't choose to be corrected on that, because that's the way I feel.
Therapist: Yes, around the kids, it is important that the two of you, on important issues, touch base with each other. That is important.
Mrs. Trezano (*interrupts*):   I think that will be done through an intermediary or the kids.
Therapist: Well, that might be. You might not be up to it, the two of you, to talk together. It won't be the first time I've seen that, but it'll be a shame because . . .
Mrs. Trezano (*interrupts*):   I don't think it will be a shame. Each case is different, and in this case it may be called for. That's no shame.
Therapist: I see how you feel. I feel you could do it more effectively.
Mrs. Trezano: I think other people could do it more effectively. Maybe as time

him advocacy and support. The triangular escape of going through the children is blocked. The therapist backs the husband.

Not to lose her, the therapist relies on what the wife said during the preparatory session.

Active blocking is now used even more pointedly as the therapist throws himself more intensely into the proceedings, matching her intensity with his. His statement is as emotional as hers, which promotes the intensity match.

The "that might be" reconfirms for her that she does have a margin of freedom. She has the right to pick the option—going through the children—that will make for more problems. The therapist modulates his pressure.

progresses we may be able to do it more effectively.

Therapist: That might be. But the point is, through the kids is not good because it burdens them, hurts them, distorts things, and gives a message to the kids that the two of you can't really take care of them.

Mrs. Trezano: Well, I don't think they think I can't take care of them. They have come to realize I am in charge. (*She turns to the husband.*) I'm in charge. I don't like to say it like that.

The issue of threat to her power and control comes out clearly. A transformation of the new issue from power to nurturance is required, since she feels exposed. The issue is moved from her fear of being thought of as not in charge, unable to take care of the children, to the certainty that the husband thinks she does the best for them.

Therapist (*again leaning forward and softly beckoning her towards him*): Dina, Frank is not questioning that issue, that you will do the best for the kids. Frank isn't questioning that.

Mrs. Trezano: The kids understand that also.

Therapist: The issue is, you do need to share information.

Mrs. Trezano (*interrupting*): I don't see that!

Therapist: Whether it goes directly between you two or indirectly.

Mrs. Trezano: And I'm saying that anything of import has been communicated to my husband via the children.

Therapist: And I know, I know (*talking very firmly*) that that is no good. And I think you know it, too.

Mrs. Trezano: I don't.

It is the fifth time that this view is put forth. The therapist holds his ground, answering her tenacity with his own.

Therapist: Then let me give you the picture. It's no good because it unnecessarily burdens them, and because there's little likelihood that it'll get across accurately to Frank. They can distort it.

Mrs. Trezano: I don't give them messages to give their father. But

Now the issue is depersonalized and the therapist shifts tactics. It is not that the wife loses power. It is not a personal attack. It is mainly that the children are penalized, somehow they do communicate everything of concern to him. So they have a free hand. They're not burdened. They're not restricted in any way.

Therapist (*mocking surprise*):   Oh, then what I thought you said was happening is not. Which was that Frank is being told. It's only if they feel like it. That doesn't sound too great. I'm talking about Frank being informed about key issues.

Mr. Trezano: Just once a year (*he laughs helplessly*). This is indicative of it. I had no idea until now, a few days ago, when the kids said something about boarding school.

Mrs. Trezano: You know quite a bit about the school.

Mr. Trezano: And Dexter [the thirteen-year-old] said he's not sure about it.

Mrs. Trezano: So talk to him about it.

Mr. Trezano: If it's once a year.

Mrs. Trezano: How would you like to be informed?

Mr. Trezano: Give me a call. "Frank, I'm thinking of putting the kids in boarding school. What do you think about that?"

Mrs. Trezano (*very superciliously*):   Oh, I don't intend to do that. I really don't. And it's not malice. I just don't intend to do that. It's not power, it's because I have the responsibility. And if I've conferred with people at the school, I see no point in asking your opinion or permission because I've very thoroughly looked into it.

Therapist: So, Dina, you'll keep Frank in the dark. He may know everything that the kids want to tell. But you're not going to. That's not your responsibility.

Mrs. Trezano: I see no point.

Therapist (*mockingly*):   No. Of course not. No point. I'll not tell him, but if the kids want to.

Mrs. Trezano (*laughs*):   At a later date perhaps.

since they have an independent capacity and tendency to distort.

The husband jumps in to offer his own defense. He has observed that the therapist has experienced the force that he, the husband, has had to contend with. While observing, he had time to recoup and make this return.

The husband is now fighting for the right to have this decision be bilateral.

The husband looks ready to retreat, and the therapist moves in, amplifying the wife's defense, going exactly in her direction in content but using a reducing tone that conveys "you know better, you do see the point." The effort is clearly

Therapist: But right now you can't tell him. You wouldn't do it.

Mrs. Trezano: I have no intention of doing it.

toward obtaining a reversal of her view, rendering explicit her most rational side which at the moment is held in check because she wants to prevail.

Therapist: Of course not. You wouldn't want to tell Frank about important things about the kids.

Mrs. Trezano: For what?

Therapist: Of course, for what? Why should you?

Mrs. Trezano: Yes, why?

Therapist: Yes, why should you care?

Mrs. Trezano: There have been no accidents.

Therapist: Yes, nothing important. They're just going to be leaving home to live in a new school. It's not important.

Mrs. Trezano: He's informed.

Therapist: But you're not going to tell him.

Mrs. Trezano: No, not at this point in time.

Therapist: In the year 2000, maybe?

Mrs. Trezano: Then they'll be adults and there'll be no need.

Therapist: Right, and then you'll be ready. So it won't happen.

Mrs. Trezano: It's not up to me.

Therapist: Oh, no, it's not your responsibility?

Mrs. Trezano: What would I say? Call him and say, "Hey Frank, the kids are on drugs. I'll deal with that." Or, "Hey Frank, Gwen got raped. I'll deal with that."

The obvious implication is that she wants to tell but won't, because it's more important not to give in. By now the therapist's message is, "Your best side is being suppressed." Her reversal of view is not imminent but is on the way.

Her tendency toward postponement is parodied until it is clearly absurd.

They are sparring. She introduces the risks one takes in bringing up children in a ghetto, as if she and she alone has the "right" to handle them. If she calls the husband, it would only be to inform him, never to ask for his help, which would require that she acknowledge that to some extent they remain a couple. Her investment in being the martyred one, the one carrying the burden, is calculated to diminish her husband's importance while rubbing in the fact that the children's growing up is full of trouble.

Therapist (*sarcastically*): But their dad shouldn't know. Only if the kids want to tell him. It's not a mother's duty.

Mrs. Trezano (*less confidently*): Er, I don't see that.

Therapist: Of course not.

Mrs. Trezano: I don't.

Therapist (*in stage whisper, mockingly*): You know it is, because you said you'll do it when you're ready.

Mrs. Trezano: Perhaps at another time. But now I see it as asking permission or advice, both of which I don't need.

Therapist (*in a bored voice, as though this has been said a thousand times*): Frank is not saying you'll be asking permission. He's not getting into that at all.

Mrs. Trezano: That's great.

Therapist: Are you saying that?

Mr. Trezano: No, I'm not.

Mrs. Trezano: But it's not my responsibility, the kids can tell him.

Therapist: Dina. Please. As you know, kids are smart. They let things out

The therapist gains intensity by sticking to his guns, this time by giving her back her own medicine, "It's not a mother's duty." The therapist traps her with her earlier statements.

The need to avoid subordination and not yield to the husband by now colors all of her decisions. From where she stands, to consult the husband about anything pertaining to the children is to lose her war with him.

The therapist allows her to see her power. His tone

selectively. So perhaps they won't tell Frank. They're off to boarding school, in which case he'll wake up one morning and find them gone.

Mrs. Trezano: But that's not what happened. They told him.

Therapist: But not all that you know. Because you have been very seriously involved in this, in a very responsible, adult way. It's different from their involvement, a thirteen-year-old's involvement is slightly different. Now I know you know this. You're very bright. But listen. There is no issue here of power, of Frank trying to take anything from you or twisting your arm. He's asking for basic information.

Mrs. Trezano: And what I'm saying is, I won't ask permission.

Therapist (*surprised*):   No one is asking for that!

Mrs. Trezano: And I'm not trying to shut him out. But he mustn't criticize or disagree.

Therapist: Who's criticizing or disagreeing?

Mrs. Trezano: He's disagreed with the plan I've set in motion.

Therapist: No, he hasn't (*turning to Mr. Trezano*). Have you?

Mr. Trezano: No.

Mrs. Trezano: Well, he has because I've been informed.

Therapist: Aha. (*He pauses.*) I'll tell you something. I wonder if you, Frank, would step outside for a few minutes.

(*Mr. Trezano leaves the room.*)

---

from now on is weary and pleading, conveying "you're a strong adversary."

She experiences any information sharing as subordination, and the therapist in asking her to surrender is implicated.

She feels ganged up on by two men, and the therapist must clarify what he is not asking for.

The therapist calls for a change in composition to cool down the participants and gain needed leverage. He realizes that the wife's rigid stance is defeating not only the husband but himself. She is becoming more effective in maintaining the impasse and in being informed about her husband's feelings by other people. She seems to be strengthened by information that she will not and probably should not disclose in the husband's presence.

Therapist: Why are you, Dina, so defensive about this issue?

Mrs. Trezano: I'm not defensive, I'm adamant.

Therapist: Hang on. Let's go through this again and sort it out. Frank is not criticizing your judgment, your decisions, your involvement with the kids, your care, your concern. He's saying exactly the opposite.

Mrs. Trezano: That is not true. That is what you are hearing.

Therapist (*supportively*): Aah. Then you're jumping beyond what he's saying. You have other information.

Mrs. Trezano: I'm hearing other things through his mother, through the children. Okay? And he's totally opposed in every way. He sees this as another broken link in the marriage.

Finally, a discovery: she is dealing with an image of the husband as it filters through the social network of his mother and the children.

Therapist (*after a prolonged pause*): Let's try. Listen to what he's saying. Not his mother or the kids. *Him.* And I really want you to try your hand, to pay attention to what he's saying.

Mrs. Trezano: Okay.

Therapist (*firmly*): Please. Do this.

The pause here conveys understanding and responsiveness. Before attempting to help her differentiate the husband from the mediated image of the husband, she needs the therapist's compassion.

Mrs. Trezano: Okay. I will.

She agrees to listen, starting a process of change that leads to an attitude of acceptance.

Therapist: I know that you and he have

This extended comment

a long history. It's a messy, unhappy history (*Mrs. Trezano nods as if in a trance*), I know that. Just around this issue, try to listen to what he's saying. (*Mrs. Trezano nods again.*) What he's saying is that he respects you as mother to his children and he respects your decisions. (*Mrs. Trezano nods.*) What he wants is to be informed as their father on the most important decisions concerning them. *Informed.* He wants to be put in the picture.

Mrs. Trezano: Why must I put him in the picture? I've not interfered.

Therapist: Because they really are not *yet* responsible for themselves. And you are in the position of making decisions for the kids for very good reasons, about which they know only a little (*Mrs. Trezano nods in agreement with each point*), and which they often distort, and which they may or may not choose to share with him in some sort of distorted way. He'd rather know it from you, who are really in the position of letting him know, in an informed way, what's going on.

Mrs. Trezano: Okay. I imagine I could do that. I don't see the point, but I do understand what you say. Okay, I don't think it's such a difficult thing to do.

Therapist: No, it's not such a difficult thing. Let me ask you, do you see this as a silly whim of mine?

Mrs. Trezano: No, not at all. I see it as you sincerely trying to help the kids and me and Frank.

---

acknowledges how justified and how hurt she has been. She is now asked to focus only on the new issue, temporarily letting go of the past. The husband is then described as he is, not as he was in the mediated image.

If the children are not yet responsible for themselves, then the implication is that she is. The therapist's comment appeals respectfully to, and reminds her of, her predominant position in the family and her responsibility for the youngsters.

Again a shift is made to the goal being pursued.

The question tests her shift and produces an opportunity to heighten and renew her commitment before things go any further; a kind of vote of confidence is obtained. She is now committed and trusts the therapist.

Therapist: So you'll tell him one thing: that it's okay to have contact on key things about the kids.
Mrs. Trezano (*nods*): Absolutely.

The therapist clearly states the directive of keeping in contact, thus setting up a mechanism for a new level of postdivorce relating, which the couple has thus far avoided.

Therapist: Your fear is he would abuse it?
Mrs. Trezano (*nods*): Yes.
Therapist: Because he maybe wants to continue a relationship with you, and you want to let him know it's over. Over! And apart from the kids, it's over!
Mrs. Trezano: Yes.
Therapist: Kids are what you have in common, otherwise, it's over.
Mrs. Trezano: Correct.

The word "over" is repeated, conveying "you will not be put back into the subordinate role in the relationship you left."

The boundary is firmed up, and the fine tuning of her preparation is by now finished. The encounter with her husband resumes.

Mr. Trezano: All I want to know is, will I be informed about major things such as this? And like the concert, I'm concerned about that. You could just call and say so and so and so, and I'll be right there.
Mrs. Trezano: I didn't feel it was that important for me to call you about the concert. I instructed him to tell you.
Mr. Trezano: Again. You're dealing with a thirteen-year-old and an adult.
Mrs. Trezano: Mmm.

The mother is now ready to deal with her husband differently, yet to hold her ground. Perceiving a change in her mood, the husband begins to say more. His waiting period has also helped. It has allowed him time to muster a new resolve, particularly after seeing that the therapist has been willing to do his share of the work for him.

Mr. Trezano: So we'll let this go at that, but in the future things of this magnitude, the school and . . . so forth . . . I've gotta know.

Mrs. Trezano (*interrupting*): *Only* things of this magnitude.

Mr. Trezano: Yes, you see, I want to be involved. Anything else that you choose to do or not do is none of my business. Just so long as no one—your friends—takes advantage of the children, then it's just school.

Mrs. Trezano: Oh, they will not have another father. No one has any say-so over my children.

Mr. Trezano: We're not getting into that. I'm just saying that anything of importance I'd feel a little slighted if I'm not informed by you because I see it this way . . . by being able to communicate it's a form of letting go, too. It's not holding on. You can talk about fifty things, and if there's still feelings, you can talk. I'm ready to talk about things concerning the children, and I'd appreciate it very much if you'd take it upon yourself as an adult and mother to inform me on major issues. Graduation and things like that.

This is the work: determining what is the scope of his business and her business. This kind of work acknowledges the reality of the divorce and is part of firming up new boundaries.

This viewpoint—that to be able to communicate is a form of letting go—was developed in the father's preparatory session. Clearly he feels more equipped to handle her and uses well all of the directives and emotional ammunition given to him in his preparatory session.

Mrs. Trezano (*looking deliberately bored*): Of course, of course.

Mr. Trezano: And as far as you and I are concerned, that is an issue altogether separate from what we talk about now. And if I can by any means put you at rest, I'm by no means going to attempt to harass you or . . . to me it's ridiculous to even think about that at this date and time.

Mrs. Trezano: Time will tell. You can't make me comfortable about that, but time will.

Mr. Trezano: Okay, you stated what you felt. That's my feeling.

Therapist: So is there agreement that on

The wife is not fully ready to abandon her mistrust, and to expect so would be unrealistic. Dialogue looks more open now and problem solving flows.

major things, Frank will be informed?

Mrs. Trezano: Oh, yes. Definitely.

Mr. Trezano: If no more than write me, postcards.

Mrs. Trezano: Oh, that's not necessary. I have no objection to picking up the phone. I have no problem talking with you. I just want to avoid unpleasantness.

Mr. Trezano: You can rest assured that you'll suffer no unpleasantness from my hands.

Mrs. Trezano: Okay, I'll say this. The first time I do, I will not call again. That's not a threat; that's the way it is. I will communicate with you things of importance concerning the children.

Mr. Trezano: That's it. That's good.

Mrs. Trezano: If I call you concerning anything else, it won't be under the guise of talking about the children.

Mr. Trezano: Let's deal with the children. You and I and anything else we'll deal with as it is.

Mrs. Trezano: That sounds great to me.

Therapist: I think that's a great boundary to draw. There really is a difference. Now this went a bit longer than . . .

Mr. Trezano (*interrupts laughing*): Either of us anticipated. (*The mother joins in laughter.*)

Therapist (*laughing*): All of us anticipated. But you've done good work.

Realistic boundaries and limits are explored.

Though she is holding her boundaries, she is making concessions. It is new for her to be so willing to pick up the phone.

The husband accepts her restrictive conditions.

Obviously, it is not the time it took them that they all laugh about. Relief follows after the distress they all went through. That is what was never fully anticipated.

Stage Three: I Did It! Evaluating the Attempt

After a modest outcome such as the one achieved by the Trezanos, reactions emerge more sharply and at first are best funneled into individual conversations with the therapist during private debriefings. What usually comes up during this stage is feedback on the affective experience that each has had, especially some new types of reference to the self or the other person. Through evaluating such references, the therapist learns—among other things—the extent to which the person is focused on self or other. The debriefing sessions also help the participants integrate the experience. Guided by the therapist, they sort out what the experience has meant for them individually.

The following excerpt is from Mrs. Trezano's session alone a few days later.

Therapist: How was it for you?
Mrs. Trezano: Oh, it went better than I thought.
Therapist: In what way?
Mrs. Trezano: There wasn't as much hostility as I thought might show up. On either his part or mine. And now I'm feeling less hostile in a sense. Actually, I see the marriage as a modern tragedy, foregoing blame. I just want it over now. And I don't feel bad about the concessions I made. I know he cares about the children, and I can imagine how he's felt left out.

Her message is, "I didn't yield more than I wanted."

Mr. Trezano also expresses positive feelings in his session alone with the therapist.

Mr. Trezano: I got quite a bit out of the last session, because it showed me that I've made some sort of positive progress from my own personal standpoint. I was able to talk! Not let feelings take over. It was a good session in that I *felt good*. To actually

The father pinpoints exactly what is required in a successful joint talk to my wife and say what I had to say to her and not feel anything other than what I said. I meant what I said and said what I meant. I felt good about it. Because for a long time I've been wrestling and unable to control my feelings.

encounter, and that is not to let feelings get in the way of problem solving.

The therapist here is sustained by knowing that the objective is not necessarily spectacularly productive problem solving, but simple evidence of better self-control and better integration between intention and action. If productive problem solving occurs, it is a bonus and will bring along a reawakening of self-responsibility. At this point, couples show pride and sometimes surprise at their accomplishments. Their separate comments reflect how good it felt to maintain self-control. Neither person said anything to the effect that "I felt good that my spouse didn't attack me." Both were monitoring their own behavior, watchful of self more than of the other. They discussed their own reactions rather than the possible attacks or other reactions from the adversary.

When work in this stage is successful, it brings out problems that are preventing progress in other areas. A clarification of those problems then makes further progress possible. In our example, when the therapist met alone with Mrs. Trezano, he found out that the husband was "not as he was here [in the therapeutic encounter]. He's really very scared that his marriage is breaking up completely. I have been told this by his mother and by his children." These comments clarified that she was relating not just to the husband in front of her but to the husband's image as mediated by the children and by his mother. Her comments also expressed her wish to reduce him to the image of the duplicitous angry man and not the one asking for collaboration. An opportunity to clear the field, to work for a new contract, came up as subproblems were clarified. The new contract called on the wife not to talk to her husband through either the children or his mother, and for him likewise not to talk to his wife through his mother or the children (or to talk about her to them). The couple was actively oriented toward tackling a different and workable issue—the problem of both being victims of other people who were inappropriately involved in the middle—and a new beginning emerged.

An important step in individual sessions right after the encounter is for the therapist to support and reward the accomplishments the couple has made in terms of direct dialogue. It is pointed out that they have survived some direct dialogue before and *will do so again.* Such reinforcement reduces their sense of threat and builds a sense of competence. The therapist reviews what was learned in the preparatory sessions and what was applied during the encounter. Each person was encouraged to focus on his or her own behavior, not on the reactions of the other. Through mastery in taking refuge in their own selves, each found the other.

Stage Four: Taking It Further

Stage Four, which comes after the therapist has debriefed each participant separately, is characterized by new attempts at dialogue, at more direct interaction between the participants. If a new contract is being forged, it will ultimately be accompanied by more instances of successful, unmediated communication between the husband and wife. Such communication takes place first in the therapy session. During Stage Four, the Trezanos' work concentrated on the need to get other people out from the middle and on how comments were sometimes taken and distorted by the children or by the husband's mother. Their shared concern—a concern that the father soon felt as much as the mother did—was that their communication not become twisted.

Some cautions with regard to Stage Four should be kept in mind. If the couple has successfully moved to the fourth stage, the therapist must learn how to keep out. The participants are expected to slip and to reescalate their conflicts, but then exercise self-control and complete the sequence on their own. This process promotes their sense of control over their interactions and should not be interfered with. Often the therapist will be tempted to intercept one of the participants who is about to spoil those precious interactions for which they all have worked so carefully. The therapist may think, "The wife is speaking too long. If I allow her to continue, her insults will be pouring out too fast and everything will be lost." Or "The husband is allowing himself too much silence. He's being crushed. If this continues, he will probably just leave suddenly." Unless the therapist's impulse to intervene is controlled, the couple's initiative will be undermined and the possibility of the process becoming autonomous will be curtailed. The therapist should convey through disciplined silence that the participants are capable of forgiving each other as they go along and that they can monitor themselves to a decent ending without warring again and having to be rescued.

At this stage, risks have to be taken, and the therapist should not expect a perfect, clear, cooperative dialogue. The husband must be allowed to do his pained routine, and the wife must be allowed her usual runaway tirades against her husband. The therapist "forgives" those slips and lets go. Such regressions are unavoidable as the husband and wife learn to use new processes without monitoring. The guiding principle at this stage is to work for intrinsic rather than external reinforcement. The participants should feel, "I almost messed it up, but I didn't do it and it paid off." The result to aim for is a rewarding exercise in self-mastery in the midst of interpersonal conflict. The therapist can easily miscalculate during this stage, but there is no simple way to circumvent errors and avoid risks.

The therapist's capacity to withdraw and let the participants try their own skills at preventing a collision was tested on the Trezanos when the wife invited her husband to visit the boarding school. The next segment starts with the therapist cueing the husband in to what should be his next move by asking a question that compels Mr. Trezano to deal with his wife in the problem area.

Therapist (*to the husband*):   Will you have a chance to check the place [the boarding school] out?

Mr. Trezano: I intend to drive up there sometime.

Mrs. Trezano (*caustically*):   If it suits you, how about the time the kids go in? I was thinking of asking you to (*she pauses*) to take them up.

The tone of this offer is aloof and reluctant, masking any signs of reliance on him.

Mr. Trezano (*stuttering*):   I, I, I . . . if it's on a Monday I can deal with it. If it's not and I know in advance, then I can. I can make arrangements.

The father's reaction is scared, and the therapist feels almost summoned to rescue him from possible rejection.

Mrs. Trezano: I'll let you know in time. I'll have the opportunity to look the place over before then. It might do you well to have that opportunity, to see the facilities, everything. And I think it's a good sendoff for the children because the week they leave I want them home with me and they've already voiced that they want to be with you before they go.

Mr. Trezano: Actually, I spoke to Gwen [the ten-year-old daughter] and she said

yes, she'd like to spend a couple of days
with me just before they leave. I said okay,
that seems fine. And then they said when
they leave they'd like both of us to be
there with them because they didn't want
to say goodbye to you, then to me. They
wanted us together.

Mrs. Trezano (*aloof*):   They didn't tell me   Her tone is cold and
that, but I don't have objections. I can see   grudging, yet she does
it's a good start for them. Going away. A   acknowledge it would be
good start.   good to do this together
    for the kids.

The wife's offer to let the husband take the children to the school was
made in a caustic manner. It was a generous moment on her part, but she
disguised her generosity by trying to pretend not to care about bringing
the children there herself. To the observer it appeared likely that the husband would decline the invitation and would counter by questioning whatever action his wife was thinking of taking. Her tone seemed capable of
disrupting any possibility of his reaching out to her and expressing interest
in becoming involved in the decision. Yet the therapist refrained from
intervening, and soon after her aloof offer, a change showed up. The husband brought up the children's desire to have them both there when leaving
for the boarding school. Since this was his weekend with the children, he
was really extending himself. To this offer of sharing she answered coldly
in the first part of her response, "I don't have objections." Her tone was
chilling, conveying her strong aversion to sentimentality or softness. The
therapist felt the husband might have been too slapped down and offended
by her tone, and again was tempted to intervene. But just then the husband
responded with a facial gesture of acceptance, relating to the more collaborative tone of the second part of her response, "It's a good start." From
such imperfect moments a new beginning was made. Obviously, the wife's
eventual concession to cooperate came not only from how her husband
dealt with her but from having envisioned the encounter as full of safeguards. She knew what themes were likely to come up, had been told there
would be a strict time limit, and viewed the therapist as an advocate and
referee in case of trouble.

The main objective in Stage Four is to launch a process of toleration and
to seek more extended dialogue. The goal is to ensure that dialogue will
remain available—to prevent dialogue from deteriorating to the point where
the participants feel they cannot try again. When Stage Four is successful,
the participants find they can more frequently be self-collected and in control while solving problems in areas of conflict.

Summary

In the four-stage procedure described in this chapter, the therapist goes from the part to the whole, preparing each participant to focus on self-monitoring during potentially hot dyadic exchanges. Worrying about what the other person may present is deemphasized; the possibility of a new beginning lies in the fact that focus is not on the other, which is declared an incidental and uncontrollable factor, but on the self. The therapist's guiding principle is that the goal of cooperation is best pursued by regarding it as serendipitous and remote. The engineering of a new reality, of eventual success in the actual interpersonal field, is considered a byproduct of self-restraint as each party comes to feel, "I mastered my emotions. I did not allow myself to be thoroughly provoked into undue attacking."

This approach builds on the notion that the most significant forces that go into play to maintain the troubled dyadic system are individuals who retain a margin of freedom for action even when caught in compelling systemic phenomena. The therapist continues to work with the participants individually, helping them organize their own resources to cope with automatic cycles that have arisen in a marriage gone conflictual. For the therapist, the long-range goal is to become more of a dispensable presence than an active mediating participant. The redundant background message to the couple becomes, "I trust that you people will take charge without hurting each other unduly." This message is conveyed through measured participation and self-restraint and by not allowing things to go too far. The therapist learns when not to tamper but to respect frustrating "in-betweens" and work that is incomplete. This "not doing" is actually important doing—it leads the couple to discover on their own their capacity for problem solving. In deciding what to do about the children's schooling, the Trezano couple exercised erratic self-mastery but created grounds for going on to more significant issues: when and how they should finally divorce.

5

Warring Couples: Frequent and Direct Fighters

SOME COUPLES have been through a variety of efforts to solve their problems with the help of marital counselors, attorneys, judges, and other authorities, with no notable success. In a sense they have defeated the experts, and they or their children pay with costly symptoms while their bank accounts are drained. Their very struggle to separate emotionally keeps these couples together; they seem hopelessly entangled in their on-going mutual conflicts. Most of these couples come to us through a court mandate. An external authority has deemed it important that an outsider step in once more. Unlike the type of couple discussed in the previous chapter—the couple that collides sporadically and then goes into hiding, working on each other only indirectly through the children—frequent and direct fighters do not avoid each other but rather seem to thrive on chronic fighting. The therapeutic challenge is to move them away from fighting and forge a new style of communication.

Since these couples are extremely committed to direct fighting, variations of the procedure in the preceding chapter are used. The procedure here requires assessing the level of stagnation of the conflict, emphasizing crisis making as preparation for the encounter, sponsoring a failed encounter if necessary, and then seizing opportunities to reorient the couple while working to anticipate sabotage.

Assessing Stagnation

After the Daleys had had repeated appearances in court, the judge referred them to the Families of Divorce Project to try to resolve their differences. Tommy, age eight, and Susan, age seven, had been living with their mother and visiting their father, who consistently wanted more time with them. The couple, in their mid-thirties, had been separated for five years.

This type of family, with its capacity for continuous direct fighting, can usually tolerate being in the room together. The therapist begins by asking the couple to explain their situation, to find out whether they have hit rock bottom and how much fight is left in them. This provides the opportunity to gauge their reality testing and readiness to problem solve.

Mr. Daley: We've spent years going back and forth on counseling, back and forth on legal expenses, and it just seems like for us to negotiate, I've really thought that we get nowhere. I don't know if you feel the same way, but if we look back at the amount of money we spent, I'm not sure exactly what you spent but I know what I spent, I just feel like it's fruitless to spend all the money that I spent. I feel like I spent money not only related to the kids but to other things in terms of our divorce that I was offering years ago. . . .

The therapist listens for what the father values, what might be likely to motivate him.

Therapist: But you're saying that you don't feel very hopeful about being able to negotiate with each other.

The therapist hears and sees that the outstanding obstacle is the feeling of having "spent" not only the money but the self. She acknowledges that obstacle while stimulating any remaining energy for negotiating which could be amplified for working purposes.

Mr. Daley: If it was the first time I would say, oh yes, and be all psyched for it, but I know what it is like to sit down and try to work something out with Kim. I just keep going back to the last four or five years, and it seems like we never work anything out and we always end up at a court hearing. (*He pauses.*) I would love to be able to work something out, I mean I proposed. . . .

Therapist (*to the wife*):   Would you like to be able to work something out together if it were possible?

The therapist is sensitive to the possibility of another failure.

Mrs. Daley (*tightly*):   We never have been able to work anything out at all. I have my feelings about why we haven't and he has his feelings about why we haven't.

Therapist: I understand that you feel pretty hopeless about the possibility that the two of you could work it out, but if you could, though, would that be something that you would like as an outcome?

Mrs. Daley: To work it out rather than go to court? Yeah.

Mrs. Daley warns the therapist against dragging her and him into another failure, since they have had too many already. Significantly, the therapist heeds the warning by acknowledging their hopelessness while rewording the question in a form more easily answered in the affirmative. The Daleys' ability to work on their problems depends on their sensing that the therapist is responsible and able to modify and pace the therapy to suit their needs and affective states.

Therapist (*turning to the husband*):   If it were remotely possible, and I'm not saying that it is, is that something that you would prefer?

The therapist goes out of her way to convey respect for the stalemate. She asks for willingness to work on another plan on an imaginary level, and not on the immediate deadlock.

Mr. Daley: I prefer, yeah, because I feel like I've asked for something that is

nothing out of line. It's not like I'm asking
for the world.

The couple describes the extent and areas of disagreement:

Mr. Daley: We went back and forth,
back and forth on one agreement, then
another agreement for five years.
Therapist: Involving the children?
Mr. Daley: No.
Therapist: Property?
Mr. Daley: Support, property, you name
it, and the children a little bit too. It seems
like everything is partitioned off,
disagreements in this court, disagreements
in that court, disagreements in another
court.

It is characteristic of the
more anxious divisive
process that no area of
interchange seems free of
conflict. This is why these
families are clinically more
complicated.

Therapist: So the two of you must be
pretty angry at each other at this point, I
would guess, after five years of that for
both of you.
Mrs. Daley: I'm just tired of it.
Therapist: Yes.
Mr. Daley: I'm tired of it, too. I feel like,
I don't know.

The anger and weariness
due to the impasse are
explored and amplified, to
fuel further the motivation
for changes.

Therapist: It must make it hard, it must
make you feel like you've been married
almost, the last five years, instead of
separated, with this much fighting going
on.

With this statement the
therapist commiserates
with the couple about the
absurdity of becoming
further entangled precisely
through their efforts to
disentangle.

Mr. Daley: I'm not sure it's fighting. I
think it's lack of common sense, sometimes
on my part and sometimes on her part. I
mean, anytime somebody spends $14,000
on legal expenses to try to get divorced
and they're not divorced yet—and I don't
know what she's spent—that's bitter, and
I'm sure she thinks so, too. It's just so
stupid.

Therapist: I'm sure late at night you must think of all the trips to Puerto Rico you could have taken with that.

No opportunity is lost to highlight the negative consequences of the current status.

Crisis Making as Preparation for the Encounter

During the first sessions with these families, the therapist tries to make the couple feel the consequences and the futility of their actions before preparing a controlled encounter. As they start to describe or live out the conflict, the crisis is relentlessly escalated until they want to soften their rigid positions. The therapist magnifies the likely consequences of the stagnation, drawing them out and dwelling upon them, to motivate the couple to want a new start. The controlled encounter is delayed until fresh motivation for shedding a pattern has reached its peak.

This delay is difficult. Most of these couples come charged with enough hysterics, honest pain, explosive accusations, and counteraccusations to make any therapist feel that the level of tension is too high already. Yet experience teaches that these kinds of adversarial displays do not necessarily reflect a drive toward change. The complaints seldom express a sense of total defeat and a wish to find a new way of doing things. The situation must become even more unbearable than the couple thought it was. Enlarging the consequences of their actions, aggressively insisting that they have no place to go, and if necessary bruising them with their own material, the therapist pushes until they feel it is important to problem solve.

In talking alone with Mr. Daley, for example, the therapist appealed to the money-conscious man who was wasting money, to the father who should have compassion for the suffering youngsters of eight and seven, and to the tired adversary who had been at it for many years and was likely to keep at it until the children were irreparably damaged. She appealed as well to the disappointed visitor to the court who sought but never found resolution. When the man tried to railroad the therapist with complaints about his estranged wife, the therapist insisted on dealing with the consequences of the fight.

But the therapist dwells not only on the options lost but also on the options that may open up if the couple resolves the stalemate. The search is for incentives, real or imagined, that may promote change. With the mother, the therapist focused on the advantages to her of the children's happiness with their father, knowing full well that the mother resented the children's having a good time with him.

Throughout this stage, the therapist is careful to assign individual responsibility, while conceding that the problem is also an interactive one involving the husband, wife, and children. The point is to avoid interpersonalizing the problem too far and thus diffusing individual responsibility. We do not want to give either the husband or the wife any excuse to maintain a rigid stance. Talking alone with each parent, the therapist affirms, "I think both of you have a part in this, but I think you might have to bend; otherwise, you might have to be prepared for this kind of fight to go on for another five or six years, and the kids will have to put up with the consequences."

Anticipating Sabotage and Securing Change

It is possible for the therapist to maintain a positive outlook about what is best in the couple while believing that the worst is possible, too. Watching couples work and rework the conclusions to their marriages has taught us that they generally go on perceiving each other in "see-saw" fashion, contrasting their own personal progress to the progress of the other, long after the official divorce. This is a deep-seated, almost unchangeable stance that reveals that at some level they remain bound to each other. Thus the therapist must necessarily maintain a skeptical bias, expecting that for most couples the resolution arrived at tends to leave a level of unrest that is unlikely to be resolved. This unrest, if allowed to sink too quickly beneath the surface, becomes a powerful potential source of sabotage. It results in a pseudoconciliatory stage that, if unexamined, may result in a perennial contest: if she becomes happy, he will resent it; if he is making more money and is making somebody else happy, she will be angry and try to take her share, perhaps taking him to court again.

Bringing the unrest and the unfinished business to the surface reduces the likelihood of delayed conflict and derailed achievements. The therapist therefore intentionally makes trouble, uncovering anger before it can be transformed into quietly building frustration. Asking couples for "second thoughts" after they thought they had already settled something is one way this situation can be handled. It works best, however, when the therapist accepts the fact that perfectly symmetrical change is impossible. The rights of the participants can be safeguarded only to a limited extent in the future. Looking for second thoughts tests initial adjustments and provides outlets for anger over unfinished business. The therapist must be ready to activate more disagreement, to escalate conflicts that presumably were resolved. The result may be considerable unpleasantness, but the alternative of letting tension continue to build is worse.

Asking for second thoughts was tried after four weeks of therapy with the Daleys. In the following transcript, we see the reappearance of friendly feelings and a fleeting return of confidence that they can work things out.

Therapist (*to the wife*):   How did the children seem after weekends with him? Have they complained less about his being angry or whatever?
Mrs. Daley: Well, you know, they haven't really complained. My daughter doesn't want to approach him with things. You know, if they're averse to his plans, I just said, well, I really think you can talk to Daddy, and Tommy can talk to Daddy, and if there's something that he wants to do that you don't want to do, I don't see why you just don't speak up to him. And you know, she said she's afraid, and I said, what are you afraid of, and she said that he'll scream and yell like he used to do with Tommy. So I just said, well, he doesn't do that anymore now, and she said, no, he doesn't. Well, I said, everybody's more friendly, and the most he can say is "no." They have to learn. . . .
Therapist: Good for you. I mean, you've been working.
Mrs. Daley: Yeah.
Therapist: Okay, I have just one concern.
Mrs. Daley: Umm.
Therapist: Things are going a little too well.
Mrs. Daley: Really!
Therapist: Yes, because you're not reporting any instances where things came

Now the therapist starts making trouble, exploring in order to resurface the crisis and the solutions thus far developed. The attempt is to check whether the resolution achieved is indeed close to going wrong, and it has to happen, and I would prefer it to happen while you're both seeing me.

Mrs. Daley: I know.

Therapist: It absolutely will always happen . . . I don't know of any exceptions. He'll come in with the wrong look on his face or he'll just say the stupidest thing or you'll be in a bad mood and you'll blow it with him or something. And that doesn't mean that it's all over. Things can still continue in a way that is better for the children and better for you, but it's not going to be just as it's been.

adequate or whether it is premature.

Despite the therapist's trouble-making attempts, the wife continues to describe only positive feelings for her husband over the past few weeks, even though there were moments of disagreement. A positive spiral has developed through the inevitable ups and downs. She can tolerate mistakes without taking undue offense or feeling that access to her husband will be closed off. The feeling is, "I can talk to him now!"

But the therapist continues to test the limits, now with the wife alone, deliberately fishing for trouble, for areas where agreement has not been reached. In our approach, the purpose is not to have them defend their gains but to have them expose areas of incomplete agreement.

Therapist: Let me ask you another thing, and that has to do with what we can do here today. Do the two of you feel ready to put some of this down for me on paper? Because you know I still have to write to the judge about what it is that you agreed on. What areas are left for us to talk about further; where do you both stand now?

Mrs. Daley: I think that most of the major things that Tom wanted, you know, have been discussed and settled.

Therapist: Is there any disagreement that stands out where you just don't want to move further on and he does?

Mrs. Daley (*hesitantly*):   There is one thing I want to ask you. I just want to

With the therapist's encouragement, the

know how flexible he is about some things. I mean, he wants to pick them up at six-thirty on Friday night, and I said, yeah, that's okay, but you know, I agreed to it because I wanted things to work out, and they have. But I was just thinking, I don't know if he heard me that Friday is our day to unwind and all, and my chance to talk to the children. And if it stays at six-thirty I guess I can sacrifice it, but on my part I'd like it to be maybe seven-thirty that he pick them up, but if you think that it's not worth discussing. . . .

Therapist: I think you certainly should discuss it. I think it's important for you to feel comfortable. Let me make a suggestion. I would like to bring him in right now. How about you two discussing that, okay?

Mrs. Daley: Okay.

Therapist: Okay, I'll be right back.

mother cautiously reveals an area of pseudoagreement with her husband. Her doubts, if allowed to remain, are the seeds that will grow to choke off the couple's achievement.

Sponsoring a "Final" Failed Encounter

In dealing with some extremely rigid blocked couples, the therapist occasionally finds it necessary to go along temporarily with a futile fight—a controlled encounter that fails—as a preparatory step. The participants do not feel accountable for their own moods. During the failed encounter, they become so focused on the moods and attacks of the other that they find themselves embroiled in typical, unproductive efforts. They fail here as they have done in the past, and they do so dramatically. Under the therapist's guidance the experience can leave them urgently wanting to bounce back, ready to grasp whatever tools and problem-solving suggestions are available in their own repertoire or that of the therapist.

This occurred with the Daleys. The therapist invited the husband into the room after the wife presented the questions, then the therapist left the room to observe; if necessary she would re-enter to intervene. The situation was organized so that the couple could experience their failure or success clearly as their own. Any remaining tendency to become stalemated and powerless when attempting to resolve conflict would now surface.

Therapist: Since I won't always be around, I'm going to leave the room now, and what I want you to do is talk about whatever concerns at this point you each have with the agreement, and see what you can come up with. And then I want you to talk with each other about what you agree to tell me, because I have to write back to the judge. Then I'll come back in. Okay?

The therapist's appeal is in terms of both responsibility to each other and their presentation of themselves to the outside—that is, to the judge, a representative of societal constraints.

(The therapist leaves the room.)

Mr. Daley: Okay.

Mrs. Daley: Well, ready? What I was thinking about was, since you're going to be picking them up on Friday nights and, you know, in the summer it doesn't matter much, but I was just wondering if, you know, maybe we could make it a little later in the wintertime, so I would have a chance to sit down with them a little and discuss how things were at school. You know, like at seven-thirty you can pick them up. . . .

Mr. Daley: Well, I dunno. Sometimes I try to make it a little convenient for myself so that I don't have to run back and forth all the time. At least at six-thirty, I hang around work a little while and then come directly from work. Seven-thirty means that I drive home from work or else I find something to do until seven-thirty in the winter. It just . . . to me it seems like. . . .

Both are genuinely concerned about protecting their own quality time with the children. Ironically, in trying to defend this quality time they jeopardize it, because their unharnessed fighting constantly upsets the children's equilibrium. The judge may be pushed to act protectively and take the time away. Defensiveness sets in. Feeling about to be denied, the mother jumps

Mrs. Daley: It's just important to me to sit and talk to them a little bit and have some time.

Mr. Daley: I feel the same, Kim. Seven-thirty I'll be rushing them home and getting them in bed almost.

Mrs. Daley: Well, it's a Friday night, they . . .

Mr. Daley: To me that was the purpose of Friday night. I could spend some productive time with them that I don't get a chance for. And then what will I do. Work is done at four-thirty. I drive home, which is one way and then drive back another way, another thirty-five or forty minutes, or I find something to do on Friday nights, to fill in to seven-thirty. That was the purpose really. To spend time with . . .

Mrs. Daley: Sometimes Fridays are a rush anyway. I have to get them back home and pack their things. I just thought . . .

Mr. Daley: I mean seven-thirty, the evening is just about shot, and in the wintertime it is dark at five o'clock, and most of the time the kids will be ready for bed by eight-thirty. I'll rush them home and they'll watch "The Dukes of Hazzard" and then it's time for bed.

Mrs. Daley (*tensely*):   You know, you have time traveling with them and everything.

Mr. Daley (*exasperated*):   I really thought . . . six-thirty to me was late, and I thought I was honestly bending a little bit. I would like to get them . . . I would like to come down after work and get them, but I realized six-thirty gives you a chance if you want to give them dinner and spend time with them.

Mrs. Daley: It just seems like by the time I get home and get them dinner, it's already six-thirty.

in and the father quickly darts back. Both become entrenched in their own rigid positions.

Each interrupts before the other has finished, so that they hardly hear each other. They insist obstinately on their own points of view, nullifying any possibility of generating creative alternatives to the impasse.

By this time they are locked into their set positions, which offer no "outs." He feels she is untrustworthy and he had better grab whatever he can get. She feels he is rapaciously greedy and she must desperately defend her position.

A powerful sense of ever-mounting tension and frustration rules the transaction, which continues without resolution. The therapist reenters the room and signals them to take control of their moods, hoping to alter the rigid set in which they are caught. She points out the absolutist nature of their positions.

Therapist: I want to point something out to the two of you that you may have noticed, which is that in discussing this, you each have gotten stiffer. You each rigidified, and that's the kind of thing that happens when the two of you get into this kind of disagreement. Okay, for example, you're talking as if the kids can never go to bed later on Friday night.

Mr. Daley: I'm not talking about that.

Multiple levels of intervention are evident. The therapist signals the couple's mood in an effort to break them away from what controls them. She encourages flexibility by highlighting their rigidity, that they talk as if the children "can never go to bed later."

Therapist (*firmly*): Wait. It sounds to me like you are. That they can never go to bed at ten. You're talking as if they can never be sleepy maybe for baseball the next morning, that things are set, that it has to be one way all the time. And it's fine that you're having this disagreement and it's fine that you're holding your own. That you're saying what's important to you (*looking at father*) and that you're saying what's important to you (*looking at mother*). I want you to see if you can resolve it. But pay attention to how, when you disagree like this, you each get very stiff.

Mr. Daley: Okay, like we're going backwards a little. I thought we agreed to something already.

By saying "wait," she refuses to let the father's move derail her; the therapist sticks firmly to her position. Their disagreement is framed as a positive endeavor. This intervention seems to work by bringing to consciousness what is automatic—that when they disagree they become rigid. But more significantly, it divides their attention. They cannot fight in the same way while they are looking at their own rigidity.

Therapist: You each have been discussing what it is you feel you can give on, and when people come to the end where they get close to putting it down in

The therapist normalizes their impasse and appeals for a last effort on an issue they are so close to writing, it is not unusual for this to happen. I want you to tell me what I can tell the judge. This kind of hassle you're having often happens outside the room, and so I'm glad it's happening in here. I'm not surprised it's happening, it's part of the process. I want you to see if you can resolve this. I know it feels like a real step backwards, after you feel you had gotten somewhere. Okay? But unless you both feel comfortable in what it is you're giving and getting, this could happen two months down the road, and you know now as well as I do that what the judge says alone is not going to make the children happy, it's what goes on between the two of you. So you've done a wonderful job. See how you can resolve this so that you don't each feel you're losing everything or getting everything.

resolving. She keeps introducing the implacable reality "outside" (the judge as an unavoidable threat). The therapist stresses what could happen later on as unresolved conflicts show up to interfere with their existence.

The intervention was of little avail. When the therapist left the room, the couple's struggle resumed immediately. The husband insisted that the wife had the evenings during the week with the children. She countered that, given their new arrangement, he too would have time with them during the week. He changed the topic and argued that the extra trip would be too much of a burden. Their dialogue became increasingly restrictive and repetitious. As the possibility of compromise or a creative solution decreased, the mood of futility grew. The fight continued back and forth for another ten minutes, sprinkled with lapses in which the participants revealed how aware they were of being stuck and at the mercy of a runaway phenomenon.

Observing such an encounter, the therapist often becomes concerned that if the failure-bound dialogue continues for too long, everything will come to naught; the couple will be unable to salvage anything and will not even be in a position to be rescued. A time-honored tactic is to have them shift their discussion to a less conflict-ridden topic, one on which they are more likely to reach an agreement. If the couple fails again with the changed topic, the therapist usually wants to intervene, out of practicality or even compassion for the couple. Yet experience teaches that the more useful way of proceeding is to intensify the crisis further.

In the Daleys' case, the intensification came with the therapist's direction to continue "downhill," as if she were sponsoring a powerful natural process, though she was really following it. What the therapist wants here is not just to maintain her leverage by ordering the phenomenon of stalemate to go in the direction it is going anyway. The therapist conveys the notion that if the disagreement cannot be harnessed, it can at least be followed through to completion, so that the couple can make a fresh start. The implication is that the therapist helps them and herself to wind up in a position of bouncing back. At the same time, by labeling the process as "going downhill," the therapist calls on them to exercise whatever measure of self-restraint is left. In this way they are buffered from feelings of failure and guilt if they can't stop, while still allowed to own the experience fully. In our experience, the therapist's intervention can fail if the request for them to continue "going downhill" is felt as just a tactical ploy. The intervention is more likely to succeed—to restore the couple's initiative—if the message is not allowed to become a calculated paradox but is indeed ushered from a nonstrategic stance of genuine deinvestment. The nature of that deinvestment is based on the ultimate impotence of the therapist as a source of influence on the couple's choice of course. They allow themselves to be convinced by the adversarial process.

Therapist: Okay, I'll tell you something. I understand something very well from watching you, and that is how you've spent many thousands on your lawyers—more than ten? Some large sum? I understand that, okay? I want you to continue. You are going downhill now. Continue! There's more than just this that you've not agreed on. You'll have to discuss all of it—the question of Christmas Day, and I don't know if you agreed yet about the joint custody stipulation. Those are the other two things that just stand out. So I'm going to give you another five minutes, but . . . (*to the wife*) you also wanted him to understand how you were feeling. But in any case, you've got three things to talk about. I'll give you another five minutes, but it *is* going downhill. You are in a sense telling me today what it is that you want me to tell the judge in terms of whether you can really solidify an agreement or not. But keep going. . . . I agree with you that it's going downhill.

(*The therapist sits back.*)

Mrs. Daley: I just try and listen and be understanding of your feelings. And I agreed to the one more week in the summer, and that you wanted to come and see them during the week and Friday nights. And I'm just hoping that you can understand my feelings on it.

Mr. Daley: I can understand a little bit. But I feel like all of a sudden something that was becoming convenient isn't really convenient anymore. You know I'm just talking about the school year. All of a sudden from September to April I'm supposed to stay at work until quarter to seven or drive home, then drive back and forth.

He thinks she has shifted ground and went back on a previous agreement (that he could come earlier Friday nights) that he had extracted from her. The word "convenience" is used, but in unilateral terms.

Mrs. Daley: Can't you just . . . you're just acting like you're going to be hanging in space for a couple of hours. Don't you have grocery shopping to do or something like that?

Mr. Daley: But I'm trying to get something convenient so that I don't do all this running back and forth. That was one of the reasons for Friday night, because I felt Saturday was running back and forth for this and that.

Mrs. Daley: But it's not my fault that you live that far away.

Mr. Daley: No, it's not. I didn't say it was. Well, that's being foolish in my eyes, and I feel like if we're living a distance, we have to consider distance. If I lived next door, it would be a lot more convenient. I would say seven-thirty, fine, I'll run around the corner and come get them. But

The husband is learning to be more careful not to come across as accusatory when negotiating with her.

that's not it. Friday nights are important to
me, but to me it's foolish for me to waste
an hour in the middle of picking them up.
Therapist: Why don't we just move on
to something else—leave this subject and
come back to it.

The husband's tone is
exasperated and the wife's
stance more rigid. Sensing
an impasse that could get
worse, the therapist
capitalizes on the blockage
to shift them to another
problem.

(The therapist exits.)

Mrs. Daley *(to her husband)*: Okay,
where do you want to move on to?
Mr. Daley: I don't know, Christmas?
(Mrs. Daley nods.) Are you willing to give
me any more time at Christmas with the
kids than one day?
Mrs. Daley: You have one day, plus you
have the weekend. . . .

(Their unproductive dialogue continues for a few minutes in the same vein.)

Mr. Daley *(interrupting)*: Wait, uh,
weekends don't always fall during the
Christmas holidays. I can pull out
calendars and show you.
Mrs. Daley: A weekend would fall
either . . .
Mr. Daley: My weekend doesn't
necessarily have to fall between Christmas
and New Year's.

It is clear that resolution is
not near.

(The therapist reenters the room.)

Again the therapist enters
and more than hints of the
repeated failures. She
continues to rush them to
where they're already
going.

Therapist: You took care of Friday nights, you took care of Christmas. You have four minutes left, see what you can do with the joint custody question. So I'm only giving you four more minutes.

Mr. Daley: On the joint custody, there's no sense even talking about it. What does joint custody mean? I'm not sure what it means. I think if I don't even have the right to have my children on Christmas and alternate weekends, is there even sense in talking about it? I don't know.

The father's frustration has reached a new peak.

Therapist: I think you won't even take four minutes to take care of the joint custody one, but give it a try. (*Looking at the father:*) You're asking for something. Why don't you explain what you're asking for and see what you can agree on, and you have four minutes. That's two down, and you'll have three down if you keep going like this.

The rushing and intensification continue.

Mr. Daley (*emotionally flat*): I'm not sure what I'm asking for on joint custody. What does it mean, what does it mean to you?

Mrs. Daley: And there were different kinds of joint custody when it was explained by the judge.

(*The mother and father then struggle to differentiate between issues of shared decision-making power and shared physical custody.*)

Seizing the Opportunity to Reorient

The therapist now determined that the participants were almost depleted—that they were feeling defeated and were anticipating that the therapist would declare joint custody another arena where they could not solve conflict. The therapist reentered the room, bringing with her a legal expert, a coworker who had been observing behind the mirror. Picking up on the theme of custody, the coworker distracted the couple with a long explanatory monologue, presumably to clear up their bewilderment about joint custody.

When couples feel defeated, as the Daleys were, they start looking for an intervention that will give them a pretext for disengaging. Each wants a chance to undergo a change of mood and be reoriented toward cooperation rather than conflict. The monologue provides just such a chance. It is purposely long, to allow the couple time to rest and an opportunity to stay disengaged long enough to calm themselves, reorganize their thoughts, and do some internal work. The therapist becomes "educational" and intellectual, and tries to focus the couple's attention on the new topic instead of on each other by speaking uninterruptedly as an expert on some aspect of divorce: what joint custody really means, how children tend to react to divorce, or how most couples resolve a situation like theirs.

Usually couples are preoccupied during this monologue. Still reacting to their recent failed encounter, they fasten their attention only lightly on the therapist. The new topic is treated as a resting station. Most couples at this juncture welcome the chance to appear as though they are attending to the outsider, while actually they are doing internal work, stepping back to reassess the situation and weigh their next move. This was clearly the case with Mr. and Mrs. Daley. As they sat quietly, their faces and eyes displayed an inner focus.

Coworker: Any questions?
Mr. Daley: No. I was just a little confused on what. . . .
Coworker: Does that clear it up?
Mr. Daley: Yes.
Mrs. Daley: Uh huh.
Therapist: Okay. Take another couple of minutes discussing that, and I also want you to talk about how you think the judge would perceive each of your positions.
Mr. Daley: Okay.
Mrs. Daley: Thank you.
Therapist: I'll be back in just a couple of minutes.

In the next segment, the father's halting small talk about the drive to the clinic signals a shift in mood and pace. He seems to apologize for his previously agitated behavior as he now begins to collect himself. He reveals a more subdued mood, which seems to elicit an equally subdued tone from his wife. The accompanying themes become personal and mundane as affect deescalates and a sequence toward negotiation and compromise begins.

Mr. Daley (*softly*):   Okay, I might be a little . . . it might be the weather and the drive down here. I've been running around all day, and I was unhappy about going in to work today.

Mrs. Daley: I know you had to. Yeah, you told me.

Mr. Daley: I didn't have breakfast or lunch. I worked my meeting right through one o'clock and I'm in a rush constantly. I just grabbed a hot dog on the way in here (*he pauses*). Okay, now I'm not happy about seven-thirty, but I'm getting sort of half of what I want. I'll just have to spend less time with the kids or spend the time doing whatever I have to do until seven-thirty.

Mrs. Daley: I was just thinking, I really feel good about . . . I thought everything was going real well and I was telling the doctor that I really enjoy talking to you and that I felt real comfortable with the situation and I thought the kids did, too. I just feel that I like to be flexible about it or, you know, maybe it wouldn't always be seven-thirty.

Mr. Daley: Why don't we compromise and say it's seven o'clock as opposed to seven-thirty, and I can find something at work to do.

Mrs. Daley: Okay, fine. If you just want to come down and have dinner with us or if we get pizza that night . . . I mean Friday night is usually a quick night because of the cub scouts, I mean you can listen to them, too. Maybe I will need to explain to you that they have tests in school, or they

The participants appear to be carried by a positive spiral (he gets softer, so she gets softer). They are, however, not just at the mercy of an automatic interpersonal process but are actively making personal sacrifices. The spiral toward cooperation represents conscious decisions to change. As he displays willingness to spend less time with his children and accept her seven-thirty requirement, she becomes elastic about time. Flexibility begets flexibility.

will want to show you their papers or
something. Or they have to remember that
they have to take something in for
Monday. It was kind of that sort of thing
that I was interested in.

Mr. Daley: Okay. That's fine. What
about Christmas? How about something
on Christmas where I get the kids on
Christmas Eve and I can bring them back,
because when they get older maybe I can
spend until ten or eleven o'clock with
them on Christmas Eve.

Mrs. Daley: Okay, every Christmas Eve,
do you mean?

Mr. Daley: Okay, I just wanted to make
sure . . . just like we've been doing lately,
we can work something out with each
other and not just be tied to this. We can
be flexible.

Mrs. Daley: I know I really feel much
better, like we can work things out.

Mr. Daley: I just feel so much more
comfortable with the fact that we can talk
to each other a little more, are a little
friendlier instead of having me stand
outside and handing things back and forth.

Mrs. Daley: Mmm hmm. I know what
you mean.

Mr. Daley: I can see a difference in the
kids.

The phenomenon of
agreement spirals now so
that they can resolve the
issue of Christmas and
visitation. As they find a
means of compromise, the
process of a responsible
divorce looks more likely.
The earlier attempt to shift
topics and to run each
topic downhill has paid
off.

(They sit quietly, looking comfortably at each other.)

Mr. Daley: I wrote a letter a week ago to
my lawyers and said that I was going to
pay them $50 a month until I paid them
off. I owe the lawyers almost $3,000 and I
need more work from them.

Mrs. Daley: I think it's $1,700 that I
haven't paid off.

Mr. Daley: And we ended up wasting all
this time and money.

Mrs. Daley: Mmm hmm. We should
have come here first.
Mr. Daley: It certainly wasn't worth it.

Resolution Rituals

Moves toward the resolution of separation are manifested differently in different couples, but in most cases one can see marked shifts in mood. One dramatic step is seen when the couple begins, without prompting, to talk about dividing up shared possessions: the stereo, the records, the chairs, the bed. As they begin the ritual of deciding the fate of their belongings, it is obvious that these objects are part of the couple's soul, and that by engaging in the sad task of dividing them they are also dividing the marriage. For the therapist, the appearance of this ritual is clear evidence that an emotional divorce is finally occurring. In this stage, the death of the marriage is in the room briefly, and the mood dramatically shifts toward melancholy. Both husband and wife mourn what they are about to lose. With a sense of loss pervading the atmosphere, the last stage is ushered in and the participants finally leave the warring arena.

The shift from warring to willingness to listen to each other—and particularly the last quick change to a sad mood and the ritual of dividing possessions—occurs voluntarily. These changes generally do not have to be extracted or guided by the therapist. They are a conspicuous, dramatic result of a process that has been under way for some time. Thus we prefer that the topic of dividing possessions should not be suggested by the therapist directly but that it be brought up spontaneously by the couple, signaling that the process of divorce has become very real.

The couple now looks capable of resolving problems on its own, and a concern for equity prevails. Yet concern for equity is seldom so strong that it deters the couple from trying to take some advantage of the newly acquired flexibility. There is often an aggressive and predatory quality to the exchanges; the participants work quickly on each other, seeking the material goods they can loot from the sinking ship. What is impressive is that because the couple is fearful of pushing things too far and jeopardizing what has been accomplished, any manipulations tend to be mindful and carefully calculated. At the same time the participants clearly want to get what they can for themselves, and they politely resist each other's parries. The overall feeling is that the participants are able to look out for themselves, a feeling that is best supported by allowing them an extended solo flight, with the therapist absent from the room.

In the next sequence without the therapist, Mr. Daley dares to ask for a share of the loot—the diamond ring. But no sooner does he mention it when he is suddenly back to talking about the stereo. The wife defends herself deftly from his perhaps unconscious subterfuge. She differentiates what he has blurred and assumes it could not be the diamond they're discussing. He evolves his own counterploy: he will try to look generous about the stereo speakers, hoping to temper her wish not to give up the diamond. He hopes for confusion about what they are negotiating—is it the diamond or the stereo?

Mr. Daley: I was going to ask you about . . . would you rather just give me some equivalent of your diamond or something like that? . . . I'll get it appraised and if it's worth too much money, I'll give you some of the money so that I can go out and buy one because I hate the idea of taking it, I don't want it but it was my brother's, but I don't want to take something off the kids either, because I'm sure the kids use it. But I feel I should get something out of it and that was the only thing material. . . .

Mrs. Daley: How much is it worth and maybe I could. . . .

Mr. Daley: The diamond?

Mrs. Daley: No, not the diamond, I thought we were. . . .

She notices his shifting of subjects in negotiations.

Mr. Daley: Stereo, you won't get a better stereo unless you want to pay big bucks— the receiver and the speakers are pretty good.

Mrs. Daley: I don't really remember.

Mr. Daley: It's a very good receiver, and the speakers are good, too. My brother paid a lot of money for them, and you won't get something as . . . you go out and buy the same grade, that is, now you pay at least $500 and not have the turntable.

Mrs. Daley: Uh-huh. I've never thought the speakers were very good. I just thought . . . I thought that he said they weren't that good to begin with.

Mr. Daley: Now what do you want to do? If you want me to take the diamond to get it appraised and find out how much we can get, and if I can get, say, $500, I'll give you $150 and take $350.

Mrs. Daley: Mmm. Yeah.

Mr. Daley: I don't care. It depends on what you want to do. If you want me to just pack up the speakers and the receiver I will. I didn't want the kids to think, hey, I'm taking something and now they're going to go without. . . . Do they have something to play their records on?

Mrs. Daley: No. Well, you can't use the turntable without speakers, right?

Mr. Daley: I know.

Mrs. Daley: Well, I was going to go and kind of price some stereos someplace, just to see. I was just going to find like a regular receiver—find out how much it would cost to replace it, and let you take it. I figured that you would take it.

Mr. Daley: Are you planning to cash in the diamond?

Mrs. Daley: I wasn't really . . . I thought . . . in case something comes up and I really have to have some money. Maybe I should just hold on . . . I don't have any emergency money or anything like that. I just thought like maybe I should hold on to it in case something came up.

Mr. Daley: If you want to, you can cash in the diamond and get $500 for it, I'll give you $150 for it, and you can keep the receiver and speakers, since you are going to have to go out and buy something.

Mrs. Daley: Yeah, I know.

Mr. Daley: I don't think you're going to get anything equivalent to it unless you're willing to pay $300 or $350.

Mrs. Daley: I don't think I'll get

The shift from speakers to diamond is swift, as if to get her off balance.

He intimates great generosity with the stereo, to soften her resolve about the diamond. But she's unimpressed by his generosity.

The husband tries again. To make her feel grateful, he swiftly fuses his request that she cash in the diamond ("if I can get $500 for it, I'll give you $150") with the offer of the stereo equipment.

something equivalent to it. I just figured I would go to Sears and see what they cost over there. You know, just to have something for the kids to play. Umm, I don't really think I want to cash in the diamond right now.

Mr. Daley: Okay, what else?

Mrs. Daley: I think that covers everything.

The wife does not fall for it. She answers him as though the stereo issue is fused with the diamond issue, and firmly decides not to let go of either. The confusion technique therefore does not work on her.

The therapist enters to reward and reinforce their independent problem solving.

Therapist (*chiding*): You want to bankrupt the psychologists? You want to bankrupt the lawyers? You're not going to give us business. You're not giving them business.

Mrs. Daley: The lawyers are the first, I'm sure we both would rather put them out of business.

Therapist: You're really to be congratulated, and you know it, don't you?

Mrs. Daley: It takes both of us to come to an agreement.

Mr. Daley: Well, we both worked it out now. But I think the lawyers made up some stories or didn't relay things the way they were supposed to relay them. And the whole thing should have been worked out five years ago. I think that maybe if the right messages had been getting to Kim then, it probably would have been worked out. Do you think so?

Mrs. Daley: Yeah, I wish. It seems like everybody knew about you people here at the Families of Divorce Project—the courts and the lawyers and all that—and I just wish way back in the beginning they had asked us to come here, before it was at the point where everybody was at each other's throats and everybody had spent so much money, and the kids got upset by it.

It is commonplace for couples to unify around the shared obstacle, scapegoating their lawyers, in order to move ahead toward completion of their divorce. The way in which the therapist can respond to this tendency depends on the way the couple wants to utilize this step, either to stagnate further or to release each other. In this situation the therapist takes the couple's attack on lawyers at face value, in the belief that it is perhaps valid and useful,

Everybody was upset by it.
Therapist: Well, you can tell the judge that.
Mrs. Daley: I'd really like to.
Mr. Daley: Do we have to go back?
Therapist: Probably, I don't know how he'll work it. I'll write him a letter.
Mr. Daley: It would be nice if we don't have to go back.
Mrs. Daley: Yeah, maybe we don't if we both say, "fine."
Mr. Daley: I don't want to take any of my lawyers there. As a matter of fact, I don't know if you would or not, I don't know if you get billed for it, I'll get billed for it. I'll go without a lawyer.
Mrs. Daley: Yeah, yeah, I think I will, too.

assisting them to divorce by uniting against a common enemy.

The couple's newly expanded capacity to cooperate is not to be confused with a transformation in the basic perceptions they have of each other. The change simply reflects a greater willingness to deal with each other directly and in a less hostile manner. At one point, Mrs. Daley said to the therapist, "Do you think I should go back and present to him that I don't want my kids to go to public school?" The therapist's best move was to become nondirective, to let the wife continue with her own line of thought. Shortly afterward, Mrs. Daley said, "Well, I'm afraid that he will put them in public school. I want them to have a proper education, and I have the money to keep them in Catholic school and I will tell him." The therapist was present when the wife brought this subject up to her husband, but she mostly kept out of the discussion, intervening only now and then to support the wife's action of reaching out to the husband. The wife handled the husband on her own.

Continuing Solo Negotiations

It is to be expected that once away from the therapist's office, the participants might have doubts about whether they gave in too much or whether the ending was real or illusory. One of the participants might ask the therapist about the consequences of a particular concession. The therapist's objective, then, is to encourage the participant to feel, "I might as well go back and negotiate." Renegotiation is possible at this stage if the participants have lowered their level of mistrust of and deafness toward each other. They do go back and keep negotiating, conveying less avoidance of sensitive issues and acting as if they have reserved just enough trust to settle remaining differences. The problem-solving flow appears fully restored when the couple is capable of negotiating successfully when necessary, without the help of an outsider.

Thinking About Outcome: The Importance of Having Reasonable Goals

The way the therapist thinks about outcome is extremely important in guiding interventions. The therapist must have a clear realization that life is unfair, that symmetrical, balanced endings are rare, and that situations where both members land safely are unusual. Ordinarily, somebody gets more, somebody gets less.

In a follow-up phone call a few months after their last session, when their truce had a chance of becoming friendlier, Mrs. Daley told the therapist that she had found out that her husband had put down a deposit on a house, which she had thought he couldn't afford to do. Predictably, her anger was reignited: she said her husband had always been "a cheat and a liar. He never changed. I always knew he was like this." Such condemnations and feelings of being misled are to be expected and should not demoralize the therapist. The wife's "I always knew . . ." involved saving face by reorganizing material retrospectively. Her perception of him as friendly and honest at the end of their therapy was as real as the new perception of him as deceptive. "If he had bought the house a year later, maybe I wouldn't have gotten so angry and so suspicious that he had the money. Now I think he was telling me he had no money because he wanted it to get a house and be with his girlfriend."

Almost routinely, the postseparation situation brings about feelings of being cheated, of being left behind, or being prevented by the ex-spouse from moving ahead. This need to redress unfairness is found even in divorced couples who do well. The nature of the marriage bond is so engulfing, extending into so many areas of life, that even long after the separation the tendency is to measure an estranged spouse's growth possessively against one's own. In the Daley family, months after our sessions with them, when the husband made a fresh start—a new house, a new woman—Mrs. Daley became acutely aware of what she felt to be her own lack of progress. Her husband had dared to go ahead. She needed time to lessen her preoccupation with her husband's moves.

Many ex-spouses are perhaps compulsive in contrasting their changes in personal relationships, material possessions, or career accomplishments with those of the other. Few take such a constant, watchful stance as to investigate, for example, whether the ex-spouse is hiding money from the IRS. With some couples, however, these feelings become the vehicle of a difficult, incomplete divorce. Such couples may have settled matters pertaining to the children but not how to react to each other's independent gains and accomplishments. To see the other person as being too happy or too successful while feeling "left behind" becomes unbearable and can lead to efforts to become extremely disruptive to the ex-spouse's life.

We work on the premise that adults generally cannot reverse cultivated hate overnight. After years of warring and hating, they are not likely to have a remarkable change of heart and become friends. They can, however, get down to doing some business. If along with that also comes a willingness to give each other a chance to prove themselves as friends, that is a bonus. We settle for each member of the couple sensing that he or she has to contain negative feelings and display only what is necessary to maintain a workable relationship. It will be enough if each feels that a polite way— sometimes an amicable way—can be used for settling differences. In other words, we aim for disciplined duplicity based on enlightened self-interest. The return of fundamental positive feelings of friendliness and even of love may be possible later. They may come after tests and more tests, during interactions in which the ex-husband and ex-wife find they can indeed trust each other again.

Neither husband nor wife can transform their carefully cultivated opinions of each other just because they went through a single period or two of avoiding head-on collisions. Yet character reconstruction and a reversal of basic views of who the other is are not necessary to reach resolution of differences and produce a nonpathological divorce.

Summary: Lessons from the Unhappy Divorce

Unhappy divorces are those that create, out of visitation or some other problem area, another acute conflict. The couple cannot resolve the conflict and thereby impairs the foundation for subsequent problem solving. For these couples, the apparent subsiding of acute conflict is no measure of change. Acute conflict is characterized by overcharged, excited explosions of anger and by the emotional involvement of both spouses. Each of them sets out simply to deter the other from taking advantage but ends up inflicting so much damage that the other decides to retreat forever. That amounts to pseudoclosure, which impairs problem-solving foundations and leaves one or both participants unwilling to try again.

These chronic fighters require special procedures to help them deal with pseudoclosure. They must work beyond the premature subsiding of the acute conflict, compelling the basic conflict to reappear in such a way that the change can be sustained. The therapist must bring out the theme that was hidden before work is completed and keep it before them, stretching out the quarrel until the residue of hard feelings is worked out so that it cannot sabotage what will come later. A central concern is to protect the fundamental relationship machinery from damage. This involves exploring how the participants attack each other in vulnerable areas instead of pulling back. Such attacks in vulnerable areas demonstrate serious miscalculations that do not enhance the couple's chances for future cooperation.

Participants who attack this way do so, of course, because they believe they have been provoked. Thus they go for the jugular, even attacking the other's basic ideas of self. Attacks such as "He's a cheat and a liar" aim directly at the other's sense of integrity and honesty. They can obviously ruin the machinery of trust and destroy any possibility of rebuilding the relationship or of keeping what is needed of the relationship for caring for the children. Couples complicate their mountain of unsolved issues while expanding their resentment and hostility, which tend to show up in the next clash if not in depression or other symptoms.

We are impressed with how hate can have a missionary zeal. We also see, however, how most couples who are entrenched in hurting each other also usually convey that they only hurt the other before the other hurts them. It would seem that the continuous and reciprocal aspects of the aggression are also maintained as a by-product of self-protective action. In our view, to appreciate the fact that people can be held accountable does not deny the fact that people are also capable of action for which they cannot appropriately calculate and control the consequences. This is seen when couples fight and cannot stop, and progressive adversarial positions develop. The self always has a margin of responsibility for its action, but the self can err. There must be a place for plain human error in the shaping of interpersonal relationships.

The therapeutic task is to sponsor realistic calculations that allow a moment of effective problem solving, in the hope of starting a positive spiral. What should develop is a history of success in resolving basic differences before additional emotional damage is done. Resolving acute conflicts improves the chances that subsequent differences will be handled well and precludes the accumulation of unsettled grievances that eventually demoralize the couple, breaking its spirit and shaping the tense divorce situation.

6

Observing the Balance: Moments of Violence Prevention

SOME COUPLES do not have to be defended or armed against each other. They know what to expect from each other and are able to calculate correctly that their spouses will not hurt them. They can negotiate in an atmosphere of trust. With other couples, however, considerable preparation is needed before they feel safe in a face-to-face encounter. They may fear, with justification, that an accident could happen: "My wife could make mincemeat out of me," or "You will not be able to field it." These couples cannot even trust the therapist to umpire correctly. They must be prepared to know what trouble to expect and to feel adequately defended against it. They must be armed with the knowledge of what to do or say in the face of counterattacks.

For the therapist this means shedding a systems-thinking idea: that if you get people to become friendly with each other, then good will grows automatically like a snowball until it fills the earth. That notion is misleading. It diminishes the therapist's alertness to the couple's need to take responsibility for keeping their relationship on a constructive track each step of the way. By and large, the couple does much better not by overrelaxing and relying on snowballing good will but by becoming responsible for the details of their own conduct. This lessens the chances of "accidental" prov-ocation. Positive movement, if and when it occurs, is usually shortlived and is best maintained by being gently steered and stretched while the therapist remains careful and vigilant. To work toward building confidence and shaping good will, the therapist must engage each participant on an instrumental, yet ungreedy, "money in the bank" approach. Our underlying attitudinal message is "handle this exchange now to build reserves for the future. Deal with him or her fairly without responding with counterprov-ocation. You may be making or unmaking opportunities for a more prof-itable exchange in the not-so-immediate future." This message inhibits unproductive fighting and generates exchanges that allow for new begin-nings. The therapist helps the participants modulate and time their com-munications in order to maintain some control over their changing rela-tionship and secure the necessary level of safety for both participants. When one person, or both, feel impotent or extremely vulnerable, a dan-gerous balance has been created. This is nowhere better seen than in work with volatile couples.

The therapist's role in the middle of conflictual and collaborative forces involves, as will be described, organizing couples toward a more productive balance, recognizing extremely precarious balances, spotting incendiary networks that tip the balance, discovering entrapments and delusions that disrupt the balance, detecting new and sudden imbalances, and finally, recognizing constantly reset imbalances.

Organizing Toward the Productive Balance

Among the routine difficulties that the therapist must contend with when dealing with divorcing couples is unharnessed anger. In one family, the husband's arrogance and self-righteous style contributed to making a very muted, inarticulate wife feel so angry yet impotent that she could only explode. Her physical reaction—punching him—was directly related to what she could not do in verbal exchanges. She was not good at verbal sparring with her husband; she would let him talk and talk, remaining quiet until she exploded in violent action. The therapist was well aware that in her silence the wife felt acutely shortchanged: "People listen to him; he's the talker; he's the one who knows how to handle words; I just sit and take it"—and from the start provided a very careful forum for this woman's grievances. Much of the therapy was organized around articulating the needs of an inarticulate woman. This meant going out of the way to sift out her wishes, her side of the story, her injured feelings, her sense of being the wronged party.

Sometimes the therapist prevented the possibility of a violent explosion by taking the man on herself, doing the inarticulate wife's job. But ultimately it was the therapist's art of using herself as part of the triadic forces and allocating reassurance between the husband and the wife that enabled her to prevent violence. By the end of the first session, the wife felt that the therapist understood and was not taken in by the verbal husband. A more productive balance prevailed, from which the therapist could work with the wife without alienating the husband.

The possibility of violence was even more imminent in another family, in which the husband had brandished a knife at the wife. He tended to minimize the incident, saying he was "just tired. It was not really a serious attempt." At an earlier session, the wife had communicated that she had been very scared when he flashed the knife. The therapist, seeing himself as part of a delicate triangular arrangement, carefully examined the event alone with the husband, analyzing the details of the knife display and finding out who might have heard about it. The session dwelled on the moment the knife was displayed, stressing that not only the husband and wife but the extrafamilial world knew that he had exercised poor judgment and had indeed been dangerous. The therapist resisted the husband's almost hypnotic efforts to lure him into believing that the brandishing of the knife was only a minor issue in the conflict with the wife—the husband's self-delusional construction of the event and his attempt to minimize the danger. Instead the therapist treated it as a possibly dangerous loss of control, not in the husband's best interest. The intense microexamination made the man understand that despite his likeability and persuasiveness, he did not charm the therapist.

The therapist continued to examine the event until the husband had a sense of being observed, of not being totally private to the watchful outside world. At the same time he appealed to the husband's self-interest: "This doesn't make you come across as really wanting some workable arrangement with your wife about visiting your child. By allowing yourself this kind of conduct, you're risking losing visits with the boy you love so much." At no point was the husband allowed to dismiss the event as an accident in the past that would never happen again. The event was kept imminent, important; it could happen again.

The therapist then dwelled extensively on whether the husband really understood how much his wife could take, in order to prevent any miscalculation. He ended the session by having the husband review in detail all that the wife was doing to protect herself, implying that if he allowed himself to step out of line he would have gone too far because she was well defended. Every intervention reminded the husband that his wife was surrounded and supported and unreachable, that it would be foolish for him to try anything, and that he had better not miscalculate. At the end of the session, a new balance had been organized between external watchful forces and the husband's impulses. This balance helped contain and check his behavior. Of course, the new equilibrium was reinforced by the therapist's work with the other side of the triangle, the wife, which involved actively discouraging her tendency to give ambivalent signals that could be interpreted as tolerating her husband's dangerous behavior.

Recognizing the Extremely Precarious Balance

The potential for violence is often associated with the sad reality that many noncustodial parents lose contact with their children sometime after the separation. In one family, the husband had severed himself from his child completely: "I would not go back there to visit my kid, because I'm going to wind up shooting somebody." On the surface this looked like just a failed case, husband rationalizing his escape: the poor man fled and abandoned his wife and child. But we learned that this man had met with painful undermining and relentless interrogation every time he went near the house to pick up his son. The wife's relatives and friends were rigidly religious people who had watched him, he claimed, as if he were "a freak." They always had been ready to interfere with his rights, ready to provoke him. He would fall for it and become aggressive. He had had no way of modifying this righteous network, and no legal help. At some point the precarious balance had broken and the husband, in lieu of violence, had used the only sensible defense available to him in the situation—he fled. Since the members of the powerful network were unwilling to come to the therapy, the therapist was unable to influence the situation.

Spotting Incendiary Networks

Situations of potential violence often include a support network that incites rather than dampens violence. Mrs. Frank was very skillful at maneuvering around her husband in dialogue (see chapter 3). She could confuse him and could excite him, and he would frequently find himself puzzled and impotent—a dangerous combination. He felt that his wife could always "get him," could always twist his words, con him, and deceive him, and in response he became dangerous. To balance the situation and prevent violence, many forces converged, among them significant counterthreats from his wife's brother and father. They eventually made it clear that if he went too far in intimidating her, they would "break his ribs."

The biggest problem in these situations of imminent violence is that often even the people used as a resource are incendiary. They are the wrong people; they stimulate and provoke in the wrong directions. For orientation, clarity, and a sense of power, Mr. Frank would turn to his brother, who only compounded the problem by arousing further hostilities against Mrs. Frank. His brother, himself in the midst of a stormy divorce, felt he was being robbed by his own wife. After a conversation with his brother, Mr. Frank would show up for a session disheveled and talking anxiously about how he was going "to be taken to the cleaners." The therapist's job became that of rapidly disengaging a distressed man from a distressed brother who was inciting him to take revenge, and that of connecting him with a lawyer.

By encouraging the husband to secure a lawyer and offering him more sessions as needed, the therapist helped him feel far less insecure. Later, the husband found himself a support group and began to experiment with dating. Only then was his wife able to feel relieved; as the husband's sense of company and safety increased, the possibility of violence decreased.

Stabilizing Around Violence: A Rigid Imbalance

Another common situation that clinicians face in divorce work is one in which a couple has stabilized around violence, experiencing it as routine and therefore dulling its import. Most frequently these couples expose a fairly rigid imbalance—one member is supposed to be the violent one and the other member the needy victim, without alternating these positions. There is an expectation of violence from only one side, and real danger always exists. Though dangerous outbursts are common, the clinician is impressed that the participants stay in the violence-prone relationship. They know it is chronic but do not try to escape.

One Latin woman had been separated from her husband for over a year, after he had taken a shot at her and left a bullet lodged in the wall just above her head. She had narrowly escaped death, yet she desperately wanted him back and was setting things up to bring him back into the marriage. She felt she had nothing in her life besides her husband and her obese seven-year-old son, whom she infantalized. Waiting for this man against all hope—since he had already remarried—she entrenched herself in a self-demeaning career as a kind of second wife. She rationalized this by thinking of herself as being the second, but most important, woman catering to an important patriarch. She found external support for her subordinate relationship to a married man in the semideviant blueprint for marriage which her mother had lived years ago in their country of origin. She kept herself oblivious to the fact that this old, traditional life style was now practiced by fewer and fewer women in her barrio.

To work against her passive acceptance of this pattern, the therapist tried to get the woman to imagine what sort of life she could create with her ex-husband and his new wife and their kids. Would she sleep in the servant's quarters? Would she—once a month, maybe—get an opportunity, a special privilege, to sleep with him? What sort of meals would she cook for him after he had finished having dinner with his wife? Would she keep her child away from the other children if the new wife didn't like him? After considerable reflection, she thought feebly that perhaps it would not work out.

The actual change began when women at work told her what they thought—that she was losing her dignity—and encouraged her to get out of the situation. She began thinking that these women had a point and that the therapist was pushing her into a situation that made no sense. *She* was the kind of woman who could not live with a man in that situation! A few weeks later, she dropped the idea of getting him back. Immense problems continued to exist between her and her son, but she had stepped out of the violence-prone, enslaved relationship with her husband.

Detecting a New Imbalance

Patterns of intimidation and violence can escalate yet go undetected until brought up by the children, who first perceive the imbalance. In the family to be described, the escalation of violence peaked in a sour divorcing situation. Its detection was classical: one of the children had stomachaches, and her sibling had discrete thoughts of leaving home to escape from what was about to happen between the parents. When the therapist started exploring the situation with the youngsters alone, it became clear that they were afraid they had discovered their mother's "concealed" efforts to acquire a gun. They were very afraid that the parents might kill each other. It was as if the children, through their alarming symptoms, were alerting the outside world that their parents' relationship had reached a new level of imbalance that required resources beyond their own.

The conflictual process leading to the separation created a situation of danger. The youngsters were struggling against recruitment dynamics, and the therapy consisted of supporting and amplifying their efforts. Separate work with the children and the parents was mandated by the children's powerlessness to deal directly with their parents' runaway conflict. The children were in no position to modify their parents' behavior, which was having a severe impact on them. The parents were blocking feedback from the children—permitting no access to the obvious signals the children were sending (stomach pains, vomiting, fear, and escape fantasies). The children's options were either to escape (live with an aunt), or to work for change through another, less direct outlet.

Once comfortable with and trusting of the therapist, even young children often become the voice of reason, cuing the therapist during periods of parental primitivity, decompensation, or imminent danger. But the therapist does not ask the youngsters to take on the task of confronting the parents directly, since that would ensconce them even more solidly in an untenable position. Instead, the therapist becomes the funnel for communication from youngsters to parents.

In this case, the couple, middle class, with one latency-age daughter and one adolescent son, had been separated for close to a year. The ten-year-old, Raquel, had been having severe stomach pains and nausea, for which no medical origin could be found. In the following segment, the therapist, alone with the siblings, explores their perception of their situation. He meets generalized confusion; all is muddled, with nothing taking precedence over anything else. The girl cryptically mentions that the mother wants her to be the "index" patient, with her name, rather than her brother Roger's, on the clinic's intake sheet. The therapist tracks his way through the confusion:

Raquel: My mamma said she was going to try to change the name of the patient to me, because she said that the doctor said when we went to the hospital that I am psychosomatic. And my mother said it's probably because of the marriage breaking up that I am being psychosomatic.

Raquel is clearly upset. The therapist especially notices an inconsistency between her rational adult content and her affect: she looks scared.

Therapist: What do you think about what your mom says?

Raquel: It might be true.

Therapist: So what is upsetting you, then?

Raquel: Because I used to, it used to really hurt me and I used to think about my father, it was about when my uncle was here . . . about. . . .

The fragmented content cues the therapist to a deeper unrest, and he tracks further.

Therapist: A couple of weeks ago?

Raquel: Yeah, I was getting real sick and my momma said it was psychosomatic and at the hospital that is what they said.

Divorce per se is often offered as an easy, catch-all explanation for signs of stress, to discourage the therapist from exploring the fundamental question of what is so upsetting.

(*Having said this, Raquel seems to withdraw.*)

Therapist: So what would you say is upsetting you most of all, Raquel? (*There is a long silence.*) Raquel, what is it?

Raquel (*tentatively*):   Did my mother tell you about the . . . er . . . income tax. . . .

The therapist encourages Raquel to go beyond the psychosomatic explanation. Just as she is beginning to drift inward again, the therapist calls her back. His manner is concerned and curious, helping her to go further.

Roger: Yeah. My mom, I don't understand her and it's really . . .

Roger is not simply trying to steal the stage. He is also protecting his sister from being the one to reveal the secret and expose the mother.

Therapist (*interrupts Roger*):   Hang on. Is it okay if Roger takes over and talks now?

Raquel: Yes, but will we come back to me, though?

Therapist: Yup.

Raquel fears that in the turmoil of the divorce her needs will again go unattended.

Roger (*indignantly*):   Yeah, I don't like this at all what my mom did, but the income tax is coming back, the income tax return. So she signs her name and my father's name so all of it came to her, and she told us that she was going to give my father half of it. . . .
Raquel: She lied on it.

Roger: Said there's more people in our family so she signed her name and forged my father's name. And $4,000 all came to us and she spent it all.

Roger's indignation is sustained by his sense of being wronged, deceived. The mother attempted to recruit him and his sister into being accomplices by telling them that she was going to give the father half.
But the attempt to deceive them is transparent and does not work. Indeed, it backlashed. The children were inadvertently confirmed in the position of having to watch over the father's interests in the face of their mother's vindictive delinquency.

And then when my uncle and all were over here, she told him to see about getting her a gun. And I asked her what it was for, and she said, "This is for when your father comes up to me for spending his income tax money." She provoked him. If someone steals $2,000 from you and they take the $2,000 for themselves. . . .
(*Roger's voice is pressured and anxious.*)

Earlier in the sequence Raquel had mentioned her uncle in the context of worrying about the father. Her uncle, it now emerges, is the one who delivers the gun.

Therapist: So you are saying that she's provoking your dad. . . .
Roger (*anxiously*):   Don't you think so?
Therapist: And what? Now she buys a gun?
Roger: Now she wants to buy a gun so she can shoot him if he comes up and gets mad. That ain't right. That's like punching some strong person in the face and then

Seeing through his mother's lie, it is easier for him to maintain the underlying coalition with some strong person in the face and then get a gun and put it to their head and then they won't do nothing, see, and if they do something, you shoot them. I don't think that was right at all.

Raquel: And I was thinking he could come over and she'll shoot him.
Therapist: How did you feel?
Raquel: I was scared.
Roger: Right, and I was scared.
Therapist: Wow!
Raquel: And I was. . . .
Therapist: You were what?

the admired "strong person," the father. And indeed there is here an offended sense of justice permitting him and his sister to react independently to the unfairness of the situation. They both alert the outside and lessen the chances of a catastrophe. However, the children's cognitive independence—their ability to not be deceived—can explain only so much. This father had "money in the bank" in his history of kindness when dealing with the youngsters, which contrasted with his wife's harshness. In this sense, the likelihood that they would use their capacity for independent, critical thinking to differentiate from the mother and side with him was preorganized.

Raquel: Throwing up all over the place.
Therapist: You were, what, throwing up all over the place . . . (*sympathetically*) I can understand that you threw up. I can understand that, Raquel. Really.

The sequence returns to the psychosomatic complaint, but with a clear understanding of the interpersonal context organizing the symptoms.

The youngster's natural fears had resulted in symptoms. She had been taken to the hospital, but the mother had been careful not to reveal the real cause. She had reinterpreted and mystified her daughter's symptoms in such a way that the physician could not discover the most evident source of the stress.

Many of the stress symptoms in children that are attributed to the loss and mourning associated with divorce are sometimes in reality related to actual but concealed violence involved in the separation. It should be routine, when "upset" is presented, that a child be investigated for more than masked reactions to the sense of rejection and sadness over the divorce. Sensitive probing should focus on the child's self-protective and interprotective reactions to actual or expected violence between divorcing adults.

The therapist correctly assessed this family's situation as extremely dangerous. The children were unable to change their mother or their father, and they could not run to him without revealing her hand. Therefore the therapist, utilizing his good standing and authority with the scared mother, moved to shift her attitude. He brought her in immediately and met with her alone. His feedback to her was carefully designed to allow her to corroborate the real source of her children's nightmarish fears. She saw how excruciatingly painful the situation was for them and how dangerous it was for her as well. He worked on her to get rid of the gun, stressing that she might be compromising herself and endangering herself and her family. She revealed that in fact she was terribly scared, which was why she had bought a gun. The therapist sympathized with her plight but was very firm that she must think about immediately removing this dangerous weapon. He suggested that she consider a letter of protest to her husband. Finally, she agreed that she really had gotten herself into a hole and that the gun was no way out. She did get rid of the gun, handing it over to neighbors.

The key to bringing about that moment of relief was the therapist's consideration for this woman. She usually felt unappreciated, and it was difficult to get her to feel that something other than just anger prevailed in the world. The first really intimate moment came in the midst of the discussion about purchasing the gun, when she had expected the therapist to be only critical. She softly confessed to feeling weak and vulnerable, and the therapist was vocal in his surprise. Like her husband, he too had confused her defensive counterhostility with implacable strength. The moments of softness with the therapist seem to have been instrumental in allowing her to cooperate with her husband. With preparation, the husband and wife managed to come together in the room without offending each other and were able to cooperate about the children.

This case reminds us that in divorce work, too much emphasis has been given to the obvious process through which parents attempt to recruit the children into taking sides and not enough to how the children resist or modify those recruitment efforts. Many children react as more than passive victims of one parent's attempt to poison them against the spouse. Like the youngsters in this particular family, they see through the parent's efforts to recruit them, and through their independent backlash (which involves their total being—cognitive, somatic, and emotional) they start a process that draws help from outside the family and transforms the situation.

The Constantly Reset Imbalance

Situations created by violent intent, which is then subsequently denied, present a most dangerous circumstance in divorce work and merit a detailed example. They are usually brought about by rather innocent-looking participants who are constantly provocative, and who organize fuming allies who feel totally righteous and justified in their actions. They always have a partner who picks up after them and protects them and possibly even encourages them. The adversary, the ex-spouse, starts to feel deeply defrauded, betrayed, and hurt, and therefore becomes dangerous.

A woman lost custody of her two children and came to the clinic two years after her separation. She had been living with her lover, Joe, for whom she had left the marriage, and had seen her children only sporadically, when they met in the neighborhood. Tension between her and her husband was extremely high. The first formal visit with her children in about six months was arranged for Christmas Eve. While waiting impatiently for the children in front of the house, she noticed a wreath on the door and snatched it, claiming, "After all, it is my wreath."

The husband arrived right after she had taken the wreath, noticed it was missing, and was furious. He ran to her car and spat on her in front of the children. "She has taken everything from me. Now she wants this, too." The woman then rushed home to complain to her lover, who moved quickly to her aid. He indignantly phoned her estranged husband and warned him to watch his step. The husband exploded, "I am going to kill you. I'm coming after you. I'm simply going to kill you." The threat couldn't be taken lightly. He had a rifle, and the lover was the man his wife had left him for.

While relating this story, the woman displayed no awareness that she had been a part of initiating and compounding a dangerous sequence, not just for her husband but for her lover. She talked as though her lover had put himself in the situation, as though she had had nothing to do with organizing and orchestrating the event: "I just went to him and told him." When asked why she had him make the call, she answered that her lover was completely free in making that decision: "Well, he decided for himself." The therapist had her look carefully at the consequences of her actions.

"Do you love this man Joe? Do you realize you are putting him in danger?" She faintly acknowledged that she did. Still, on her way out the door at the end of the session, she casually dropped another message, analogous to the provocative wreath incident: "Do you think I should stop paying child support?" Clearly, she could not do one more thing to her husband without prompting a dangerous outburst, yet she was ready to do just that.

The therapist in such cases must be unambiguous if violence is to be prevented, firmly warning and directing the participants. In this case, the therapist told the woman that it was a bad idea to stop child support and that if she did not keep her lover out of it she might get someone killed. The therapist's advice: "Use your lawyer instead of Joe for protection and support."

The therapist then told her that he would be in touch with her husband. The husband was at first extremely suspicious, wondering if this were not another of his wife's tricks. But the therapist said that he needed the father's side of the story—that the welfare of his children was involved—and the man listened. The therapist made clear that he knew only the wife's interpretations, that he was available and open to both sides, and that he was not interested in becoming part of a triangle or taking sides with the wife. Looking for a chance to warn the husband, but without warning him openly or breaking his confidence with the wife, the therapist asked the husband to describe his wife. As the man did so, the opportunity showed itself. The husband began to describe her as bizarre and crazy. "What do you mean? What does she really want you to do?" asked the therapist. "She wants me to beat her up," he responded. The therapist quickly seized the opportunity to sponsor self-restraint and care: "You can't fall for it."

The balance of power between this husband and wife had been radically upset. Even though her lover was taller, bigger, and stronger than her husband, she enlisted her friends to help support and protect her, making her husband feel even more cornered and provoked. He felt that she had everyone on her side, while he had no one. He felt so far down that he might well try a desperate move to come back up.

The imbalance was made worse by the match between the wife and her lawyer. Some people show an uncanny skill in finding a lawyer who will actualize their wishes. This compounds the problems immensely. In this case, the therapist was brought the news that the wife had finally found a lawyer who really understood her plight, a lawyer "who never loses a case." The lawyer had instructed her on ways of collecting evidence to indicate to the judge that the father was an incompetent parent. She was to carry a tape recorder inside her coat. Everything he said would be recorded to use as evidence against him. Her goal would be to set him up, to provoke him, to reveal poor parenting, to bring out any way in which he was acting contrary to court mandates. Her lawyer also explicitly suggested that she get back into the house, which still legally belonged to both of them, so that she could tape his evicting her from the house.

The woman set out to do precisely this. She watched the house and waited for the husband to leave. Once he had left, she tried to get in. The children felt compelled to follow their father's instructions and refused to open the door for her, while she stood outside begging to be allowed in.

When the mother persevered in trying to get into the house, the children telephoned the police, who escorted her away. In the middle of it all the youngsters may have called the father and gotten some support, but even with his support, being put through the dirty work of rejecting their own mother was obviously damaging to the children. Thereafter, the mother pathetically pursued the teenage boy in the streets on his way to school, telling him "I love you. I love you." From then on the boy tried to stay away from her even more, not only because he believed his father's version of the separation but because he felt deeply embarrassed. She would approach the youngster at odd moments, such as when he was with his friends, and start rubbing his back. In one particularly demeaning moment the son threw a stone at her. Instead of relating this to her son's feelings about her behavior, she interpreted it as further evidence of the extent to which her husband had turned her son against her and as one more reason to go on with the radical tactics of her new lawyer.

During the early phases of the therapy, we had been impressed by this woman's complaints that the legal profession did not understand her because, she claimed, they continually emphasized that she should reconcile with her husband. In order to examine her complaints, we asked her to bring in letters from her lawyers. The letters were found to be very different from her description. Far from suggesting a reconciliation, the lawyers were simply suggesting that they would help her get visitation or custody: they were not interested in becoming committed to an endless battle with her husband. They were, in fact, trying to restrain her. The majority of lawyers saw through this woman's ascendent wish not to stop until she could demolish her husband by taking everything from him.

The extent to which obsessions with gathering damaging evidence can go was illustrated a few weeks later. The son had for the first time had a grand mal seizure, and telling the therapist about it, the mother expressed glee and satisfaction. Now she had further evidence that her husband, in not contacting her immediately after the seizure, had been a negligent parent; he might have brought about the seizure in the first place. She was oblivious to the real danger to her son. The angry collector of evidence in her had totally taken over.

Since this woman appeared to be committed to the polarizing tactics of her new lawyer, the therapist attempted to impress two messages upon her. First, he was not convinced that this way of working was in the best interest of the children. While possibly winning a battle with her husband, she would lose the war to get the best for them. The second was that her lawyer needed to be informed that she was concerned about the effect that his approach would have on the children. It was her responsibility to let him know immediately that she wanted the kids unhurt, unscared. She was misleading her lawyer in not indicating to him how dangerous, provocative, and irrational she could be with her husband, how she might incite him to violence. The therapeutic aim was to change her fixed notions that her husband was always and exclusively to blame.

The first message, about the children, hardly registered. She was so absorbed in her vindictiveness that she was only minimally tuned in to the children's needs. The second message, about her responsibility and the necessity for her to communicate how she provoked her husband, got through. She was at first upset by this, complaining that the therapist didn't understand her, and protested that he, like the lawyers, doctors, priests, everyone, took her husband's side against her. Nonetheless she did speak with her lawyer, and evidently she was aware that she was scaring and dangerously provoking her husband, because she did reduce the provocations. The husband was more malleable in coming to see that it was not in his best interest to respond to her wild provocations. Although the skewed situation was never stabilized, the minimal goal of containing violence was accomplished.

More often than is attested to in the literature, the problems of relationship imbalances that lead to dangerous conflict in divorce couples prove beyond the capacity not only of therapists but also of lawyers, whose involvement often complicates rather than harnesses the situation. To learn how to manage those special complications, the field requires a more developed network theory than is now available. That theory should explicate how social units become constructive or incendiary units. The necessity for societally sanctioned and especially empowered institutions such as the court as an ultimate authority must be invoked to deal with these difficult networks. In chapter nine we will describe how such family networks move to the courts for assessment and last-resort resolution.

7

The Children's Work

CHANGES in families are often hard-won. The therapist utilizes observations of and interviews with both children and parents to facilitate postseparation change. Many options exist. Sometimes the therapist focuses on and works through the youngsters, helping them deal better with their parents; sometimes the therapist more directly works to cancel out the parents' destructive behavior. Typically, the therapist works concurrently and sequentially through a variety of avenues, seeking to understand the way the participants are positioned vis-à-vis each other. With such knowledge, the therapist can attempt to shake whatever positions are accounting for dysfunction in the total system, expand each individual's range of alternatives, and lead the family to more viable arrangements.

The therapist maintains the prerogative to work strategically with different groups at different times. There are times when it is advisable to reduce contact between the generations, perhaps with an overt declaration to the parents that contact is presently counterproductive. The therapist then works with the parents and children separately, motivating change while preparing them for future encounters with each other. At other times the generations are brought together to deal with each other face-to-face in interactions monitored by the therapist. Thus, the therapist forms a triangular relationship with the children and the parents, sometimes blocking undesirable processes and other times facilitating and amplifying the family's interactive efforts.

Among the processes the clinician must handle when dealing with the children in divorcing families are the phenomena of pumping, poisoning, and brainwashing, all of which represent a parent's efforts to recruit children into devaluing the other parent. Pumping, the most natural and elusive of these activities, is the spouse's sometimes calm, sometimes desperate effort to learn or size up the situation of the other spouse without dealing with that spouse directly. The child is asked direct questions or encouraged to drop revealing information about the other parent. Too often the aim of pumping is to collect and develop ammunition for more poisoning innuendoes and brainwashing of the child against the other. All of these processes amount to recruitment and make the children's lives the arena of the parents' conflicts. These recruitment processes, however, generally surface in direct observations of parent-child interaction or become conspicuous through anecdotal revelations as the therapist speaks with the children or their parents.

In the family to be described, organizing a face-to-face encounter between the generations was a feasible and necessary first step. The youngsters in this family were late adolescents, and they could expedite the removal of obstacles that had created an emergency situation in the stagnant separating process. By virtue of their age, personality development, and sibling-group affiliation, the youngsters were in a position to respond actively to the parents. They could be expected to initiate controlled feedback of their own that would directly free the parents to deal with their process of separating.

We will present transcripts selected from a number of primarily sibling-focused sessions with a family over a ten-month period. The discussion goes beyond the use of a special procedure in the crisis period, into the changing sibling relationships and hierarchical reorganizations that follow the initial crisis.

The Garceaus were a lower-middle-class, devoutly Catholic family with four children—Bruce (age twenty), Debbie (age nineteen), Cathy (age eighteen), and Peter (age sixteen). The two eldest children had been living outside the home for about a year. The children had been living amid extreme conflict for at least eight years, despite their parents' efforts to improve matters by participating in marital therapy and pastoral counseling. The strain of the situation was compounded by the family's image of itself as a model family within the Catholic community. The parents were sleeping in separate rooms, the mother on a mattress on the floor of the living room, and they did not eat together. Over the years Mrs. Garceau had been beaten a number of times by her husband and had left the home; on one of those occasions she had landed in the hospital. But she had always returned. Her anger and fear were of such proportion that she had recently gone for a knife with which to stab her husband. He was nevertheless adamantly set against the idea of separation, claiming that the children would be hurt by such a move and would oppose it. Although the mother overtly wanted the separation, she covertly shared, with ambivalance, her husband's conviction that they should stay together for the sake of the children. She therefore did not directly oppose his argument but instead contained her rage. She was barely able to control her homicidal impulses and sense of entrapment.

The event that triggered the family's entrance into divorce therapy was an explosion of violence on one of the children's part; Peter had punched his mother and pushed her to the ground. Peter had been having difficulty in his own life: his school grades had slumped and he had become increasingly withdrawn and depressed.

At the first session, which lasted approximately three hours, the whole family was seen together briefly and then in different constellations. It was clear that the parents were locked into a massive, long-term conflict. Imminent danger prevailed, and, with good reason, the children were afraid that someone would get killed. To varying degrees they were all embroiled in this conflagration. In particular, Peter, by his own and everyone else's admission, was unambiguously in the father's camp. As Peter stated when seen with just his siblings, "I'm on my dad's side. That's my problem. Cathy and the others, they jump back and forth and make out better. But not me." Clearly, he was the father's bodyguard and champion and was acting out his father's anger. Consequently, he was simultaneously obsessed with protecting his father and depressed over this burden and over the fact that he was dangerously jeopardizing his relationship with his mother, his siblings, and his friends. The sibling subsystem was sharply divided, and Peter was isolated.

The Confrontation Parade

To deal with this stuck situation, a procedure can be used in which the youngsters, one at a time and in a controlled format, tell the parents what they have told the therapist: that they are suffering more from the parents' staying together than they would if the parents separated. We call this procedure "the confrontation parade." The organized and cumulative input from the children debunks the homeostasis-maintaining parental myth that the family should stay together for the sake of the youngsters—that the youngsters would oppose and be seriously harmed by the separation. This procedure works when the youngsters have become the main arena of detour for a failed marriage and the alibi for not changing. With the rationalization for the status quo removed, the possibility of change is enhanced and the separation can finally come about.

It is sometimes argued that in matters pertaining to the continuation or dissolution of a marriage the therapist's ethical stance should be to stand by conservatively and maintain neutrality. Other clinicians argue that the therapist can never be neutral and that leaning either toward continuation of a marriage or toward its demise, depending on the circumstances, is an acceptable position. In using the confrontation parade, the therapist may rationalize that he or she is simply eliminating detours to the breakup, removing a roadblock to the separation, not steering the family. But this viewpoint ducks the ethical dilemma.

With this family, the therapist was well informed of a long history of escalating violence and the many failed efforts of helping professionals to save the marriage. The probability of still greater violence was high. Our decision to promote the separation in this way was helped by the mother's emphatic stance that she wanted out of the marriage and by the youngsters' pain and turmoil. Obviously, a conservative stance of neutrality in a situation of such grave danger would have been clinically incorrect and unethical. Standing by passively would have licensed stasis and promoted the likelihood of physical danger. The option was to employ the confrontation parade.

Another purpose of the confrontation parade is to begin the process of releasing the siblings, who are caught in the middle. That is, when youngsters are in that position, the therapist can use this procedure with the family members to redraw more appropriate boundaries between parents and children.

The confrontation parade is best employed with older adolescents or young adults. The steps involved in the procedure must be followed carefully. We will describe them in detail, along with safeguards that should be observed at each stage.

Having made the clinical assessment that the homeostasis-maintaining myth ("We don't leave each other because of the children") must be dispelled, the therapist meets alone with the siblings to explore with them whether or not they want their parents to stay together. Usually, each sibling has one of three possible points of view: wanting the parents to separate, not wanting them to separate, or feeling that he or she could live with either possibility as long as stress is reduced. To prevent any contagion phenomenon, in which one sibling might coerce or influence another, the therapist avoids addressing the siblings collectively. Instead, the therapist emphasizes each child's freedom to choose a stance, tracks each one's point of view, and differentiates among the different responses. The careful tracking of the siblings' attitudes clarifies their alignments and reveals the extent to which they are controlled by or differentiated from the parental myth.

If the siblings agree that the parents should not stay together on their behalf, the therapist carefully prepares them for the next phase. They are told that it would be useful for the parents to learn of their feelings in this regard. There is a risk, if this phase is poorly handled, that the siblings might feel they are being asked to turn their backs on their parents and run from them. If the approach is correctly handled by the therapist, however, the suggestion merely builds on their true feelings. The idea is conveyed that they are asked only to express their feelings regarding their parents' staying together for them; they need not take a stance for or against continuing the marriage for other reasons. What they wind up saying to their parents amounts to, "Don't suffer on my account," or "You have helped me grow strong enough to make it without your living together."

The therapist also informs each sibling that he or she has the clear prerogative to choose not to participate in the confrontation parade. If any one sibling feels that the parents should stay together for his or her sake, or does not want to participate for some other reason, the idea of the parade should be scrapped without further ado. The therapist must be careful to avoid coercing a youngster into going along with the therapist's agenda, and must intervene if one sibling coerces another. Pseudoagreement or equivocation must be distinguished from true agreement; both types of reactions commonly occur amid the desperation of crisis, as siblings seek to please the therapist. In short, each youngster should have the unambiguous right to veto the confrontation parade, and it is incumbent on the therapist to be sensitively attuned to signals of reluctance.

If there is full agreement from siblings to go along with this procedure, each is briefed on the exact format that is to be followed. They will enter the room one at a time, make a brief statement to both parents, and then, avoiding any discussion of that statement, leave the room. Holding the parents back from responding protects the youngsters and creates some security for them during what is inevitably a stressful experience.

Before the confrontation parade, the parents are seen together, without their children. In a tone of grave expectation appropriate to the circumstances, which is intended to maximize the likelihood that the parents will hear what they are going to be told, the therapist says that their children have something of crucial importance to say to them. But before they hear from the children, they must first agree to two conditions: they must refrain from discussion or dialogue and simply listen to what their children have to say, and they must refrain from punishing the children in any way for what they say and from discussing it with them later. Parents almost always accept these conditions.

The siblings are then led in one at a time. The one-by-one entrance builds tension and prolongs the message so that it can be heard. Each sibling says his or her piece. The therapist blocks any further discussion or argument so that the intense affect created—which is fundamental to cracking the defensive myth that holds the couple together—is not diminished through qualifications and counterarguments. After the children have been in and out, the parents are asked to think deeply about what they have heard. The session is then abruptly terminated without any effort to calm the parents. It is important that they leave the session feeling that the seriousness of the situation continues.

This procedure capitalizes on subsystem composition and employs careful monitoring of moods. The process is designed to control the intensity and clarity of the key message, and to ensure that it penetrates.

When seen at the initial session, the Garceau family was considered to be in an extraordinary situation. It was not the threat of violence per se that was unique (extreme violence in families is increasingly commonplace), but the level of imminent violence and homicidal risk that prevailed. For two and a half hours of this marathon session, the therapist listened while the parents, both together and alone, and the siblings as a group described their fears about the escalating level of violence.

In the segment that follows, the therapist begins the process of change by puncturing the reified myth—that the children would oppose and be hurt by a separation—that maintained this dangerously dysfunctional system. The siblings are discussing whether they want their parents to stay together. The two boys feel the situation is unworkable; they want their parents to separate. The sisters are less sure. Continuing this discussion, the therapist moves quickly.

Bruce: Cathy, what was your opinion on it? Do you go toward them separating or do you go toward them trying more still?
Cathy: I can see a temporary separation.
Therapist: But you're not clear on a final separation at all. But you know, Cathy, that is your parents' decision. (*Cathy nods in agreement.*) Now listen. I really think that you need to think more, be talking more about it, and I will be happy to talk

The therapist does not make an unrealistic attempt to disengage the siblings from their parents' marriage; he sanctions their interest in and desire to discuss the parents' marriage.

more with you about this, too. What I am going to ask you to do is this, and you can—you must—say "no" if this doesn't meet with your approval. If you feel that I am twisting your arm, say "no!" What I am going to suggest is that you tell your parents this. That they should not stay together for you, for you, for you, or for you (*looking in turn at each of the siblings*). If they need to separate, that is okay with you. But they mustn't stay together on your account or your account (*looking at the two sisters*). How do you feel about that?

Cathy: I can understand that. That's okay.

Therapist (*looking at Debbie*):   How do you feel about that?

Debbie (*nodding*):   Okay.

Therapist: You sure?

Debbie (*firmly*):   Sure.

Peter: It'll take a load off their minds.

The therapist emphasizes their veto privileges.

Note how this is stated. They are not being asked to recommend that their parents separate.

The therapist avoids talking collectively to the siblings. He emphasizes differentiation among the siblings' viewpoints and their individual responsibility for their positions. This approach avoids the diffusion and avoidance of individual responsibility that can be bred by a misguided family therapy format.

Therapist: Now, are you all comfortable about saying one at a time to your parents—for you, for you, for you, Cathy, and for you, Peter (*looking at each of the siblings*)—that they should not stick together on your account? Just keep it to that.

(*All of the siblings nod and say "okay" in unison.*)

Therapist: Okay.

While the therapist and siblings talked briefly together about what was to ensue, their parents waited in the lobby. The siblings then left the room, and the parents entered with the therapist. Together and separately with the therapist, they had already spent over an hour and a half discussing their rage at each other and the hopelessness and futility of the situation.

Therapist (*in a grave tone*): I've been talking to the kids. They're fine kids. Each has something they want to say to you, and I would like you to listen very carefully because it's important. (*Both parents nod.*)

The therapist's simple, pointed statements and request, delivered gravely, create intense anticipation.

Mr. Garceau: Fine.

The therapist briefly obtained the parents' agreement to the two rules of no dialogue and no retaliation described earlier, then brought in the children.

One at a time, dramatically and amid much tension, each of the youngsters enters. Standing, each says his or her piece and leaves. The therapist stands supportively beside each as they speak.

Bruce (*his voice choking with emotion, his jaw trembling*): The only thing that I have to say is that I don't want either one of you to feel responsible that you must maintain the marriage because of me. Okay? (*He leaves rapidly, clearly in the grip of strong emotion.*)

Debbie (*speaking slowly and fighting to stay in control*): I don't want you to stay together on my account. (*She breaks down and immediately leaves the room.*)

Cathy (*speaking with urgency and passion*): I want what is best for both of you, and if it means separation, whatever, then do it, because I can make it on my own. Okay? But I can't live like this, and you know . . . last night . . . I can't, you are just tearing me apart. So, just do it and make it quick. I can't stand this. (*The father, shaken, moves to hold Cathy, who continues talking.*) I love you both, but this is for both of you. Okay? (*Cathy leaves.*)

Notice the multiple messages delivered here. Cathy (1) differentiates herself from her parents' marriage: "I can make it on my own"; (2) conveys that she is profoundly affected by the quality of their relationship: she cannot endure the status quo; (3) emphasizes the

Therapist (*to father*):   Just keep listening.

Peter (*speaking slowly, solemnly, courageously*):   I just wanted to tell you that if you want to break up, don't stay together on my account. All right? Because I will be able to make it. I just want you to do the best thing for you. All right? (*Peter leaves.*)

Therapist (*gravely*):   Okay, that is how it is. The kids are not helped by this. It couldn't be much worse for them. I want to end right here, and you both have a lot of thinking to do. (*The parents nod grimly.*)

temporal dimensions: change must occur now, not later; (4) in response to her father's move for coalition, insists that she not be trapped between them: "I love you both." The parents, of course, believed resolutely that the youngsters would not be able to "make it."

To avoid the intensity becoming diluted, the therapist prohibits discussion and ends the session in an atmosphere of deliberate crisis.

When using this procedure, the therapist must expect consequences and be available to deal with them. These consequences must be weighed against those of the parents' remaining together. In this family, the procedure was effective and spoke strongly to the mother. The stalemate was broken, and a few days later she left the home. Simultaneously, the husband, who had already been depressed, predictably became more depressed. Peter, his father's ally, also became more depressed.

Bringing about a crisis within a crisis must be the beginning of a journey. The procedure is not the entire therapy, by any stretch of the imagination. Its merit lies in its effectiveness in initiating a first step in changing a clogged and rigid family system. In fact, this procedure, like most others, is only as good as the therapist's skill in working through the consequences. Therapy with the Garceaus continued for another ten months, while the consequences of the initial intervention and the reorganizational dynamics that ensued were monitored.

After the first session, the therapist met regularly with the wife and husband, both together and alone, without the children present. He also met with the children as a group and periodically with either the mother or the father and the youngsters. Not long after the separation, the mother moved out of town. In the remainder of this chapter, we describe our work with the siblings and the father, highlighting the processes that interfered with their adjustment after the wife left the home. We further illustrate how the therapist can help to realign coalitions after a separation.

Blocking Inappropriate Cross-Generational Coalitions and Strengthening Sibling Ties

In the Garceau family, Peter was linked with his father in a tight and exclusive cross-generational coalition. This coalition both burdened him and isolated him from his siblings, and his depression reflected this unfortunate position. A task of the therapy was to weaken Peter's coalition with his father and strengthen his ties with his siblings and other people with whom he might identify outside of the family.

The therapy was therefore designed to firm up sibling solidarity and disrupt a process in which Peter was jeopardized. The essence of this process was that Peter felt that he was alone in protecting his father, that no one else was standing by him. Since the other family members identified Peter with his father, this also implied that no one stood by Peter. The real risk was that Peter would become rigidly entrenched in the role of the father's savior, and in so doing, would stand alone. As his siblings indirectly attacked their father, took positions in their mother's camp, or superficially reassured Peter that their father could cope, Peter experienced a "crisis of faith." He worried about whether anyone but him would stand by his father and about whether anyone would stand by him. In the following segment, notice how this process unfolds.

Therapist: Let's figure out what it is that concerns Peter.
Bruce: I think he is worrying about Dad.
Peter (*in depressed voice*): I don't care about Mom. It doesn't even bother me that she's going. I think it is better.
Therapist: But you are worried about your Dad and what's going to happen to him?

Peter: Yeah. Because he worked all his life to get, what, $20,000 a year, to live in a nice house, now what? She's screwing it all up.
Therapist: But why do you think he is going to lose everything he worked for?
Peter: He's not going to have what he worked for: a nice house, a nice family, retire. . . .

Peter's coalition with his father leads him to place unilateral blame on his mother for the dissolution of the marriage. His coalition also leads to complaints against change.

Peter voices the father's theory that the marriage is fine—it is just that his mother wants out. Part of the therapist's job is to dent unuseful mythologies.

Therapist (*softly, supportively*):   But is it a
nice family?
Peter (*very sadly*):   It was.
Therapist (*in tune with Peter*):   Yes, it was.
Bruce: I see what you are saying from a
guy's point of view.
Peter: He's working nights, he's working
here and there, he's not even home half
the time.
Bruce (*sympathetically*):   Peter, something
you don't see, probably because you don't
remember it . . .
Peter (*defensively*):   Mom, I know . . .
Bruce (*still sympathetically*):   No, no, not
that. I didn't say Mom. It was Dad's own
free will to change jobs.
Peter: So what, so? Why can't he change
a job?
Bruce (*angrily*):   There is no reason he
can't, but he also had a chance to go in the
office and work.
Peter (*attacking*):   He doesn't like the
office.
Bruce (*trying to be reasonable*):   Okay, but
if he was in the office, he could be making
more money than he is making now and
working a nine-to-five job.
Peter (*attacking*):   So, why isn't Mom
working, then? She's a secretary.

Peter accommodates
briefly to the therapist's
injection of reality.

Bruce begins an attempt to
assign their father realistic
responsibility for the
change.

Peter interprets Bruce's
statement about their
father having made the
job decision on his own as
reflecting Bruce's tendency
to side with their mother.
Peter's coalition with his
father is reflexively
activated as he perceives a
criticism being made of his
father. Conflict between
the siblings arises, with
Peter being isolated and
his coalition with his
father reinforced.

Cathy (*harshly*):   Dad won't let her.
Bruce: Dad wouldn't let her.
Peter (*hopelessly*):   Oh, you don't
understand. (*He subsides into depression.*)

Brother and sister move in
tandem against Peter.

There are many ways to intervene to weaken a coalition such as Peter's
with his father and strengthen sibling ties. One therapeutic approach involves careful subsystem orchestration and thematic control. Five basic
stages and strategies are employed.

STAGE ONE. SOLIDARITY THROUGH REAPPRAISAL:
HELPING ENEMIES BECOME FRIENDS

One aspect of Peter's coalition with his father was that he felt (and in fact was) alone in recognizing how vulnerable his father was and in supporting and protecting him. Peter's siblings did not see their father's vulnerability. Precisely because Peter was carrying the burden, the other siblings did not need to, and their standing aside was an important facet of the dysfunctional system. The task of securing sibling solidarity included breaking through the sibling denial of their father's vulnerability and thereby mitigating Peter's isolation and burden.

In the following excerpt, the therapist takes the first step in making Peter's fears and concern for his father explicit.

Bruce (*trying for reasonableness*): Now we have to realize that Mom feels that she has to be happy, too.

Peter (*bitterly*): I hope she is.

Bruce: Okay, I hope she is too.

Therapist (*quietly*): What do you think is going to happen to Dad?

Peter: I don't know.

Therapist: What is your fantasy about it?

Peter: He is probably going to sell the house. I don't know if he's even going to stay here. I don't know. There are so many things.

Therapist: How do you think he is psychologically?

Peter (*immediately*): Pretty messed up. I don't think he knows what is totally going on here. Or he can't deal with it. . . . He's messed up.

Therapist: What do you think could happen to him?

Peter: I don't know. He's got high blood pressure, he's got a lot of messed up things. He's overweight.

Bruce: What is your biggest fear about your dad, Peter?

Peter (*immediately*): Death.

Therapist (*softly*): Do you think he can die? How?

The therapist attempts to break through Peter's rigid defense of his father to his underlying fears for his father. He carefully tracks Peter's fantasies.

The issue is not the ventilation of these fears in the safe presence of a trusted therapist, in order to decondition them and render them manageable. The immediate purpose is to bring out these fears in the interpersonal context of his siblings so that they can share with him the protective burden of fearing for the father's health and how he will cope alone.

Peter (*nodding*): High blood pressure and psychologically and mentally just getting on him. Overweight, the way he eats and all. It will all catch up to him at once, plus this. It could just put him in shock, because what does he have to live for now? Because I'll be at college and everybody else is gone.

Bruce: But he still has us to live for.

(*Peter shakes his head negatively.*)

Therapist: No? Why not?

Debbie: Because we're all getting out on our own. We are all becoming individuals and independent, and although we are home most of the while, it's not like he is still raising us. He's got to take a lot lesser role with our lives.

The fundamental reality of the family crisis is now explicit: the family is in the midst of two simultaneous separations. Even the continuation of parental responsibilities is diminished because of the increasing autonomy and imminent departure of the adolescents.

Therapist: Yeah, but he's got to watch you guys get into relationships and marry.

Peter: Who cares? He's got to worry about himself.

The therapist attempts to challenge Peter by reassuring him that the father will continue to be involved in some ways. Unwittingly, the therapist has been inducted into the same unuseful pattern that the siblings themselves attempted, and is immediately rebuffed by Peter, who is like a brick wall.

Therapist: And that, too. I mean, how old is your dad?

The therapist suggests that the father has a future for himself.

Peter: Fifty-three, fifty-four.

Bruce: Don't you see? When they had us they knew that eventually they were going to get older.

Bruce suggests that their father was prepared for the separation. He might be ill informed, however, as he is further from his father's psychic reality than is Peter.

Peter: But they were going to get older together.

Bruce: I don't mean that they were going to get older together. I mean that they knew that as they got older, we would leave eventually.

Peter (*angrily, defensively*): But they would have each other.

The therapist now disrupts this divisive dialogue. He confirms Peter's perception of his father's depression and his fears for his father. This confirmation will be elaborated and repeated many times throughout the session. Through this process, the therapist spreads concern for the father among the siblings and opens their eyes to what Peter is going through.

Therapist (*interrupting*): It's true what Peter says—that he is going to have a hard time, he is having a hard time, and that is the reality. But he has a life ahead of him, and that is the other side of the coin.

Debbie (*questioning*): He doesn't see it that way?

Therapist: I'm sure he doesn't now. You're right, he doesn't.

Debbie: So, what are we supposed to be doing? How can we help him get through that? Because I hardly even see him, and he doesn't talk much even when I am home, you know.

From this point on, the changes associated with the confrontation parade begin to unleash a powerful affective experience of fear, sadness, and mourning among the siblings. The therapist encourages expression of these emotions and deals with them.

Therapist: This is going to take a while, because this is happening now. It's not as though it happened a week ago or two weeks ago. The situation has been locked and rigid like stone for years now. And all of a sudden things are beginning to crack, and he feels that his life is falling away from him. This is the worst time.

It is a bad, tough time, "the worst time." The therapist joins in the full recognition of the father's undeniable pain, emphasizing that it has its boundaries and its own course to follow. He does not rush to prescribe how they can help. This formulation speaks to the father's pain as stage-specific, dulling their feeling that their father is trapped terminally in his depression, unable to move beyond it.

Cathy: Does Dad realize this?
Therapist: Probably not, but he's hurting. This is the worst moment. Things are going to be difficult for a while, and there are certain things that you guys can do, and I think it's a good idea to talk about this. But the journey is quite a long one, and it isn't over for him. It's just the

The therapist's extended comments reflect his acceptance of his role as guide. Throughout, the therapist frames the father's struggle as transitional and therefore time bound. The core message is, "it will pass." In the process, the children's own fears also become time bound and ameliorated.

beginning. He has a way to go, and he has things to work out. I'm here, and there's a lot of advice and support and help that I can give him and that you guys can give him. What you are seeing now is the worst. It's the height of the storm. It's where all the pain and all the fear is. This is where it is, and Peter is absolutely right

Though the therapist is careful to assign them some helping function, the main thrust of his message is that this is the emotional work of the father. The central metaphor that the turmoil is a passing storm when he says he sees it in your dad.

Peter (*in a softer voice*): I think the worst part about the breakup is that Dad is going to have to move out and live in another house and pay Mom money and all. He can't afford that. Why should he?

Therapist (*firmly reassuring*): This they will have to work out. Your mom may have to go and work herself. This is something that they will need to work out with lawyers, and this takes a while. I've seen many, many parents in exactly the same situation grappling with this and sorting it out. Even when they have less money than your dad has. You know, I've seen fathers who are sole wage earners and mothers who are sole wage earners and mothers who really have nothing, no profession, and where all the kids are much younger, and they make do. They somehow do it.

Bruce: What my brother is saying is that the one thing that Dad always wanted, as far back as I can remember, is a big house, and his thing is the big house and not only because we were a large family. It's a thing to Dad and now I can see. . . .

Therapist (*softly*): But, Bruce, he also wanted a happy marriage and it didn't work. And your mom wanted a happy

puts the father's reaction in a broader perspective while validating the son's perception.

The therapist provides a normative frame for what Peter sees as a hopeless situation. Notice the multiple directives and messages. They are deliberately long-winded and aim at extricating the youngsters: (1) This is the turf of your parents and the outside experts; stay out and do not trespass. (2) Do not expect a quick fix. An easing of the situation will occur only with time. (3) Your parents can cope. They do not stand vulnerably alone. The therapist invokes his experience and authority to reassure Peter about issues, such as money, that are of particular concern to him.

Bruce sympathetically brings out the father's shattered dream. He is beginning to disclose that he has been moved by Peter's presentation.

The therapist acknowledges compassionately the son's

marriage. It didn't happen. And you wanted that for them.

reading of his father's symbol of marriage and family. He answers that defeat and periodic disenchantment are a part of life. He offers no facile, false reassurance; the world is partially made of things that do not work, things that do not happen.

Bruce: Yes, that's true. This is part of the reason that Dad right now is . . . I was amazed to talk to my father on the phone the other day, because of the same thing he [Peter] said, I thought of his blood pressure and stuff because Dad has always been, he's never really been an outgoing person, but Dad has always been positive. He's always been on all of us to be everything we can, as much as we can, and for the first time ever I heard my father defeated. I heard my father really depressed and I was absolutely amazed. It's like he wouldn't talk. I personally went out of my way to get Dad to talk. . . .

Bruce initially denied his father's depression and tried to convince Peter not to worry about him. But by now Bruce has been enlightened and has grown by being exposed to Peter's concerns. The two brothers are now in tandem; Peter is no longer alone.

(*There is a long, sad silence.*)

As the siblings begin to include Peter and gather as a group concerned about their father, the therapist frames and puts in perspective the father's depression—and Peter's—as an appropriate, logical, and even healthy response to a great disappointment. He emphasizes the need for the siblings to rally to their father noninterferingly, so that it not be Peter's exclusive responsibility. The therapist does not hesitate to indicate that he will take some of the responsibility for helping the father in this time of crisis, implying, "I am part of this system now, let me handle this. I'll take your burden." This relieves Peter of some responsibility and enables him to join his siblings even further. Theoretically, one might worry that if the therapist takes on this caretaking function, the siblings might completely avoid this task, or that their efforts might be crippled. In actuality, his involvement helps the siblings become closer and more helpful to each other. It is also consistent with his overriding aim to take charge in guiding the acceptance and reinterpretation of the father's depression, shifting its meaning toward a prospective orientation.

Therapist: Yes, you're seeing what is happening. He really is depressed. In some respects, though, there is an important, positive side to that. He is recognizing the reality of the struggle that is ahead for him, which is a good sign. Because what we also see is that some people have a bland "no-response" to a situation which is difficult, like this one, and these are people that we get really concerned about. Because then they are not even beginning to consider the tasks at hand. It seems to me that your dad's depression is related to seeing what it is that he is losing, and he's losing a lot of dreams. Dreams about a marriage that failed, that didn't work, a house, and beginning to recognize the struggles that he has to face. That he has to meet people, he has to make new friends. That he has a lot of work to do with your mom to work out business, financial things, property, and also a good arrangement for you guys for the future. That is key. And his depression, I am sure—even if he can't think about it this way now because he is right in the middle of it, is related to all this. And this is the reality. And from my little contact with him I think that he is a bright man, and I think that he has some objectivity about his life and will manage, but it is going to be hard. I have a role to play in helping him through this, and I think you guys have, too.

The father's depression is framed as a positive thing that is readying him for life's demands ahead.

To be convincingly reassuring, the therapist must be careful, detailed, extensive, thorough, and precise in his attention-getting presentation of the tasks that follow relentlessly upon more tasks. Through the untoppable discharge of the demands awaiting their father, the therapist conveys that he is intimately familiar with the territory that must be traversed. His credibility as guide is thus enhanced, and he immediately heightens the possibility that the youngsters will let go, giving him some of their burden and moving on to disclose their own personal hurt. When the extensive authoritative monologue is effective, it frees what is behind the youngster's move toward the parent—fear for his own injured and defective self. Fear for self can now be expressed, no longer masked by fear for the other.

Peter: It's that I feel like I lost all my drive to do anything. I used to do a lot. I used to love school. I used to really get into work, friends, and everything. I just lost all my drive for anything.

Therapist: But you know what is happening, and I don't think you are absolutely alone with this in this family. You are damned worried about your dad, and I'm not surprised that you can't concentrate on things at hand for yourself. For you to concentrate on work, and what is in line for you for the next couple of months, really falls away when you think about your dad. You said you thought that he might die. I'm not the slightest bit surprised about what you are talking about. It makes absolute sense to me. You are worried. You think your dad might not make it through this. He's in the midst of one huge crisis, probably the biggest of his life. And you are scared for him.

(*The therapist leans forward and touches Peter reassuringly on the knee.*) Let me tell you something. I am concerned about your dad and that is why I am going to be here for him. That is a big part of my role in

Peeling off one depression, the father's, has revealed another, Peter's. The therapist can now move to reframe Peter's depression as logical, natural, appropriate, and transitional. By normalizing it in this way, he offers new meaning to Peter's symptoms, which increases Peter's self-tolerance. And self-tolerance is crucial to managing the understandable stress-related reactions that must be endured during the family's reorganization. Lack of concentration, fear the parent may die, being scared—all are declared understandable reactions. The therapist inserts himself even more fully by explicitly emphasizing that he will carry Peter's burden. The message is this. I have experience in this area. . . .

not just reassuring in itself. It is timed to further release Peter from his lonely task of caring for his father and enable him to join and share the burden with his siblings.

Peter bows his head and starts to cry. Everyone sits quietly. Peter covers his face with his hands and then gets up and rushes out of the room. Bruce looks at the therapist, who nods, and Bruce leaves the room to follow his brother. In the lobby they hug, and Bruce sits quietly with his arm around his brother comforting him. The therapist sits with Peter's two sisters and joins them in silent commiseration and mourning.

After this session the siblings were more sympathetic toward their father and more understanding of Peter, who nonetheless remained depressed and closely tied to his father.

STAGE TWO. SOLIDARITY AND DIFFERENTIATION
THROUGH GRIEVANCES

Peter and his siblings now tended to interpret as pathology the natural process of mourning in which their father was engaged, and they treated him accordingly. The risk was that they would dwell on his vulnerability, treat him like a patient, and place him in the "sick" role. A second risk was that Peter might be placed in a similar position by his siblings. The therapist worked to disallow this by highlighting the disharmony, conflict, and grievances that exist or potentially exist in any relationship. This meant carving out and capitalizing on whatever disagreements they had with their father.

The goal here was to facilitate the father's and Peter's recovery and to consolidate the sibling group around being able to get angry with their father. By doing so they signalled that he was strong, rather than helpless and weak. If they only pitied and feared for their father, they would be swallowed up by him and his problems. By helping them identify grievances, the therapist created distance between them and their father and helped them, particularly Peter, to back off. Of course, this was not meant to imply that they should ignore their father at this difficult time. Compassion and loyalty required that they should help him as best they could.

In the following excerpt, the therapist seeks to move the siblings from concern over the father's plight to consideration of how they could best alter an unsatisfactory situation. Bruce missed this session because he was out of town on business.

Therapist: Peter's got a good point. You are being pulled into the middle. And Peter's point is, how can you talk to your mom, how can you talk to your dad, so that they realize that you don't want to be part of this? That is a key question. How can you talk to them so that they will hear you?

Peter: I just feel like coming home and going to my room. I don't even feel like . . . I'm just so depressed all the time. I don't feel like anything. I have no initiative anymore. I just feel like going upstairs, sleeping and waking up and going out and coming home. There is nothing to it anymore.

Therapist: It's a depressing time, it is. But how can you speak to your dad so that he will give you some space? So that he won't intrude onto your personal territory?

Peter: When you start talking to him, he just changes the subject and it starts all over again.

Cathy: Yeah, he brings it all back. You try to be nice and he comes back to the subject you're trying to avoid.

Therapist: Debbie, you're a bit out [of the house] and maybe a bit more distant. Do you have any counsel for your brother or sister on this?

Peter's depression operates at two levels. First, it immobilizes him, creating inertia; but it also operates interpersonally to draw him into maintaining his coalition with his father.

The therapist perceives that depression and failure to express grievances go with staying with the father, and he works to mitigate that too-close tie. The therapist tries to render the depression interpersonal, so as to avoid the threat that it will become intrapersonally encapsulated.

Notice how the siblings inform and advise each other, utilizing the many resources they collectively possess.

Debbie is asked to operate as a cotherapist. Since she is the eldest sibling present, this is appropriate. The therapist's move also correctly places

responsibility for dealing
with the father on the
children. They are united
by a joint responsibility.
They must deal with him
well so that they don't
wind up "carrying" him.

Debbie: I don't know. So you can't talk
to Daddy. It all comes back to this.

Peter: It's home stuff. Like today, I told
him I'm going to do this and then I'm
going to go out. And he's sitting there, and
he says, "I've got dinner made." I told him
that Mom would say, "You want dinner;
you make it yourself." She was right. She
would make a dinner and nobody would
be there. So like, she was just saying, it's
easier for her and us, so we don't have to
be there. But Dad's like, five o'clock is
dinner. You'd better be here. He has got to
let us be ourselves.

Debbie: What do you say if maybe we
get him to sit down tomorrow, after the
football game, after he's had a good dinner
and he's in a good mood? What do you
think, Pete?

Peter: I don't know. That's the thing. I
don't even feel like, I don't want to talk
about it. I don't . . . nothing's wrong . . . I
just don't feel like talking to anybody. I
don't want to do nothing. I don't want to
be home. . . .

Debbie: But the thing is, if you let it go
like that, if you are passive, right. . . .

Peter: I'm not passive, I just don't want
to talk.

Debbie: . . . no change is going to come
about. You know what I am saying? That
if we don't talk to Daddy and let him
know what you are feeling, goodness
knows he'll let us know what he is

Peter is referring to the
preseparation efforts of the
family members to
minimize contact with one
another.

Peter's depression again
manifests itself as an intra-
and interpersonal force
operating to maintain
homeostasis.

Debbie's concern, like that
of the therapist, is that the
father might totally prevail
and crush the youngsters'
initiative. She goes for

feeling. . . .

Cathy: Yeah, but it always ends up in an argument. It's a waste of time. Then he says it's my house, don't tell me how to run it. Go live with your mom.

Therapist: It sounds like Cathy and Peter might have another idea about how to handle it. Find out from them, Debbie, whether they have any other ideas.

Debbie: What do you think would be a better way?

Peter: I think just time, because he was never here and Mom knew what to do. I think he just has to learn that we're not always going to be there to have dinner at five o'clock and we can take care of ourselves and all that. Right now, he thinks that Mom must have had dinner at five o'clock and that your clothes were folded all the time.

Cathy: I like to let the wash go for three days and prove to him it can be done.

Debbie: Well, how did Mom get to know how these things. . . .

Peter: Years ago, I don't know. It's just the way it is. I think Dad has to learn, you know, that meals are getting wasted because we're not there to eat them. . . .

discussion as a way of revising and adjusting the routines to fit the new situation. She describes the father's attempts, made in his usual tyrannical style, to avoid conflict and revision of routines.

In trying to help, Debbie has met with solid resistance. Now the therapist suggests that Cathy and Peter participate and help their sister. In part, this might move them closer to a solution. At a process level, the therapist is encouraging such a dialogue to facilitate sibling cohesiveness around effective problem solving.

The possibility of new routines is seen as the vehicle through which to disengage the father from them.

Much family reorganization is essentially a mundane process: the father expecting from the children what he used to expect from the wife, and the children searching for ways of answering those expectations while salvaging their autonomy.

Discussion continued for another ten minutes, without resolution. The three turned periodically to the therapist for help, but he avoided being too helpful. It was important that the siblings deal with one another on this. The therapist, who had stayed peripheral to the interactions throughout the session, only nudging the process along periodically, now disengaged even more completely by leaving the room to observe the siblings from behind a one-way mirror. He hoped that his absence would further facilitate and consolidate their unity.

With the therapist watching from behind the mirror, this therapeutically sponsored "dialogue of grievance" continued and became more focused. As the dialogue unfolded, a particular subsystem phenomenon occurred, one for which the therapist had aimed but over which he ultimately had no control—namely, a real shared intimacy. In the excerpt that follows, the youngsters were mimicking and ridiculing their father's rigidity. Notice the esoteric examples they generated, the immediate mutual understanding, the code-like language, and their light, buoyant affect. This all reflected their growing distance from their father. One might worry that Debbie, the eldest, would stand apart from Peter and Cathy and play only her role of older sister. She clearly had, in fact, assumed this position thus far, partly as a result of the therapist's directive comments. But while she at times seemed to be continuing in the role of cotherapist, she also managed to leave this role and laugh with her brother and sister, a sign of healthy flexibility.

This segment begins as the youngsters mock their father's tendency to drill a message home laboriously. Though there is affection in his making fun of his father, Peter's initiative is extraordinarily effective here in rallying his siblings around him at the father's expense.

(Peter imitates his father speaking, and his sisters laugh.)

Peter: But it gets the point across. (*They agree. He then talks very fast, almost inaudibly for an outsider.*) But like when you are serious and you're talking to him. It irritates me so. Like he'll say something and then he'll say it again, and then he'll say, "wait a minute," then he'll start talking r-r-r-real slow like. . . . (*Peter drags out these few words, mimicking his father.*)
Cathy (*smiling broadly*): Like we haven't grasped it.

Peter (*laughing*):   Yeah, that's it. And I
scream inside "shut up!" (*They laugh.*)
Debbie: You mean he's trying to drill . . .
Peter (*interrupting*):   Yeah, to drill it in
your head (*he makes a drilling motion*) and
it drives me crazy, I just feel like getting up
and . . . (*he makes strangling motion*). (*They
all laugh.*)
Cathy: Or he tells us how to organize
your mind, or about the dog's mess, he
says "Clean it up!"

They share a common
experience. Their
exasperation at the father's
rigid authoritarianism
enhances solidarity. They
are enjoying sharing this
experience of having lived
under his drilling.
Laughter in and of itself
acts here as
counterdepressant,
powerful in their difficult
situation.

Peter: Oh, yes. He says, "Clean it up,"
and I'm getting the paper towels and he
says, "Aren't you going to clean it up?"
within thirty seconds.

The father's impatience is
rendered legendary.

   Their conversation continues for ten minutes more as Peter and Cathy
explain laughingly to Debbie how impossible their father is. Through this
process, the father's depression and ridigity are rendered less menacing as
the youngsters reassure themselves that they are above it.

Peter: And this morning for this therapy.
He says, "I think the clinic wants you to
go a little early today." I get home, he says
it again, "It's about time to leave now,
right?" I say, "Oh, Dad, I'll leave five
minutes late, just to stick it in your face."
Debbie: What you guys are saying is
when he does all this, when he is trying to
run your life and drill all this into you, it's
really getting you upset.
Peter: If he'll just leave us alone.
Debbie: You got to try and tell him, to
let him know. Because even if he sees the
look on your face and he hears the anger

Notice Debbie's
incisiveness. If Peter and
Cathy do nothing to
change their father, then
he will only remain the
bad ogre. She knows full

in your response, he probably doesn't assimilate, he doesn't grasp onto the fact that he is running your lives like a dictator.
Peter (*teasing her with a pompous voice*): The psychological aspects of what we're trying to do, blah, blah. (*They laugh.*)

well how her siblings like to complain but fail to confront him effectively.

Debbie spearheads an attempt to deal differently with the father, but Peter wants to escape his sister's injunction by a return to fun-making. It is easier for Peter not to assert himself if the father remains the unmodifiable figure. By ineffectually complaining, he can remain the worried son.

Cathy (*also teasing Debbie*): We can't read between the lines (*more laughter*).
Debbie: So you got to find some way, right, or am I way off base in saying . . .

Debbie persists.

Peter: We cool man. I want to see that movie.

Peter tries to escape again.

Debbie: What movie? *Scared* . . .
Peter: No, it's with Richard Pryor and . . . he walks into jail saying, "Cool man, we bad." What's it called . . . *Stir Crazy.*

Peter has found a good metaphor. Pryor's "cool" act in the movie masks his fears of a terrifying world.

While the youngsters' dialogue did not lead to a resolution of how best to deal with the father, it did solidify the siblings as a group and help them maintain their distance from him.

STAGE THREE. DIFFERENTIATION THROUGH COALITION REARRANGEMENT

At this time during the parental separation, the therapist must monitor familial structures that have been shaken up and are starting to settle into new patterns. The therapist must work to prevent the formation of bizarre or difficult arrangements and to facilitate appropriate, helpful ones.

In the case of the Garceaus, the objectives were to break the rigid father-son coalition and to allow Peter's brother and sisters to reorganize their relationship with their father. In the following excerpt, which took place at a time when Peter's rigid coalition with his father was beginning to soften and his tie with his siblings was strengthening, a rebound phenomenon occurred that jeopardized the gains that had been achieved. The father, perhaps sensing Peter's move toward his siblings and away from him, had inappropriately drawn Peter into a major conflict between himself and his son Bruce. The father and Peter had together decided that Bruce, who had been assisting his mother in the move, should not be given a key to the house. The therapist convened a session with the father and the siblings. He used the issue of the key as an opportunity to loosen further the rigid father-son coalition.

Note that Peter begins with the conviction that he is right in participating in the decision not to grant Bruce a key:

Peter: Put yourself in our point of view, Bruce, because you gotta trust me—you either trust me or you don't. Two years you've been out of the house. You come back and you're still part of the family, but look at what's happened. Put yourself in our position. There is a lot of mistrust on everybody's mind. Bruce, you have to trust me.

Cathy (*upset, to Peter*):   You got a key to both places [to both the mother's and the father's houses]. Bruce doesn't.

Therapist (*very loudly and firmly*):   But why is this something that Peter is involved in? Mr. Garceau, this is your issue. It's your house, not Peter's house.

The therapist vigorously challenges the father to take responsibility. His aggressive tone leaves no doubt that he sees the father violating generational boundaries.

Mr. Garceau: I thought Bruce was coming over one night to talk it over, and he never showed. The opportunity is still there for him to come over and discuss it.

The father avoids responsibility by insinuating that had Bruce only come over, he would have changed his mind.

Therapist: No, no. We're talking right now. This is not Peter's issue; this is not your son's issue. You are in charge of the house. It's your issue (*softly*). Don't get Peter involved in this. It's not fair.

The high affect is necessary here to drive home the point that the reorganization of the

Mr. Garceau (*clearly touched by the therapist's words*):   Okay.
Therapist: And it's not useful, either.

Mr. Garceau: It's between Bruce and me, then, okay?
Therapist (*firmly, turning to Peter*):   And for you to get into this is really no good for you, because it's between the two of them, it's going to muck up your own relationship with your brother, and you don't need that.
Peter: Okay, I see what you mean.

family hinges on maintaining these boundaries.

The father has accepted giving priority to boundary maintenance. Seeing the coalition between the father and Peter as a reciprocal and mutual process, the therapist now moves to Peter, trying to dissuade him from involvement in the problem between his father and Bruce.

The therapist then made a seating change. He moved Bruce to Peter's seat next to his father, and Peter moved next to the therapist. This physical rearrangement became a vehicle for the relational goal of the rest of the session: to increase the proximity between the father and Bruce and increase the distance between the father and Peter. In addition, the therapist was now well placed to intercept and inhibit Peter's automatic intrusions into the father's relationship with Bruce. Soon the father and Bruce entered into a long, honest, and forthright dialogue to revise their relationship. The following excerpt, which took place some twenty-five minutes into that dialogue, highlights how the process of realignment of relationships following the parental separation tends to entail reworking past hurts and unsettled business with each of the participants. There were bad feelings between Bruce and his father that had to be cleared.

Mr. Garceau: The reason I stopped talking or shut up is because you didn't do it and I lost my temper. I don't want to lose my temper. Do you think any man wants to live losing his temper? I certainly don't.
Bruce: It seems to me you like it.
Mr. Garceau: Absolutely not, Bruce. No way. No man wants to live constantly losing his temper, but if I told you things, have you listened to them? The response I get is, who the hell are you to tell me these things, I'll just do what I goddamn well please anyway!

Bruce implies that his father has used this angry, silent stance to such an extent that it cannot be incidental or just for coping with occasional anger. The father implies that this angry, silent

Bruce (*very upset*):   Have I ever said that to you? (*He is on the edge of tears.*) Have I?
Mr. Garceau: Bruce, I do not believe . . .
Bruce (*finishing the father's axiom*):   . . . in what you say, I believe in what you do. I know.

stance was brought about by his son's disrespect and rebelliousness.
Bruce implies that his father's actions are oppressive to him and that he doesn't trust his father's words.

Mr. Garceau: So, I listen to talk ad infinitum, but it's the actions. But do I love you? I certainly do.
Bruce (*clearly not yet convinced*):   It's nice to know.
Mr. Garceau: Sometimes have you hurt me? Certainly you have, Bruce, and the more you hurt me, the more I shut you off.

The father explains that by his silent anger, he is just responding to his son.

Bruce: Okay, going by that I must have hurt you so bad, you don't listen to me, you don't even want me. I feel like an outcast member to you. Peter and I get along better recently than you and I ever had. I feel outcast to you, I feel like you want nothing to do with me.

Bruce implies that his father claims that he, Bruce, is powerful and can hurt him yet also that he is powerless in that he cannot have an impact on him. His father turns him out.

Mr. Garceau: That's right, Bruce, because many times you just run over me. I've asked you things or told you to do things, and all you've done is what you want, nothing that . . . or very infrequently have the things I want been done. Bruce, let's go back to when we moved to New York and I said go to school, study, get a job to support yourself socially. Have some social life. And you moved out?
Bruce (*his voice cracking with emotion*): Do you know why? Did you ever ask me why? I have felt like a twelve-year-old at home. I've felt like a twelve-year-old. You never treated me like you are treating Peter

The father implies that he renders Bruce powerless because his son always rendered him powerless as a father.

Bruce's account reveals the specific ways in which he has felt frustrated and shortchanged by his father. The sibling rivalry now. I'm not bringing him in. Or the way you are treating her [Cathy] now. You never treated me like an adult. You never treated me like somebody you respected. I felt like a grade schooler going to college. I wanted to rebel. I didn't want to do this. I don't like this, and I was made so uncomfortable at home and I had to get out of it. I had to do something. I couldn't live at home any more.

surfaces as he reveals that he is jealous of how the father treats Peter now. We can infer that much of the father's angry, silent stance was exclusively toward Bruce and was not shown to the other siblings. It is also evident that long before adolescence Bruce was locked into this position of being at odds with his father. The father's angry stance grew stronger after Bruce's emancipatory move (leaving home), a move he made after consulting his implicit ally, his mother.

Peter: Can I say something? Please, I've gotta.
Bruce: No (*firmly blocks Peter from intruding*). And it's not that I didn't want to go to school, I just couldn't stay home under this pressure and it wasn't only you. It was Mom, too. (*Peter becomes very agitated; the therapist leans over to him and quietly talks and jokes with him while Bruce continues to talk passionately to the father.*)

As Bruce moves into Peter's turf, Peter attempts to intercept the process but is blocked by both Bruce and the therapist. Here, Bruce makes a gesture of exoneration by apportioning some of the blame to the mother. The therapist restrains and detours Peter from Bruce and his father, intercepting his contribution and paying close attention to the insight Peter was about to offer his father and brother.

I told Mom and I said, it can't be this way
anymore. And so finally I just had to leave
school. I left. And at the same time I left
school, I left home. They were very closely
tied together, as I recall.

Mr. Garceau (*skeptical*):   Bruce, there's a
little bit of bullshit in this, too.

Bruce (*firmly*):   No, there's not, there's no
bullshit there.

Therapist (*to the father and Bruce*):   If I
can stop you, Peter had an interesting
insight here.

Peter: Can I say it? I'll put it real nice.
Please?

Therapist (*playfully*):   No. But I'll tell you
something. Even though Peter's insight is
really interesting, I think the more
important thing is, you guys are talking. So
what I am saying is that the most
important thing is (*therapist looks at Peter*)
that you in fact are staying out and they're
talking together.

Peter (*touching his collar, which he had
gnawed on when the therapist suggested that
he remain quiet*):   This thing is wet.
(*Everyone laughs.*)

The therapist, having
acknowledged that Peter's
insight was worthwhile,
nevertheless continues to
focus the family on the
new processes that are
emerging. Peter did have
an idea, but the structural
ploy is to keep him out of
the father-Bruce
interaction.

STAGE FOUR. HIERARCHICAL REORGANIZATION

Soon after separation it is common for the protecting or coalitionary
child to insist on peer status and refuse to accept the authority of the adult.
If this process escalates, the protector usurps parental power. Further escalation can lead to a runaway reversal of the family hierarchy and tyrannical acting out.

In this family, Peter's coalition with his father at its worst had just such
a spinoff. To avoid its escalation, it was necessary to monitor the hierarchical
rearrangement. In the dialogue that follows, the therapist encourages the
father to take a position of leadership and defend his rights, and makes it
clear that Peter will have to accept a less grandiose idea of his position.
The issue of washing dishes masks a process where the children attempt
to lay down the rules for the father.

Peter (*brashly to father*):   There were five glasses and a couple of forks and knives.
Cathy (*to father, picking up on Peter's brashness to him*):   You left the frying pan.

Peter and Cathy's brash manner of speaking to their father reflects the blurred hierarchy and the extent to which the father is a hollow leader.

Mr. Garceau: I did that intentionally, Cathy, because I cleaned out the sink when I came on Wednesday and I . . .
Therapist: Let me check something, Mr. Garceau. Is your feeling that the kids know the way in which you want the house to be kept over the weekend and simply aren't doing it? Or is your feeling that they don't know what you have in mind?

The therapist intervenes to reveal the issue as the hierarchical-power confrontation that it is, and not a communication-information issue. The question is to the father and not to the siblings. This centralizes him, asks him to pass judgment, and thereby begins to restore him as the key executive in the system, where he sets expectations.

Mr. Garceau: I think they know . . . I think they know. I've told them frequently enough and they don't do it. Also, one of the things that irritates me is when something has to be done. I've asked them to do it and the response is positive, but the commission of the act occurs when they get a chance, if they remember. And if they don't remember it, I get an apology. I'm sorry. Then it ends up with my doing it.

The father protests having to be the one who must accommodate, who must do it himself. This protest reflects the first step in moving from a sense of impotence to a sense of being a leader who has been taken advantage of.

Peter (*brashly*):   What's wrong with that?
It gets done.
Mr. Garceau: No, it doesn't.
Therapist: The thing is, Mr. Garceau,
that these are perfectly okay issues that
you have to work out with them. We're
talking now about issues of a family.

Father and son argue as
peers, at the same level.

The therapist encourages
the father to deal with his
youngsters, and
normalizes the issue of
their conflict. The issue is
defined as common to all
families. The insinuation is
that these conflicts must
be resolved in all families,
including the single-parent
household.

Peter: That's something that bugs me.
When he comes home, he's nagging,
nagging, nagging.

Peter attempts to regain
the center of attention and
bump his father from it.

Therapist (*ignoring Peter and turning to the
father*):   What I would like you to do is
work this out with them. What are your
ideas about how the family should be—
how things should be in the house, what
their responsibilities are—and work it out
with them.
Mr. Garceau: Okay, the same thing . . .
(*turning to the therapist*).

The therapist pointedly
interrupts, breaking the
sequence in which the son
could usurp the position of
the father, and returns and
holds the father in his
central position. The
therapist's move models
some of the aggression
and forcefulness that the
father will need to muster
if he is to assume
leadership.

Therapist: Work it out with them.
Because this is absolutely relevant to your
living together.

The therapist insists that
the father solve problems
directly with his children.

Mr. Garceau: It's to be worked out but
not just the way they want to do it?

The father is unsure of his
authority. He seeks
guidance from the

Therapist (*firmly*): Certainly not. You are in charge of the house.
Mr. Garceau: Okay.

therapist, who doesn't hesitate to take his side. Here the therapist is in clear coalition with the father. He lends his authority to the father to facilitate the arrangement of a clear hierarchy.

Cathy (*to therapist*): Whose side are you on? (*There is laughter, which the therapist ignores.*)

Cathy's laughter reflects her recognition of the therapist's leaping around, his having shifted sides, to fulfill his commitment to the well-being of all family members.

Peter (*to his father*): What is wrong if we clean up the kitchen when we have the time? We're not a time machine, okay?

The negotiation begins.

The family members talked further, but Peter continued to address his father in a brash, loud, and disrespectful way. The therapist next altered his strategy, intervening directly to join even more strongly in coalition with the father and utilizing the strong connection that he had already established with Peter to assist the father.

Peter: It's like I don't do anything that is totally provocative or rude to my father's rights or privileges. All right, I don't do it. . . .
Therapist (*looking Peter straight in the eye*): I think you are rude.
Peter (*shocked*): Do you really?
Mr. Garceau: You answer back and debate with me. Sure, I'm very offended. Why do you think I raise my voice and lose my temper?

Peter tries to get this one by fast. His con is charming and emphatic.

Consistent with earlier modeling, the therapist goes out of his way to continue to break through posturing and subterfuge. This is particularly important now as father and son try to reorganize their relationship, finding a new way of problem solving. The implicit rule injected here contains

Peter (*looking accusingly at Bruce*):   I don't think it's all me.

Peter and reminds him that honesty is necessary for problem solving.
Peter tries to pull in Bruce.

Mr. Garceau (*looking at Peter*):   If you're doing it to me and I'm talking to you, it is you. You're not the only one who does it. Yeah, that is correct. But now I'm talking about you.

The father successfully keeps Bruce out, a good sign for future problem solving.

Therapist: You see, I think that there are ways of talking to your parents that really don't have to be rude or disrespectful. The fact that you have ideas that are different than your dad's is the way things should be. That's what being sixteen years of age is all about. The fact that you are bright, have ideas, and disagree with your dad, that's fine. The way in which you do it is very often—most often—rude and disrespectful. That's not fine.

The therapist is careful not to blur the issues. He emphasizes that adolescent differentiation from a parent is appropriate but that respect must be maintained.

Peter (*amazed*):   Wow. I didn't realize.

Peter's response is genuine. It also has additional meaning in that he is grateful that the therapist has stopped him from being disrespectful to his father. The sense of gratitude may emanate as well from the fact that as the therapist protects his father, he is relieved of that interpersonal task.

STAGE FIVE. DIFFERENTIATION THROUGH INDIVIDUATION

One aspect of facilitating Peter's differentiation from his father was helping him individuate. Peter had to do more than become a sibling, he had to become a person. In part, this entailed Peter's use of identification models both within and outside of the family. To aid these processes of differentiation and individuation, the therapist met alone with Peter, who was the sibling most absorbed in the conflict. What follows is an illustration of Peter's use of the modeling aspect of therapeutic interaction and his attempts to draw from the therapist's experience.

Peter, who was then finishing high school, was thinking about what he wanted to do after graduation. He was trying to decide between doing what his father wanted him to do (immediately begin pursuing an accounting degree) and what he wanted for himself (take a brief moratorium to travel and consider alternatives). Peter asked the therapist whether he had taken any time off before going to college. The therapist told him that he had traveled and done odd jobs for a while, but he then put it back on Peter. As the sequence begins, Peter is in doubt as to what course to take. He would prefer to take a break before going on to college, but he is unsure.

Therapist: So who do you have to convince, then?
Peter (*a little unsurely*):   Myself.
Therapist: Not me you have to convince?
Peter: I think it's really myself.
Therapist: I think so. And I'm sure that you'll do well, whatever you do. If you go to college now, you'll do well because you have the ability to do well. And if you decide to take a bit of time off and do it later, it will make no difference. You have to decide what you really want . . . I think that is the key thing—you (*pointing to Peter*) have to decide what you want. This is basically what it's about. Not what your friends want, not what your dad wants for you, but you, you, you because there is only one you, and you have to live with yourself for the rest of your life.

The therapist's questions help Peter shift from doubt to a point where he affirms that the decision is not for anyone but himself. Once he reaches that point in heightened receptivity, the therapist offers support that will guide him through the uncertain territory ahead. The therapist emphasizes Peter's confidence in his own abilities and his free choice and options.

The emphasis on "you" demarcates and differentiates the self that has tended to get lost in the business of rescuing the father and in the realignment hassles with the siblings. He is encouraged to become, in a way, his own generous parent.

Peter: That's true (*looking amazed and shaking his head*). It's a bitch living with myself (*he laughs*). That's the truth. Jesus. I never thought of it like that. . . . (*There is a long pause. Peter is deep in thought.*) . . . I can't believe you took a year off.
Therapist: Why not, Peter?
Peter: It seems . . . I don't know how we got into that discussion, but it ended that you did the same thing. Did you feel you wanted to take off time, or was there pressure there too to go straight to college?

Peter takes in the message and appreciates its truth. He uses this moment to comment upon himself, laughing at the fact that he is more than a handful. This is soon followed by surprise at the fact that adults such as the therapist can indeed take time off, not get lost, and still achieve later. This notion is obviously incongruent with what other authority figures have told him.

The family was seen for another six months. During that time, Peter tried accounting briefly and then shifted to medicine, where he was doing well and was happy. Just prior to the termination of therapy, Peter wanted to leave home and move to a college with a better reputation. The idea of leaving his father still raised unsettled issues for him. By this time, however, his father's life had expanded and was well grounded in the extrafamilial world. This reassured Peter, and with his father endorsing his plan, he could confidently go ahead with this move.

After separation, families must reorganize, if possible without lapsing into ways that are dysfunctional. The basic structural changes in the family cannot be separated from the necessary affective tasks—working through natural themes of transition such as sadness, loss, fear, and anger—and the necessary establishment of new rules among members. The therapy just described respects this connection and harnesses the powerful resources of a sibling group to reduce dysfunction.

8

Arresting Abdication Dynamics

THE PROCESS of separation often results in at least a temporary decline in adequate parenting. Discipline may become erratic; a child's needs may be neglected; and conversely, excessive or even obsessive attention may be given to the structuring of the child's day. Inevitably, the child's behavior shows that the custodial parent has lost control. This development is especially serious in the case of the adolescent, who is already exploring boundaries, experimenting with outside relationships to organize the normal departures from the family. The adolescent who is aware of tensions between the parents often attempts to manipulate and outflank the divided executives. For parents in personal trouble, it is easier to rationalize leaving the adolescent alone to fend for himself. But extreme distancing and disengagement from the custodial parent may result in the adolescent being left uncontrolled and unsupervised, and even in the adolescent's precipitous—and premature—departure. The adolescent therefore requires special consideration because of the almost unique potential for personal and social pathology that such a premature departure entails.

In a postseparation situation, it is common for both parents to become depressed and preoccupied and to cease to meet the adolescent's needs for structure and nurturance. Usually, this is only for a brief period, however, and either with or without minor adolescent acting out, parental functions are recovered or reinstated. It is when parental functions remain dormant and paralyzed, when even escalating acting out does not restore the parents to their necessary position, that dysfunction—generally known as abdication—occurs.

We use the term abdication to describe parents' almost complete failure to carry out the usual socialization functions: taking a tender interest in the youngster's everyday triumphs, struggles, and disappointments; consistently checking curfews and actively appraising the adolescent's girlfriends and boyfriends; meeting periodically with teachers and other school officials; and making occasional but necessary checks with the other parent. The youngster is left to make it alone. Two levels of the abdication phenomenon can be differentiated. The first is the absence per se of indispensible parental functions because of parental depression, obsessive preoccupation, or physical absence. This level might be analogous or similar to parental absence due to illness or injury. The second is more directly linked to the spousal battle. Here, abdication serves to sustain a parent-adolescent, cross-generational coalition that undermines or excludes the other spouse.

If the period of abdication is not a long one and if the adults have previously been competent and responsible parents, this brief abdication need not create undue disorganization or stress. But if the abdication is prolonged, and especially if it is associated with a high level of parental conflict, the youngster's development will be jeopardized, regardless of the preseparation quality of parenting.

This scenario of parental abdication and adolescent acting out has been identified frequently in the families seen in the clinical service of the Families of Divorce Project.

Four processes were seen to operate: (1) parental nurturing functions had diminished or collapsed; (2) parental guiding and controlling functions had been allowed to lapse; (3) the view of family reality had become distorted; and (4) parental cooperation and unity had disappeared. These common processes will be illustrated by transcripts from the treatment of one family, excerpted from a total of twenty-eight sessions over a period of approximately eight months.

In this family and others we have seen in the Families of Divorce Project, a combination of these sometimes overlapping processes was associated with serious adolescent acting out.

The Jarret Family: A Preliminary Diagnostic Picture

The Jarrets were an attractive, bright, upper-middle-class family with three daughters. The mother (the custodial parent) applied for treatment five months after she and her husband had separated. The couple's marital difficulties had increased during the last three years of their twenty-year marriage, culminating in the wife's discovery of her husband's involvement with another woman. Soon thereafter he had left to share an apartment with a male colleague near the home of his much younger girlfriend, whom he saw often.

When the wife and her daughters were first seen together, the wife stated that she wanted to "improve communication," especially with the middle daughter. She explained tearfully that she had "been incapacitated because of depression, and they [the children] have been very kind to me and very good during that, but I think they also have been neglected because they had problems, personal things that came up with each one of them, and didn't have anybody to come to. And, I feel very guilty because I wasn't available when they needed me." When asked what contact her daughters had with their father, Mrs. Jarret stated that they didn't see him. "To be quite honest with you and all the girls, I'd love it if they never saw him again. I would like it if when he did call, they would just say, 'Forget it, I don't want to see you.' "

In this family, Karen, age seventeen, was upset by the separation but strengthened by her relationship with her steady boyfriend. She maintained good grades in high school and avoided becoming a parental substitute. Sue, age sixteen, however, was badly shaken and depressed. She had no steady boyfriend and had previously been close to her father. She was now breaking rules and having difficulty with school and social relationships. Fourteen-year-old Janet was somewhat depressed and angry but generally able to stay within the rules, although she was also having some difficulty at school.

The picture that emerged during the first interview was of three daughters who had each, to a greater or lesser extent, been abandoned as their parents moved into orbits of their own. The mother, for her part, had experienced her husband's affair and subsequent departure as a profound narcissistic blow that precipitated a clinical depression. She suffered deeply, was enraged, and was preoccupied with revenge. She exposed her daughters to continual tirades against her husband, partly because she lacked self-restraint and partly because a previous therapist, oriented toward uncensored sharing, had advised her that such behavior was "good communication." Clearly, the mother gave her daughters little support or structure and few limits.

The husband, for his part, had abandoned the parental turf and was enjoying his "release" from the family. His backing away also stemmed from guilt and confusion about his postseparation role. His wife strove to keep him away from the children, and only the eldest daughter kept up contact with him, despite her mother's prohibitions. The family, previously close, had become fragmented.

Forging Connections

In this situation of family fragmentation, common strategies employed by an adolescent are disengagement, distancing, and attempts to connect elsewhere. The adolescent might be seeking to escape from the toxic escalation of parental anger, depression, and neediness or simply trying to find sustenance in the absence of parental support and supervision. When the noncustodial parent has also been a friend and a preseparation ally (or coalitionary partner), the adolescent may have to use distancing to escape the retaliatory wrath of the custodial parent. The distancing adolescent may find an anchorage in socially acceptable areas—schoolwork in preparation for college, sports or religious activities, or a stable relationship with a boyfriend or girlfriend. But there is also the strong possibility that he or she will latch onto delinquent groups and activities or drift perilously alone.

ESTABLISHING MOTHER-DAUGHTER CONNECTEDNESS

In the Jarret family, the first therapeutic task was to reduce fragmentation by reestablishing crucial affective connections. This step most directly involved the mother and her second daughter, Sue. Sue's profound depression was obvious, and in therapy she was seen alone to explore the specific sources and depth of the depression and to assess the suicidal risk. She revealed that over the past six months she had had an abortion, which her mother knew of, and continued to be sexually active without restraint. She described, amid sobs, how she felt: "Like, why am I here? You know, what's my purpose here in life? I'd just rather be dead sometimes." She felt desperately lost, without support or direction.

There was no question as to the specific course of action needed. Sue was seriously vulnerable, needy, and alone. The task was to galvanize the family to connect with her and sustain her. This process was initiated immediately in a meeting with Sue, her siblings, and her mother. The singleminded intent of the session is clear.

Mrs. Jarret (*angry*): Your grades are very, very poor, and I don't think that changing to another school is going to change your grades all that much. You have to do it.

The therapist is immediately struck by the mother's angry tone. The mother attacks.

Sue (*defending herself*): I know, Mom, that's what I have been trying to tell you. I want to do it, but I don't want to do it in that school because I don't like being there.

Sue defends her position.

Mrs. Jarret: Well, what I was emphasizing then, was that you have to. . . .

The mother again attacks.

Sue: Well, it seemed like you have no confidence at all in me.

She defends herself and asks for affirmation.

Mrs. Jarret: Well, I was just adding to the fact that what I am saying, Sue, is . . . (*her voice rises in anger*).

The mother continues the attack, and Sue's request goes unheard.

Therapist (*softly and leaning forward*): Can you hear, though, what Sue just said there? Because that's quite important. She feels that you don't have any confidence in her.

The therapist's tone of softness is an attempt to counter the prevailing angry affect. He leans forward to create proximity and intimacy with the mother. The therapist views the content and affect as a vehicle to redirect the mother toward support.

(*Silence.*)

Mrs. Jarret (*more softly but then increasingly angry*): I guess I don't, Sue,

The mother briefly accommodates herself to

because you haven't demonstrated it. You're a very capable young lady and very smart and you just fritter away your time.
Therapist (*softly*):   Something's happening here, Fran. You're concerned, I hear it, and your concern is coming out sort of angrily . . . You're worried for your daughter, I can hear that. But somehow or other the concern is not really getting across—the concern and the care—and that's what Sue needs to be hearing at the moment. . . .

the therapist's softening, but then she attacks again.

The therapist again modulates mood and content, indicating what is required. He first positions himself alongside the mother, acknowledging her worry. He then clarifies how she comes across, pinpointing her anger and encouraging her to respond differently.

Mrs. Jarret: But right now. . . .
Therapist (*softly but firmly*):   Well, right now I really have to emphasize this, Fran. Sue really has been depressed, and I think is depressed, and school is important, you're right. But you're the most important person for Sue. She only has one mother, and Sue needs you bad, very bad! She really needs your support and your care.
Mrs. Jarret: But she's got that and she knows it.
Therapist (*with emphasis*):   She doesn't. That's what she needs to hear from you.
Mrs. Jarret: But she's . . . I do, I don't know what else I can do to demonstrate that.
Therapist: Maybe you can find out from Sue, because that's what Sue is questioning. She's scared about whether you are concerned, whether she can get from you what she needs. She's really scared. . . .

The therapist supports and resists simultaneously. He presents Sue as frail and needy and the mother as the one who can protect her.

The mother feels helpless.

The therapist suggests a simple source of knowledge—that Mrs. Jarret can find out what she needs to know from her daughter—and encourages the process of connection. But the pattern of redundant conflict rapidly recurs.

Therapist: Let's stop this for a second. Try it again. Try to get Sue to say to you what it is that she needs so that she knows that you really care and support her. Because right at the moment I know she's doubting that, and you are terribly important for her. She's got to know clearly, Fran, that you're with her. Try to find out from her. Try to get her to express what it is she needs. And Sue, help your mother with this.

The therapist again intercedes to increase the proximity between the mother and Sue. But in addition to challenging the mother, he asks for Sue's help, implying that she is a participant in the fragmentation. This makes it clear to the mother that it is not all up to her, and strengthens her willingness to cooperate.

Mrs. Jarret: Sue, is there anything else, other than my show of lack of confidence in that conversation, what else can I do? (*Tenderly:*) And Sue, I do have all the confidence in you, all the confidence in the world. Because I do know that you are capable. Is there anything? What else can I do to show you?

The affective shift is marked as the mother links with her daughter and breaks the fragmentation.

Sue (*sobbing softly*): Sometimes, I'm afraid to talk to you. I don't . . . I don't know how to come and start it.
Mrs. Jarret (*softly*): Why?
Sue: I don't know why. Maybe if we just sit down sometimes and you start talking to me.
Mrs. Jarret (*softly*): I do. How many times have I just come up to your bedroom and sat down on the floor with you and talked with you?
Sue (*softly*): Not so much.
Mrs. Jarret (*tenderly*): Sure I do.
Sue (*softly*): You don't come up to the third floor too much, Mom . . . I know I don't come downstairs too much where you are. I just want to be able to talk a little bit more easily with you and I just need help in starting that.

She acknowledges that the process between them is stuck.

A positive spiral has been released between mother and daughter. It continues in a self-sufficient way and the therapist can stand back.

Mrs. Jarret: Is that what you need, is that
what you're afraid of . . .
Sue (*choked up*):   Starting it, yes.
Mrs. Jarret: And I can be more
supportive starting conversations. Is there
anything else, any other areas? Can you
think of anything else where I might be
supportive for you? Sue (*with deep feeling*),
I do love you and care about you so much.
(*The mother's eyes fill with tears.*)
Sue (*whispers*):   I know, I love you,
too . . .

(*Both are silent.*)

Therapist: This is tough stuff, it's hard.

> The therapist facilitates the
> continuation of this
> process of reaching out
> while simultaneously
> validating that it isn't
> necessarily an easy
> process.

Sue: I'm going to try . . . (*with conviction*)
hard.

(*The mother reaches her hand out to Sue, who responds. They hug, then kiss.
Their connection has moved beyond the verbal to the physical. The session ends
on a more hopeful note of closeness.*)

   This was clearly a stressful session, full of intense emotion, drama, and
tension. The mother was urged to begin to transcend her own sadness,
anger, depletion, and neediness in order to sustain her daughters. This
message was repeated relentlessly, with increased intensity. The request
was mostly one-sided—the mother must change—but in reality, both contributed to the situation; Sue was to some extent withholding herself from
her mother. Although aware of the complementary dynamic, the therapist
intervened mainly on one side, in order to stimulate change. Other aspects
of this complementary dance could be worked on later.
   It would be naive to assume that this single session would puncture,
once and for all, the youngster's isolation or break up the rigid, unuseful
exchanges that she had with her mother. This was only the first step. Later
sessions with the mother and daughters, the father and daughters, and the

siblings alone reworked the same themes and consolidated change in this area.

A session like this can occur only when the therapist has already consolidated a therapeutic alliance with the parent, in which the latter feels understood and valued. This was accomplished in earlier contacts with Mrs. Jarret alone. Without this preparation, she probably would not have been able to tolerate the stress of the maneuver. In families of divorce, this prior connection, or rapport, is especially important as a prelude to the successful use of often stressful procedures. Too much haste in moving on to more compelling child-focused issues generally increases resistance and the probability of dropout later in therapy.

This approach is somewhat at variance with a more traditional systems approach, in which the therapist is oriented to the whole. Here, the therapist connects strongly with the part (Mrs. Jarret alone) in order to be in a position later to maneuver the whole or its subsystems. It is not only during this early phase that the therapist meets alone with the wife. Solo sessions may be held throughout the therapeutic process, and the therapist is careful not to limit the therapy to issues of parenting and the wife's dealings with her husband.

Mrs. Jarret had not worked outside of the home since the birth of her first child. The therapist expressed an interest in the details of the jobs she once held, to mobilize her hopes and aspirations. Initially, Mrs. Jarret was uncomfortable talking about herself as separate from her children or her husband, but the therapist drew on those separate aspects of self through the careful use of asides, the small talk as he walked with her from the clinic lobby to the therapy room. Later, she started a job and spontaneously began to bring material from that experience to the therapy. She shared her simple discoveries: her pride in new accomplishments and the stirring of feelings of mastery at work. He listened to her faint thrill of independence on boarding a bus alone, not knowing anyone on it, and deliberately prolonged the discussion of that feeling. On another occasion he prolonged her description of pleasure in being with two new women friends, drinking beer and telling racy feminist jokes. The therapist operated on the assumption that if the woman cannot emerge, the mother probably cannot emerge either, and this will handicap the family work.

REENGAGING THE FATHER

Central to the process of forging connections was the task of reengaging the father. A basic axiom of work with postseparation families is that children do better when they maintain regular contact with the noncustodial parent. The Jarret children's access to their father had been virtually severed, and at the least they had lost a potential key source of support.

Once a therapist has determined that the severance was not the result of real danger (that, for example, the father is not homicidal or dangerously psychotic), he or she must intervene to shift the mother's way of thinking about the father and his continuing parental role. In the process, the therapist must draw clear generational boundaries to remove the youngsters from the parental battle. The goal is for the mother to allow, and preferably to encourage, the children to have contact with their father. The therapist delivers this basic message to the mother: "You lose, you do not win, if you succeed in keeping your children from their father." This message shakes the mother's vengeful belief that withholding the children benefits her because it is a mortal blow to her ex-spouse. It is usually sufficient to detail the various consequences to the children if their father has no contact with them. The therapist can resonate with the mother's rage by pointing out that "the children will never learn how difficult he really is; then they're yours completely, and he gets off the hook; then you will get no help from him, while he enjoys himself and takes no responsibility for their care." Another argument resonates with her genuine wish for the best for her children and her guilt if she does less than this: "A girl (or boy) needs a father to learn how to relate to men (or how to be a man)." Fear and threat, too, are powerful persuaders: "If they have no contact with their father, they'll blame it on you and hate you. It will destroy your relationship with the children." Permeating this approach is the principle that although the two have divorced as husband and wife, they should not divorce as parents. The goal is never to divorce one's children; the father needs to stay involved.

The strategy of looking at the consequences was used to shift Mrs. Jarret to permit the father's involvement in the therapy process with the children. Once invited by the therapist, he readily agreed to participate. The involvement of both parents in therapy, although not yet meeting together directly, and this first effort to restore the nurturing component of the hierarchy are the first counters to the parental abdication of their indispensable functions.

At the point when the father is invited to join the therapy, the therapist must make a clinical decision either to make contact with him directly or to put the onus on the mother to obtain the father's participation. Unquestionably, the goal is to obtain the father's participation. If the mother successfully makes that initial contact and if the parental relationship is thereby enhanced, so much the better. But there are risks in placing the initiative on her: she might feel rushed or coerced by the therapist, she might be overstressed by the task, or she might be turned down by the father. When these risks are judged to be high, the therapist should obtain the father's participation.

Therapists sometimes fear that doing so sets up the therapy to become a losing battle, either because the therapist will come between the parents irrevocably or because the responsibility for initiative in treatment will shift from the parents to the therapist. But this need not be the case. With a highly volatile separation, the therapist can start out by respecting the distance between spouses and secure the involvement of each parent, later placing responsibility squarely on them both and bringing them face-to-face. In this format, the therapist works from part to whole, and that is not necessarily a false start.

When the therapist phrases the request carefully, very few fathers are reluctant. If there is reluctance, the therapist must attempt some understanding of the reasons behind it. A father may fear that he will become the victim of a coalition or conspiracy of his ex-wife and the therapist, he may misunderstand the purpose and duration of the therapy, or he may want to stay away because he is afraid he will be provoked and become physically violent if brought face-to-face with his ex-wife. He may, then, see abandoning ship as the lesser evil. The therapist must learn to dismantle these objections and deal with the fears. It usually suffices to explain that the therapist, out of respect for the father's position in the family, needs his help to understand the plight of the youngsters in full perspective. If necessary, the therapist reassures the father that he will not have to become friendly with his ex-wife, and that he will not have to face her right away.

Sometimes the therapist refuses to begin therapy until one spouse can get the other in. This intensifies the crisis and puts total responsibility on the available parent to invent some new ways of resolving the impasse and involving the other parent. Sometimes lawyers or the judicial system are used to secure the other's participation. Options such as these are considered before deciding that the focus can be on only the single parent. With these various approaches, we have obtained the collaboration of both parents in 82 percent of our cases.

If it is clear, however, that a spouse will not participate, either now or later, the focus of therapy must shift. Crippling preoccupations and dependence on the ex-spouse will then be the target. The message becomes, "You cannot afford to wait for his help in dealing with the youngsters. You are it."

Restoring Executive Functioning

When dealing with emotional fragmentation within a family, the therapist must be keenly aware of a complementary phenomenon: the extent to which the youngsters are out of control and out from under parental vigilance. In the Jarret family, the daughters—Sue in particular—were running wild and unsupervised. At the same time that the family's nurturing capacities collapsed, so too had its guiding and controlling functions, the power element of the hierarchy, collapsed. Sue's fear and depression came not simply from deficient family nurturance but from her harrowing everyday existence. Still upset and confused by her recent abortion, she was cutting school, smoking a great deal of marijuana, periodically ingesting LSD, and coming home at all hours of the night or not at all. Unless she was given structure and control, her depression would be perpetuated and she would remain at high risk, a danger to herself.

With the Jarrets, the therapist had begun by emphasizing nurturance, because a focus on issues of power in this family, which was evaluated as characteristically conflict-avoiding, might have overstressed them prematurely, and because Sue was truly alone. Supportive contact with her parents and siblings was missing, and she was no longer seeing her boyfriend. The therapist started out with support issues in the hope that when controls were later applied she would be more open to them. The assumption is that issues of support and control are synergistic and not antithetical. Matters of love and power coexist as aspects of hierarchy and most often are worked out simultaneously in the therapy. In the Jarret family, control issues were brought to the surface only after themes of nurturance had been worked on.

The therapist often does not know which of many possible dynamics is operating to maintain the renunciation, neglect, or failure of parental executive functioning. A parent preoccupied by anger or depression might be immobilized or unresponsive. The custodial mother may be unaccustomed to assuming the executive role formerly filled by the father or may be ineffectual without his image of greater power and authority to back her up. Sometimes this is a covert parental contract licensing abdication; each parent absolves the other from having to take responsibility. Alternatively, a covert or even overt abdication contest may operate in which each parent refuses to pick up responsibility until the other does, or in which each avoids responsibility in order to heap it on the other. A mother may abdicate because she fears becoming competent and self-sufficient; if she appears to no longer need her ex-husband's help, she will lose both her ex-husband and her control of him.

Adolescents may be active and resourceful participants in these processes. Often angry at their parents for breaking up the marriage and exposed to their frequent two-way battles and demeaning criticisms of each other, they revise their perceptions of the parents, stripping them of automatic authority. Of interest to the therapist is how the tension of the separation and the lack of parental cooperation allow the adolescents to prey on, divide, manipulate, and outflank the executive system.

COUNTERING THE SIBLINGS' CHALLENGE

The restoration of a parent to an effective executive position in the family hierarchy is seldom easily accomplished. In the Jarrets' case, the wife, who avoided conflict, found it difficult to challenge her daughters. Dealing with her daughters by herself was a new experience, because prior to the separation her husband had either been the first executive or had backed her up with his image of authority. For the wife to feel competent with her daughters and to continue her psychological separation from her husband, she would need to accomplish alone the task of guiding and controlling the girls. The task was made more difficult by the fact that Sue had grown to cherish her freedom, harrowing though it was. She had been totally and prematurely unfettered for close to a year, and in seeking emotional shelter she had become immersed in a delinquent subculture that had become her primary group. She was not simply dropping out of her family because of the parental collapse; by now she was being pulled strongly by this extra-familial world of peers. She could not be expected to submit easily and surrender the freedom to which she had grown accustomed. Furthermore, if Sue submitted, she would then be entrusting her mother with her care—and therein loomed a threat. Sue had already been abandoned once when her mother became absorbed in her own problems. To test her mother's resolve, Sue challenged her repeatedly. Only by withstanding her daughter's salvos could Mrs. Jarret prove herself trustworthy.

Therapist: I think that this really is an important thing, and I know Sue is going to be pretty mad with me. (*There is laughter.*) But I really think that rules are required, and that some of the fear that you've been talking about (*looking at Sue*) has to do with really being free and very vulnerable. Rules are protective, and that's where your mom is coming from. Now precisely what the rules are, is something for you people to negotiate with your mom. . . . But rules are a necessity, even though they can be a little tough. Okay, why don't you go ahead, Fran, and work it out.

By anticipating the daughter's defiance in a playful way, the therapist hopes to lessen it while putting the mother on guard.

The therapist uses the value of parental protection to encourage the mother's boundary making and the creation of a family hierarchy. In the process, the mother is provided an avenue of repair for her guilt at having abdicated her caretaking functions.

Mrs. Jarret: Well, I just gave you a compromise at a time of one o'clock.
Janet: Who, all of us?

Sibling opposition begins immediately, and the mother will be besieged.

Mrs. Jarret: Well, let's talk about that.
Karen: Well, I think that, not often do I stay out till two, but when I do go to a party or something, it's an older group of people I go out with, and they don't have a time and so the parties don't really start until. . . .

The siblings' skills in resisting their mother should not be underestimated. They use a variety of strategies—for example, pragmatics and logistics.

Mrs. Jarret (*countering appropriately*): Well, you do . . . you have to think of your age in relationship to them. You can't. . . .
Sue: Why?
Mrs. Jarret: Because she can't keep their hours.
Karen: Two o'clock is not too bad. They stay out till four or five. I'm not asking for that. But whenever I'm out, if I'm driving I'm going to leave when I get tired. . . .

They point out the reasonableness of their request, and their own maturity and sense of responsibility.

Mrs. Jarret: Well, how about two for Karen . . .? (*She rubs her head as if in pain.*)
Janet: One-thirty for Sue and twelve for me.
Sue: No, I don't think it's fair, the age thing, I don't think it's right at all.

They also use fairness—morality, in effect—an effort to paralyze the mother by using guilt.

Mrs. Jarret: Why?
Sue: Because it's just not fair, we all do the same kind of thing, we all go to parties.

The siblings then try to shift their mother's criterion for determining curfews away from age to activities.

Mrs. Jarret (*her voice like that of a little girl*): No, you don't do the same kind of things. . . .

In the face of this collective counterforce, the mother begins to remove herself from the executive position. Her voice signals that she is not holding firm.

Therapist: The issue, though, is what you feel is safe for them. The position that you're coming from is a concerned, protective one, and for them to say that's what we do is not good enough, because you now are determining what they'll be doing and what's safe. So you're going to be calibrating for them how far they can go. And your judgment is sound.

In other circumstances it is likely that Sue would have prevailed. The therapist intervenes to prevent that. He again delineates the necessary hierarchy, supports the mother's stance, and extends the struggle.

Mrs. Jarret: Unfortunately, they don't think so.
Therapist: They're going to challenge it, that's for sure. They'd be silly if they didn't. They're not going to let you get off the hook lightly. They know you well, exquisitely well, and they're going to give you a tough time. But your judgment's good, so go with it. And they need your protection. . . .

The therapist's intervention emphasizes, for the first time, the power element of the relationship. Simultaneously he indicates the normality of this facet of the parent-adolescent relationship. The mother, encouraged, asserts herself. The power struggle reemerges. Will the mother meet the confrontation and stand firm, or be toppled? The test is severe.

Mrs. Jarret: I do feel very strongly about the times. I really can't see any justification in your being out any later. I think it's plenty of time for you to have a good time and it's a decent time for you to get home.

Karen: What time is that?
Mrs. Jarret: Two o'clock, one-thirty.
Sue: But, Mom, Karen's going to have to be picking me up a lot now, until I can at least get my license.

Mrs. Jarret: Well, then, you'll have to work that out with Karen.

Sue: I still don't think it's fair.

Mrs. Jarret: Sue, you do have friends who drive.

Sue (*shouting*): I can't have my friends driving me everywhere.

Sue rejects her mother's reasonableness and fights her.

Mrs. Jarret (*in a girlish whine*): Why? I drove them everywhere.

The mother knows she is competing with Sue's friends for respect, and notes the injustice.

Sue: No, you didn't drive all of these friends everywhere.

Mrs. Jarret: Not this group of friends that you're with, but I certainly have driven other kids around (*she sighs*). What about Merle? Someone from her family . . . her friends drive her all the time. (*With resolve:*) Sue, the thing is that if you really wanted to, you'd get a ride, and you will. You must have your rides arranged before you go. And if you don't have somebody who will bring you back on time, then you may not go. . . . What time were you getting home when you were down at Mary's?

The mother asks that Sue impose on her own friends and then that she take responsibility within her peer group. Because the therapist has extended the transaction beyond its usual endpoint (Sue refusing, mother retreating), the mother changes her tone completely. Going beyond her usual range, she makes a firm demand.

Sue (*mumbling*): One-thirty or two.

Mrs. Jarret (*firmly*): So you have to leave that party a half hour earlier . . . is that clear, is that all right with everybody now? Is everybody set on that? (*All but Sue nod agreement.*) Sue, are you?

Sue (*with resignation*): There's nothing I can do about it.

Mrs. Jarret: Okay.

Sue accommodates to her place in the hierarchy. She is persuaded by her

mother's firm
reasonableness, but she
won't show it.

Generally, as the parent begins to take the executive position and the new vertical structure slowly emerges, the youngster predictably tests the new arrangement. Over the following weeks, Sue tested and her mother held. The father, now participating in the ongoing therapy, did not hold. His parental stance remained minimal, sporadic, and insufficient; rule-breaking continued. His abdication needed to be countered.

COUNTERING RIGID COALITIONS

There were many possible reasons for why the father was not holding to his executive position. For example, his withdrawal might have been a misguided attempt to prevent his competence from undermining his wife's tentative efforts at limit-setting, or it might have been precisely designed to undermine her efforts. Having already transferred his allegiance and commitment to his new girlfriend, he may have felt totally disengaged from his spouse. Or possibly he was operating in coalition with his daughters by default, by failing to counter their acting out. During parental separation and divorce, it is common for cross-generational coalitions to be exacerbated, to be made dysfunctional, and to block necessary executive functioning. In the Jarret family the husband's coalition with Sue had in fact already been noticed in the therapy sessions.

The following transcripts illustrate a combination of the second and third possibilities listed previously, indicating a complex father-girlfriend-daughter troika. The husband had left town for a week on business and returned to his apartment, which he shared with his friend Don, to find it virtually ransacked. Mr. Jarret and his daughters were in the session.

Mr. Jarret (*angrily*): Sue, you know I was really, really ripped!
Therapist: What happened? Just put me in the picture.
Mr. Jarret: Well, Don came back from being away—he was away also—to find both toilets blocked up, overflowing, one on the second floor, down through to the first floor. His room, all his clothes which were on the bed thrown on the floor, his shade twisted and tied to the bicycle. The

The father is angry because Sue has defiled his place and disturbed his peace. His anger is narcissistic. This will be therapeutically utilized.

tapes all over the floor in the living room
and some of his . . . a significant amount of
his Valium taken. There was only one
person who has the key to that place and
that is Sue.

For approximately forty minutes, the therapist keeps the father angry
and sharply focused on this particular incident. The aim is to convert him
from a protective to an attacking position, in order to elevate him to a
position of authority.

Mr. Jarret: It seems to me, Sue, that you
can think right now about who was there
with you on Friday. (*Angrily and very
firmly:*) This is not a hard question.

Encouraged by the
therapist, the father
demands information and
takes an uncustomarily
firm stand.

Sue: Dad, I'm not sure if Ben was there.
I'll find out, I'll find everything out for you
this weekend.
Mr. Jarret: This weekend is too late!
Sue: How about tomorrow, tomorrow
night?
Mr. Jarret: Before this weekend!
Sue: Before this weekend, I'll go back
and we'll talk.
Therapist (*looking at his watch*):   Okay.
We're running out of time. What's the
arrangement, then? Sue will get back to
you before this weekend and then you'll
have an explanation. Okay, and then
you'll take it from there.

The father is now in a
clear executive position,
and a generational
boundary has been drawn.
The therapist decides to
punctuate the experience
at this point by ending the
session.

Mr. Jarret (*nodding*):   Yes.
Therapist: Okay, I want to talk to you
(*looking at the father*).

His intention is to meet
briefly with the father
alone, to help him
consolidate this
experience.

Karen (*looking at therapist*):   Wait.
(*Rushing:*) I think there's another issue that
has to be talked about.

The pull to maintain
homeostasis is seen as
Karen and her sisters

compete with the therapist for control of the session's end. The other siblings pull together behind Karen, attempting to topple the father from his recently assumed executive position.

Therapist (*warily*): Okay?

Karen: Sue, should I start it for you?

Sue: No. It's just . . . one time I slept over there, Dad, and you went out and wanted to know what time I wanted to get up in the morning, and I said about seven-thirty . . . er . . . the telephone rang at seven. It was Janet calling me. You weren't there, and I heard you coming in at seven-thirty.

Mr. Jarret: That's right.

Sue: And you hadn't been in all night.

Mr. Jarret: That's right.

Therapist: Okay.

Sue: Why didn't . . .

Therapist: We really don't have time here. There are other things I really want to do. We can handle this next time. I know that you had things to bring up. (*Pointing to Karen:*) We got caught in something that I think is very important.

The therapist sees the challenge coming and attempts to block it by refocusing on the specific theme of the session and its importance.

Janet (*firmly*): No, I think this is important, and I'd really like to know where you were. Really!

The therapist's effort to block is rebuffed.

Mr. Jarret: I was at Eileen's [his girlfriend's] house.

Janet (*very upset*): Well, that's wonderful, that you leave someone who's under your responsibility for the night with nobody. (*Her voice rises in an anguished cry.*)

They accuse the father of delinquency.

Mr. Jarret (*shocked*): With nobody?

Sue (*softly*): Don was there.

With the father now under attack, Sue's coalition with him emerges as she tries to defend him.

Karen: Well, the thing is, we're expected
to come home, so you should be expected
to come home. You can go out, but you
should come home at night.

> The eldest daughter
> disciplines her father.

Mr. Jarret: Yes, I told Sue what
happened. I told her we were working on
something that had to be in, we worked till
three in the morning.

> The father is on the
> defensive.

The therapist then halted the session. The siblings left the room and Mr.
Jarret was seen alone briefly.

The above sequence reveals a powerful dynamic. Sue's extreme acting
out, together with the therapist's relentless highlighting of this event in
the session, forced the father to take a firm hierarchical executive posture
in which he was no longer proximal with Sue. By taking this position, he
broke the silent agreement with his daughters: if he lets them get away
with things, then they'll let him get away with things. The father was
stung, his authority undermined. He was ready to retreat.

At this point the therapist had to take charge. He welcomed to some
extent this runaway event in which the siblings dressed down their father,
for whom it was possibly a corrective experience. Although sympathetic,
the therapist would not join the youngsters. Rather, his role was to support
the father as an executive. He had a number of alternatives: sympathize
with the father's self-destructive skill at making himself vulnerable to his
daughter's attack, ask how the father's own father might have handled a
similar situation, or refocus and restore the father to his parental position
by playing on his fear, guilt, and sense of parental responsibility. The therapist chose the latter.

Therapist: I'm really pleased that this
happened. So now you have some sort of
idea as to what the hell is going on.

> The therapist frames Sue's
> acting out as a positive,
> useful learning experience
> for the father, who should
> now clearly see the full
> dimensions of her
> behavior. The therapist
> purposely arouses his
> indignation.

Mr. Jarret (*shaking his head hopelessly*):
No, I don't have any idea, I really don't. I

> Mr. Jarret is still
> preoccupied with the

don't know if I have an idea. I know Eileen and I had to discuss something that night.

Therapist: Well, I'm not talking about that.

exposé that has occurred. He has been derailed and relinquishes his appropriate executive stance.

The therapist ignores the father's preoccupation and begins the process of reinstating the hierarchy.

Mr. Jarret: Well, I'm . . .
Therapist (*interrupting, talking seriously*): I'm talking about Sue (*pointing to Sue's seat*). Over those days it sounds to me that she was pretty much, totally delinquent. You were guessing about drugs a couple of weeks ago. . . .
Mr. Jarret: I know she had a long talk with Don. He told me about it. Sue said she has a couple of beers now and then. She may smoke a joint now and then, but no drugs.

The father moves to exonerate Sue. He readily accepts this reassuring secondhand account. His attitude is a further manifestation of his coalition with Sue and his proclivity to abdicate executive responsibility.

Therapist: Do you believe that?
Mr. Jarret: Well, I don't know, she's been pretty. . . .
Therapist (*leaning forward*): The Valium was missing. She doesn't even seem to know what the hell is going on. It's outrageous. I mean your description of the way the house was is pretty incredible. She's bullshitting you, and she and her friends are into delinquent stuff. I think this is a message loud and clear that you should not be surprised by anything that she gets into. . . . And that's why I'm pleased.

Noticing that the father is in the process of fooling himself, the therapist sharply attacks his perception and stance. He leans toward the father, speaking in a very definitive manner, as he vividly repaints the incident, trying to rekindle the father's sense of indignation. He suggests that this is only the beginning, forewarning the father.

Mr. Jarret: I won't be surprised anymore.

Veridicality, Distortion, and the Intergenerational Dialogue

A basic parental function is to socialize children to see the world relatively accurately. During parental separation and divorce, this task requires that parents talk with their children and provide relatively clear and consistent information. Parents gear this information to the age and needs of the child. The goal is to provide them with a useful way of understanding their parents' divorce. At a minimum, there should be an effort to allow the children to continue to love and respect both parents, to relieve the children of responsibility for the breakup or for reuniting the parents, and finally, to reassure the children of continuing parental involvement and protection. Most parents are able to accomplish this task, and the children, although upset by the separation, begin to accept it or at least to recognize the futility of fighting it.

In the more disturbed, conflicted situation, this necessary process may not occur. Instead, the child's perception is sacrificed to the internal, vindictive needs of each spouse or to the view that one spouse is blameless while the other spouse bears the onus of the separation. Adolescents, like younger children, often receive contradictory explanations or highly skewed, hollow, and distorted family myths. Such distortion is a bilateral process. On the one side, a spouse values having in his or her camp an adolescent who might speak out against or harass the other spouse, or might provide reassurance in moments of private self-doubt. On the other side, adolescents—especially those in dysfunctional situations—become greatly interested in their parents' perceptions as they seek data from both sides to make sense out of the chaos. The dislocation of the separation process entails threats to the stability of their external and internal worlds at different levels. The disruption affects their interpersonal alignments and also their introjections—their relatively stable ideas of who their parents, their family, and they themselves are and will become.

Some adolescents, in the face of contradictions or skew, retreat: "The hell with it." But in a clinical population, it is more common to see adolescents embroiled in and distressed by the contradictions. They tend to get hooked to a single, skewed mythology: one parent is "right." The advantages of this view are simplicity and freedom from ambiguity, characteristics that may be welcomed by the anxious adolescent whose life is so much in flux. The adolescent may feel more secure when in a coalition with one parent even though it jeopardizes the relationship with the other parent.

In this situation of contradiction and distortion, the therapist often must facilitate a dialogue between each parent and the adolescent children. The adolescents generally participate eagerly, and the dialogue usually contains recurrent and predictable themes: how the separation came about, who will take care of them, how both parents will behave after the separation, and what the new family will be like. For the adolescents to question— indeed, vigorously interrogate—their parents is not uncommon. Their priority is to cross-validate and untangle the webs of parental accusations, conflicts, and rationalizations for the marital separation. They judge the situation for themselves and will quiz the parents about the various property, child support, and visitation arrangements that are being negotiated.

In the following transcript of a session with the Jarrets, the husband talks with his daughters about the breakup of the marriage and attempts to clarify for them his own and his girlfriend's participation. The therapist sponsors this dialogue, which helps determine how the husband and his girlfriend (later to be his wife) will be perceived by his daughters and what sort of postseparation relationship he and she will have with the girls.

Sue: But see, Dad, we didn't know everything that was going on. Mom is certainly to blame. But it was just that we saw you saying "I'm leaving" and Mom saying to us that she wanted you to stay around so that you could work out your problems and everything.

The children declare they had insufficient information. On the basis of what their mother had told them, it is their understanding that their father is ultimately to blame for ending the marriage.

Karen: Yeah, also, from what I understand, Mom was trying to make the marriage work. But she didn't want Eileen in the picture. And you weren't ready to give up Eileen. So therefore, I do see it as your fault, because you didn't want to give up Eileen to try to make the marriage work.

The mother was virtuous. There is a denial of the serious difficulties of the marriage. The girls' blaming their father is an aspect of their coalition with their mother.

Mr. Jarret: That's right. I didn't want to try to make the marriage work any more

The father moves to correct their perception

than I had tried for eight or nine years. The trying had stopped as far as I was concerned. The marriage was over, as far as I was concerned. Does that make sense?

Karen: No. Because. . . .
Mr. Jarret: I guess that's what I don't understand. Why doesn't it make sense to you?
Karen: Because you didn't try again.
Mr. Jarret: Well, I guess there's a point when you just say to yourself that it's not worth it. I am not an unintelligent person. I am a reasonably reflective and thoughtful and caring person who does not usually make impetuous decisions. I do make some impetuous decisions, but this was not an impetuous decision. This was simply not this carefree, casual kind of thing that you intimate it was.

Karen: Well, that's the way I see it. Soon as Eileen comes on the scene, that's when I see the problems.
Mr. Jarret: But you didn't see the problems?

Sue (*addressing Karen*): You weren't there, you (*her voice rises*) . . .
Therapist (*interrupting Sue with voice and hand*): Hang on, hang on, your dad can talk for himself. Karen . . . Karen, are you saying that when Eileen entered, the

and fantasies. The structural aspect of the process is that he disrupts their coalition with the mother. Thematically, he attempts to answer their queries about his commitment to the marriage, whether he had acted responsibly or not, and whether in fact the marriage was over.

The father is apparently candid in his answers. He is consistent in his viewpoint and demanding of respect. He maintains his adult position and prerogatives in the hierarchy while showing flexibility. This will strengthen his position with his children.

This is the first explicit statement of the role of the father's girlfriend in breaking up the marriage. The therapist will soon pick up this theme. Sue tries to assist her father.

The fantasy that the father's girlfriend is

problems started? Is that essentially what you're saying?

Karen: That's my understanding.

responsible has significant implications. If allowed to stand, it would kill the possibility that the children could ever have a good relationship with her. The father would be seen as a floating cork—passive, buffeted, and at the mercy of outside influences. The children would be unable to respect him. The fantasy also would allow responsibility to be projected away from the parents' real marital difficulties.

Therapist (*turning to Mr. Jarret*): Is that so?

Mr. Jarret: No.

The therapist refutes the notion that the father was pirated away. This is a fantasy that the father might be expected to foster, given his guilt feelings and his proclivity for avoiding conflict and responsibility.

Karen: That's what you say. That's not what Mom says, and it's not what I see. It's not that you didn't have problems before. She didn't think this was ever going to happen until Eileen came into the scene, and it probably wouldn't have. If you didn't have somebody else to turn to, you wouldn't have separated from Mom.

Karen clings to her (and probably her mother's) idealization of the marriage and probably to a fantasy that her parents would reunite.

Mr. Jarret: I would probably still be living in the same house, going through the same forest, that's what we have been doing.

Therapist (*expressing surprise*):   Is that so? You would really have continued living there?

Mr. Jarret: Well, I don't know how long or how much longer it would have lasted, because it was just getting worse and not better. Every time we'd sit down, we'd go over it and we'd try different things . . . it just didn't work. I don't know how long that would have ended up going on. If anything, I would have stayed there for you guys so that there would have been that semblance of the family. I don't know how long that would have lasted.

Karen: Well, I'm sure it would have been easier for me to accept the divorce if no one else had been involved. Because I see it as Eileen's fault that the marriage broke up.

Mr. Jarret: But don't you think that's a little strange, though, Karen? By Eileen's fault, I assume that you mean it's my fault.

Karen: Well, yours and Eileen's.

Mr. Jarret (*pointing at himself*):   Mine.

Karen: No, she knew what was going on. She knew that you were married.

Mr. Jarret: Yeah, she did, but whose decision was it to walk away?

Karen: Yours and Eileen's, probably.

Again, the therapist calls on the father to take responsibility for his actions.

To the father's credit, he takes responsibility for the decision to end the marriage. It is likely that the daughter's fantasy of the father being snatched by an evil witch is being dented. This increases the possibility that he will be seen as a substantial figure and that the girls could further develop their relationship with him (and with his girlfriend) in the future.

Mr. Jarret (*with great emphasis*):   It was   The father indeed takes
mine. It was mine.   responsibility for the
                                                                  closure of the marriage.

The therapist must prevent this dialogue from becoming interminable. Efforts toward clarification can yield obfuscation and continuing fog; challenges can be met by repetitious, defensive counterchallenges. The imposition of firm time limits will usually contain the discussion, preventing it from generating extreme anger and anxiety or from serving as a red herring that diverts attention from difficult issues. The dialogue may also be dysfunctional when it becomes a forum for perpetuating cross-generational coalitions—the youngsters speaking for their mother, blaming their father, and retaining for themselves the right to determine whether the marriage is over. To avoid this, the therapist should carefully monitor the exchange to ensure that it is respectful. If it appears that siblings are scoring with impunity and that a parent's authority is being jeopardized, or if it threatens to topple an executive parent or precipitate the disengagement and flight of a parent, the therapist must intervene and make sure the session ends with the parent still appropriately in charge.

Reuniting the Parental Executive System

One indispensable task for divorcing families is to establish separate parental hierarchies that allow for both protective limits and emotional connectedness. Such hierarchies not only provide the beginnings of the parental cloak the children need but increase each parent's sense of parental mastery and competence. However, the parents' individual achievements will be insufficient so long as they remain divided. It must be expected that the adolescent will skillfully exploit the division. It becomes mandatory, then, to reunite the parents as parents. This process is often delicate and requires careful preparation and pacing. In a high-conflict divorce, a conjoint session prematurely convened is often counterproductive.

In the Jarrets' case, the parents had not seen and had hardly spoken to each other in the eight months since the separation. The mother dealt with the youngsters, and the father dealt separately with the youngsters, who now visited him regularly. Here, the process of reunion is initiated as the therapist asks the wife to contact her husband.

Therapist: But I'm interested in you and Michael working something out (*waving his hand between Mrs. Jarret and the empty seat beside her*). You have to have. . . .

The therapist indicates both verbally and nonverbally the necessary task.

Mrs. Jarret (*shaking her head firmly*): I can't, I can't. No, I just don't know how I could sit in a room with him.

The mother's worst fears surface immediately. It is too early to bring the two face-to-face.

Therapist: No, I'm not talking about necessarily . . . that's one alternative, sitting in a room. But there are other ways of doing it. In Africa they do it with drums (*the therapist, smilingly, drums on his knees*). Can you . . . you any good at it?

The therapist uses humor to decrease the mother's anxiety and to suggest alternative strategies.

Mrs. Jarret (*smiling*): I'd have to learn. I don't know, I. . . .

The mother remains skeptical.

Therapist (*waving his hand in a spiral in the air*): Smoke signals . . . letters.

The therapist lightly coaxes the mother on.

Mrs. Jarret: Much later, I think maybe . . . um . . . I can't think of anything but um . . . anger with Michael.
Therapist: But how are you going to communicate to him that you want the kids in at twelve o'clock, twelve-thirty, and one-thirty?

The mother procrastinates.

The therapist ignores the mother's protestations, refocuses the discussion, and reminds her of the task.

Mrs. Jarret (*smiling*): You'll have to do it . . . um . . . I don't know.
Therapist: I think that you have to find a way, even if it's a letter.

She dodges responsibility.

Responsibility is returned to her with a concrete suggestion.

Mrs. Jarret: Well, the girls already know.

By utilizing the youngsters as go-betweens, she dodges again.

Therapist: It needs to go from you to him. This is going to keep cropping up, and you're going to need a way of passing him messages that concern the kids and where you want his cooperation and agreement. It's necessary. I don't know how you're going to do it (*very firmly*) but it has to be done. . . . Also so that he can be held accountable. If he comes in next week, and he says he's spoken with you and the agreement we have agreed to is this, then he has to answer to that. As long as there's no real agreed and stamped arrangement, he's not accountable for anything. He can just keep switching and changing eternally.

The need for appropriate generational boundaries is punctuated with a firm statement.

The therapist is unconvinced of her commitment to the task. To motivate her, he draws on her anger and implies that she does not hold her husband accountable.

Mrs. Jarret (*nodding*): Uh, huh.

Therapist: And then he won't meet his responsibilities, which he needs to do for the kids. It will help you and it will help the kids if you could have some sort of way to communicate what you want from him.

Mrs. Jarret: That's going to be most difficult right now, but I . . . you're right, it does have to be done.

Agreement is obtained.

Mrs. Jarret followed through and called her husband. Thereafter they spoke to each other occasionally, remaining a tentative parental unit. Their sense of being parents together was still fragile and tenuous, however, hindered by a measure of continuing anger, mistrust, and fear. Their moves were uncoordinated, and they still used the children to carry messages. This is an expected transitional phase, and the therapist anticipated that the parents would be motivated to consolidate what they had begun when the divided parental unit fell easy prey to their daughter's manipulations.

This scenario of continued, although diminished, acting out heralded the important final stage of the therapy: the parents were brought together face-to-face for the first time since the separation. The children were not present. Preparations for this meeting had been made throughout the therapy; the necessity for one or more joint sessions had been mentioned periodically to desensitize the parents' anxiety. Both spouses had by this time developed a sense of their own individual parental competence, built around their withstanding Sue's onslaughts. For the wife, recovery also was fueled by her working with the therapist to expand her interests. This individual work had not been necessary with Mr. Jarret. Both spouses therefore entered the joint session feeling relatively good about themselves. They were first briefed individually on what would take place during the session. Since the mother was the more anxious, the therapist employed light imagery exercises to prepare her for the session: she was terrified of dissolving in front of her husband, so the therapist coaxed her to summon the fantasy of "kicking him in the butt," thereby mobilizing some self-confidence and lessening the tension. Because she feared her own rage and envy, should her husband arrive for the session looking good, the therapist joked with her about how she could beautify herself and what she should wear.

So that the spouses would not collide in this first joint venture, the therapist focused their attention on the skill of their youngsters at outmaneuvering them, and away from each other as spouses.

Therapist: Let's now go through possible scenarios. Things that might happen with Sue. And we're focusing now on Sue because quite frankly Sue is the one that I think is at highest risk. I think she has a lot of potential. She's bright and can do well, and I think she has great potential to fail. She can be irresponsible, and really loose. And she's smart. She really knows how to exploit differences between the two of you. So the two of you have got to be together on this. Let's go through some possible ways in which she bypasses you or plays one against the other or puts something over on you. I know a few things she does to you, but let's just go through them so that you are aware. (*Following a short silence, he turns to Mr. Jarret.*) Do you want to start?

The therapist defines the task of the session as that of helping Sue to succeed. To this end the parents will need to cooperate. He is deliberately longwinded as he recruits them to the task. He watches their moods, helping them collect themselves. He demonstrates that he will be an active participant and in charge of the session. He will end the monologue only when he feels that they have moved from themselves to the task at hand. He frames Sue's behavior as calculated and divisive. They are her victims. Both spouses are asked now to participate in a concrete, goal-oriented process intended to join them as parents and differentiate them from Sue.

Mr. Jarret: Well, she does a lot of last-minute calling. She creates a crisis situation and then needs an exception to a rule to bail her out, whether it's a ride home or coming home late. Not her evening curfew, she's real conscious of that.

Therapist: Okay, so it's last-minute stuff. What's the problem with that; what are the implications of that?

Mr. Jarret: Well, I think she is not assuming the responsibility to plan something, and there seem to be things that she probably could plan more easily.

Therapist: Does it mean, then, that arrangements are made that are loose and you don't have the details?

Mr. Jarret: I have the sense, I don't have enough details of this dance group that she is in. I was concerned when they had a rehearsal and I felt I learned about it real late.

Therapist: Do you know what Michael is talking about?

Mrs. Jarret: Yeah. It leaves you wondering, is that in fact what she is

doing . . . (*her husband begins to interrupt*).

It leaves me wondering that.

Mr. Jarret: I think I wonder less, although as those items build up. . . .

The husband picks up on the therapist's framing. As he talks, the wife sits attentively, waiting her turn.

The therapist asks for elaboration. The objective is not only to obtain further necessary information but also to reinforce the husband's new alignment as an executive who is no longer in coalition with Sue.

The therapist here implies, "Do you agree with your husband?" This promotes parental cooperation.

The husband's interruption is in reaction to the wife's including him with her "you." "Wondering" here becomes an indicator of good parenting—that is, well-founded skepticism is part of being an effective parent. The husband's "wondering less" reveals his coalition with Sue. The

Therapist (*pointing to the husband*): I think you *would* wonder less, because in relation to Sue you can be pretty gullible.
Mr. Jarret: Well, I think you've said before that I could be pretty gullible in relation to all of them.
Therapist (*looking the husband in the eye and suggesting an intimate knowledge*): Yes. You might well wonder less. I can understand that. I know. Okay. But this is something that she does.

wife, he implies, is silly to wonder. This indication of the coalition may have emerged in reaction to the therapist's first move to forge parental cooperation. This dynamic is at the core of the dysfunction.

The therapist moves rapidly to curtail the drift that the husband has initiated and that could undermine the goal of the session. Respecting the fragility of the parental relationship, the therapist does not ask the wife to confront her husband. The therapist remains in control through most of the session. This is a necessary intermediate step.

Mr. Jarret: Yeah. . . . Okay.
Therapist: All right. What can you do about it? Because if this is recurring, if this is the pattern, then this is a maneuver. This is one of the things that she is doing to bypass you in some way. What can you do about it?

The husband appears to accept the idea for the moment. He subsides. The therapist reiterates the framing of the parents as victims of Sue's calculated manipulations.

Mr. Jarret: Well, one of the things that makes me be less doubting is that I have a sense that school operates on a "let's do something" basis. I don't perceive as much planning and as much structure in that school as there are in other schools. The school decides at the last minute, that kind of thing.

The husband again exonerates Sue, maintaining his coalition with her. The therapist is impressed with the husband's deft attempt to transfer blame from Sue to society. This dynamic process, which stunts conscience development, is camouflaged by the husband's reasonable concern with how "liberal" schools operate.

Therapist: But you said yourself that this is happening to both of you, so let's not try to whitewash it.

Mr. Jarret: No, I don't mean to whitewash it.

The therapist again struggles with the husband to halt his rationalizing. A clear tug-of-war is operating between them.

Therapist: You said yourself that the dance thing was probably planned a long time in advance. How come you were only notified just before? I think that what you need to do there is find out what's going on. Be intrusive. Phone up whoever needs to be phoned.

In order to develop the kind of probing specificity that an executive parent must display in relation to the breaking of rules, the therapist's questions plant the idea that the youngster is using "selective notification." She is out to obtain the upper hand. The therapist goes out of his way to imply that intrusiveness can be a good characteristic of parenting. His message is in direct opposition to the husband's readiness to avoid looking closely.

Mrs. Jarret: Those kinds of things come up a lot. She did a lot of this around the prom. She wanted very much to be allowed to stay overnight. First it was, they were all going to the beach right after the party. I said no. The next thing it was staying overnight at Mary's house. Again I said no. Then she had brunch immediately following the party. It just seemed she was creating situations one after the other.

The mother's response here indicates a potential payoff of the joint session. She details Sue's clever attempts to outmaneuver adult control. By so doing, however, the wife tends to elicit her husband's indulgent side taking.

Mr. Jarret: I don't mean to be an apologist for Sue. But it is just a shade over a week before Karen's graduation, and Karen doesn't know what parties there are afterward, and this, that and the other thing.

The patterns of collusion between father and daughter are becoming exposed.
Predictably, after the wife takes a critical and demanding executive position, the husband disqualifies her by supporting Sue. The system is delicately but rigidly balanced.

Mrs. Jarret: I don't know what you're saying.

Mr. Jarret: Well. . . .

Therapist: What you're doing is you *are* being an apologist for Sue. Let's really try and simply acknowledge that this is one of Sue's strategies. You know it's happening too often.

The therapist again confronts the husband, asking him to transcend his current stance. The move is confrontational and aims to expose fully the father's general tendency to line up with the daughter against his wife.

(Mr. Jarret shakes his head, obviously dissatisfied.)

Therapist: What's wrong, Michael?

Mr. Jarret: Well, I have problems handling that. That is, I don't have evidence that shows me that that is exactly what's happened.

Now his position is totally flushed out, making it possible to confront the conflict.

Therapist: You know, you're not going on terribly much evidence here, because, first, Sue is smart, and second, you're not following it up. You need to be following up.

Mr. Jarret: Okay. Let me ask you this. If

Sue comes in with a situation like the prom and says can I stay at Mary's and we're going to sleep for three or four hours before we go down to the shore, should we acknowledge to Sue that we don't trust her as far as we can kick a fire plug? If Karen did that, my guess is that we wouldn't follow that up.

Therapist: Well, two things. First, Karen is older, she's eighteen, and she really has not had the sort of difficulties that Sue has. Now we're talking about Sue, of cutting school, of the Valium incident where she really ransacked your place. (*The therapist looks toward Mrs. Jarret:*) I don't know if you want to throw in anything more, Fran?

The therapist decides it is mandatory to provide the "evidence" that the father is asking for and that the mother has concealed. He now turns to her. She must confront the father. The therapist could have asked this of her earlier, but he has worked throughout the session to create an atmosphere of nonavoidance, of dealing with raw reality. She has seen him wrestle with her husband. The therapist has tried his best for her. Protective of her boundaries and defenses, he gently invites her contribution.

Mrs. Jarret: I think that. . . . I do. . . . And I will have to ask you, Michael, that this will be in strict confidence. I think that I have to tell you this just to show you where my fear comes from. Sue has had an abortion.

Mr. Jarret (*stares at his wife, shocked*): Well, that sure does change things some. That's something I didn't know.

Mrs. Jarret: She was supposed to have told you.

Mr. Jarret: Well, she didn't.

Mrs. Jarret: She wanted to wait until a better time. And when I asked her if she

had discussed it with you, she said that's
in the past, let's let it alone. And it is in the
past. But I am very much afraid for her.
Therapist (*after a period of silence*):   I
think it's the responsible thing to let
Michael know about that.

Mrs. Jarret: I had thought that too, but I   The wife acknowledges
also left it up to Sue to tell him, and she   her moment of abdication.
hasn't.

    The husband anxiously taps the floor. He is visibly shaken. There is
silence, then he asks his wife some further questions about when the abortion was and who the father was.

Therapist: But this is some of what's   By summarizing the
been going on. An abortion, Valium   situation graphically and
incidents—that might just be the tip of the   emphasizing its lethal
iceberg—cutting school and probably lots   potential, the therapist
of things that you simply don't know   tries to capitalize on this
about. But these are powerful, telltale   moment to have them
signs. You can't go back to that and harp   close ranks further.
on it. Sue is right. This is stuff that has
gone by. But at least the two of you need   The past cannot be erased,
to know what the risks are, the direction in   but they must now take
which she is moving. She has potential to   responsibility for dealing
do well and potential to self-destruct. And   with their daughter in the
that's it. . . . So the two of you really need   future.
to be together on this. And you need to be
intruding into her life to find out what's
going on. . . .

Mrs. Jarret (*anxiously*):   How much   The wife's fears surface as
control can you have without her turning   she anticipates her
the whole thing around?   daughter's defiance. The

Therapist: How do you mean?   therapist will address
                                                 these fears and weave a
                                                 twosome out of the
                                                 parents' shared experience.

Mrs. Jarret: I mean if I hold her back and   The fear of the girl's
say you can't do this and you can't do   defiance quickly gives way
that, she'll defy me in other ways. I lose   to the more outstanding
something if I do that to her. She'll quit   fear that the youngster

confiding in me, she'll quit talking to me altogether. You know. She'll use a lot of things.
Therapist: This is another one of her maneuvers. What she says to you quite simply is, "Mom, you do that and I won't talk to you. I'll be very angry with you." And that scares you, you're going to lose contact with her. (*To the husband:*) Does she ever do that with you?

will reject her altogether. It is this ultimate fear, that "my child won't love me," that tends to paralyze. But more significant, as the wife is complaining she looks over not just at the therapist but at her husband, linking with him as he looks at her and agrees with her. Their interaction continues to show attention to each other at the nonverbal level as the therapist addresses the fears (which the wife articulates and the husband shares) by normalizing them.

(*Mr. Jarret nods in agreement.*)
Therapist: Same thing?
Mr. Jarret: She did the whole thing with the trashing of the house.
Therapist: Yes. Well, that's the way she goes on that one. And you get scared, both of you. You feel really guilty, and she rides on that. You think, "Maybe I haven't done enough for her, maybe she's justified in being angry with me." That's the line she uses. And I know it twists your guts. I've seen it happen with you, Fran. . . .

Asking "Does she ever do that to you," brings the husband in more fully and points out that they share the same plight as parents. The therapist builds on their nonverbal linking. As the husband agrees, the couple is no longer in conflict and is able to start the process of working toward successful problem solving. By grasping the significance of how the youngsters prey on the parents' guilt, the parents are supported and prepared to deal differently with their youngsters.

The session proceeded for another twenty minutes, during which the parents spontaneously began to talk to each other, anticipating Sue's resistance and searching for new ways of managing her. A new level of parental cooperation was beginning, and the therapist backed off. Toward the end of the session, the therapist moved to consolidate the gains.

Therapist: Okay, these are some of the things that you're really going to have to be very vigilant about and keep checking in with one another about. We're going to have to pull this to a close now. I think you have a fair idea of some of what's ahead of you. It's going to be quite a long thing, but in a way it's going to be quite a short thing. She's now sixteen and a half or something. She's probably going to be out of the home at eighteen. So it's two years you are talking about. Some seven hundred days.

Mr. Jarret: Less than that.

The therapist gives them a confused time frame. At its core is the notion there is no time to waste. But he expects the husband to disagree as usual so as to have the last word. He thus plays down the urgency, allowing the father to step in and emphasize the urgency himself. This is precisely the note on which to end the session.

Therapist: You're talking about very little time. But my guess is there's going to be round after round. So relax. Roll up your sleeves. You can expect this to keep on happening for a while. Don't be surprised by that, okay? Let's stop now. I'm very impressed by the way you two handled this. I'm really impressed.

The therapist banishes any fantasy that this will be a quick fix.

The goal of the session was achieved. The couple had begun to accept the necessity of taking a stand and working together as parents, although in the face of other resistances this acceptance remained fragile and needed to be therapeutically consolidated. Further sessions were held with both parents together and with the parents and Sue. As the parental alliance was gradually forged, the therapist began to move from his previously central position, increasingly facilitating more parental interaction and encouraging their own self-directed initiative. This shift is important because the tendency toward parental abdication can be unwittingly encouraged if a therapist is too helpful. All efforts to keep the therapist in charge must be dodged.

Sessions were gradually spaced out and convened only after the parents had come together on their own and felt they had resolved problems with their children. These problems now occurred with diminishing intensity. Therapy was then terminated. An eighteen-month follow-up session gave evidence of enduring positive change. Sue had graduated from high school with good grades, was holding a responsible job, and was considering going to college. The parents had not become amicable, but they continued to check on Sue and were pleased to find that they could trust her more. Sue too was pleased with the changes in her life.

Conclusion

Not uncommonly, spousal separation gives rise to familial splintering of varying degrees and precipitates pain and psychopathology among the children. The case described in this chapter demonstrates a useful way of viewing intrafamilial processes and working with postseparation families with adolescent children. The guiding principle of the therapy is to facilitate the restoration of parental functioning and a rearrangement of the post-divorce family. Separation and divorce need not herald the death of the family. For some, separation can be a transition and not an end. The well-being of parents and children can be enhanced as the family—albeit considerably changed—attempts to remain a viable, self-propelled, and inter-protective unit.

9

Expediting Court Processes

CLINICAL EVALUATIONS for the court generally fall into two categories: those requested by one attorney for his or her client, and those requested by the court itself (or by attorneys from both sides) to assess the overall situation. Evaluations for single attorneys may pose serious questions of ethics for mental health professionals. It can be very difficult to do a fair assessment of family functioning when the evaluator is called in to support one side, is paid by that side, and is presented only one side to assess. An attorney fighting for custody for a client may be asking for an evaluation with the sole purpose of supporting the client's position in court. The fees come from that parent, and to satisfy the referral source (thereby insuring future referrals), the evaluator's job can become "making a good case" for that parent.

The best custody evaluation includes both parents. Without working with both parties, the professional can be biased from the start, being restricted to information coming from a person who is in an adversarial stance to the absent parent. The children subjected to such evaluations often find themselves in a compromised situation. Taken to the "doctor" against the wishes of their other parent, their loyalty conflicts may be exacerbated or consolidated.

Nor does meeting with all members of a family necessarily solve the problem of fairness or guarantee a systemic evaluation. The question of who has hired whom is fundamental, though it is often downplayed. The request for a systemic evaluation must come from, or be hinged on, a source outside the warring parties. The field shows experimentation in a variety of directions. The court may order a family evaluation from an outside source. Some courts also have their own family evaluation units. The trend now is toward circumventing the adversarial stance by having both parties agree on one evaluator. Moreover, there is increasing awareness that a longer, more family-based evaluation may in the long run turn out to be more cost-effective for all involved.

This chapter is concerned with the evaluation ordered by the court. The judge uses such an evaluation to help decide which parent should be awarded custody. Today's judge often is aware that more than a child's relationship to the mother or the "favored psychological parent" needs to be considered. What most judges and attorneys still expect, however, is that the mental health professional will interview the participants, take a history on each of the parents, do a mental status examination, and assess each parent's thoughts about child rearing. They expect the report to cover the physical facilities available to each parent, such as whether the child will have a separate bedroom, the characteristics of the neighborhood surrounding each home, and each parent's plans for schooling and after-school care. They expect that the evaluator will interview the child and gain an understanding of the child's preference while assessing whether the child is mature enough for the court to take the stated preference seriously. Finally, the evaluator is expected to weigh all of the data and make a recommendation, not just as to who should get custody or who is the better parent but as to what living arrangement is better for the child and what time the child should spend with each parent. It is expected that the recommendation will be fully substantiated in the report submitted to court.

In such a traditional evaluation, the interviews are usually individual. The parents might not be seen together, and the children might not be seen with either of the parents. The reason is that most evaluations tend to center on intrapersonal issues. The evaluator considers each parent's assets and liabilities as a parent only: closeness to the child, emotional warmth and stability, ability to nurture and set limits, and knowledge of the child. The parents are then compared, the wishes of the child—particularly older children—are taken into consideration, and the parent who comes out ahead is recommended in the custody arrangements.

Toward a New Family-Based Evaluation

While all of these factors are certainly important, an evaluation that stops here misses the influence of five outstanding dynamic considerations involving the total family unit. These are: (1) the powerful effect of the couple's ongoing fight; (2) the kind of participation other members of the social network have in the ongoing fight; (3) the degree of commitment each parent has to cooperating with the other parent, to setting boundaries in their respective networks, and to promoting the other parent's relationship with the children; (4) the willingness of each parent to deal directly with the other about the children and to share crucial parenting information; (5) the willingness of both parents to curtail the reciprocal destructiveness that often accompanies divorce and litigation. It is by teasing out these five dynamics, a process that requires considerable professional expertise, that the clinician can make an informed prediction as to the viability of different custody options for particular families.

Every clinician and every divorce lawyer is familiar with the situation in which the parent who looks best "psychologically" and with whom the child obviously wants to stay is in fact overtly or covertly blocking the child's relationship with the other parent. Also commonplace is the situation in which it becomes clear over time that a child's insistence on living with a particular parent is based on the belief that he or she must save that parent from falling apart. Such situations call for a new manner of evaluation that moves beyond the issue of who is the better parent to an exploration of the total family situation, and that actively uses the dimension of time. It is important for the court to understand that this kind of evaluation involves more than a static reading, an X ray of the family forces. It tests not only the current conditions but the potential for change.

This kind of evaluation, which can come either before or after a custody decision is made, examines how the custody decision relates to the balance of power between the participants. Priority is given to learning about how shifts in that balance may be used to bring core conflicts to the surface, so that they will not be buried to corrode the relationship later. It looks at how the kind of custody and the living arrangements are likely to play upon the way the conflicting parents distribute responsibility for nurturance and control, improving or worsening the situation to come.

EVALUATING THE POSSIBILITY FOR FAMILY CHANGE

When the court is the ultimate decision-making body, the parents have yielded their parental authority. This places the child in a highly distressing situation. Once the decision is made, the losing parent is likely to sabotage the court's decision or to appeal it, thus leaving the child in limbo for some time. The first order of business in an evaluation, therefore, is to attempt to move the parents away from the court—a move that the court is always eager to see happen—and to help them come to some agreement on custody and living arrangements on their own. Though the likelihood of success might not be great, since parents coming to us via this route are already chronically entrenched in battle, it behooves the evaluator to make this the first step. The parents are invited to use the evaluation to begin to behave differently and are motivated toward this end by the pressures of their childrens' needs and the unending drain on their pocketbooks, as was the Daley family, discussed in chapter 5.

In this manner of evaluating, the main goal is to ascertain the degree of malleability in the system and the consequent likelihood that the participants will be able to collaborate about *anything* in the child's life. Our first diagnosis concerns their potential to collaborate in some measure. If they are unable to cooperate, this kind of approach will bring out that fact immediately and prevent a recommendation for an unfeasible arrangement that later would have to be painfully dismantled. (In fact, many of the most disturbed families that came for help through the courts had once or twice in the past worked out arrangements that turned sour because they were based on an overestimated and untested potential for flexibility and collaboration.)

To assess the possibility for change, we need an orientation that taps the family's potential to reorganize itself in a more optimal manner around the child and that tests elasticity in the system. The parental job of upholding a custodial arrangement entails too many tests of flexibility to be made on static information—that is, information gathered on the status quo, without challenging the family members to change their destructive status quo. The couple will need to coordinate their parenting and negotiate unforeseen events. Judging the couple's capacity to coordinate therefore entails some measure of restrained and professional tampering with the familial system. Such an evaluation takes longer to complete and costs more than the court may have had in mind. It is helpful to spell out as clearly as possible to the court the nature of a systemic evaluation procedure, its emphasis on looking at the whole family, and approximately how many meetings will be necessary.

EXAMINING THE CUSTODY DECISION

The period in which divorcing parents negotiate custody and living arrangements is usually one of severe emotional stress, in which they are involved in the turmoil of the separation and often are unable to anticipate the evolution of their own postdivorce lives. Their capacity to anticipate logistical problems, geographical shifts, the shuffling of the child back and forth, and changing parental schedules is therefore impaired. Yet only to the extent that these details have been anticipated and handled will a long-term arrangement be workable. Even parents who do not show great friction or animosity in making the custody arrangements and who initially appear to be thinking only of the best interests of the child may not be ready emotionally to look closely at what is coming ahead.

Moreover, parents often do not consider that the arrangements may have to be modified in the face of unforeseen developments. Those developments will test the couple's capacity to collaborate on adaptations to changing circumstances. Parents must remain on some kind of workable terms—not too hostile to each other, and willing to compromise when an arrangement has to be changed.

One family decided upon a so-called birdnesting arrangement with joint custody, where the children stay in the house and the parents alternate, shuttling back and forth from apartments nearby. For the youngsters, this arrangement created a difficult situation. At the start of her week, the wife would get angry to see the condition in which her husband had left the house. To avoid their mother's anger, the children would try to clean up the house themselves, before their mother's shift. The children were responsible for maintaining the nest and for finding out how to live with demanding logistics.

Eighteen months later this arrangement broke down and needed to be changed. The husband, who earlier had not been ready to give up his wife and had found the overlap in the birdnesting arrangement essential, had begun to develop new resources. He had lived for a while by himself and no longer needed his wife. The birdnesting arrangement was no longer comfortable. The couple now established a more workable joint custody arrangement in which each parent had a separate home.

EXAMINING FOR PSEUDOCLOSURE

The possibly defensive purposes of the custody decision being considered by the participants should be a target of any good evaluation. Unfortunately, these defensive purposes are sometimes seen most clearly in retrospect. The failure of parents to predict the consequences of a custodial arrangement may stem from the tension and anxiety surrounding the negotiations. To lower the tension, one or both parents may agree to an arrangement that they later reject. Cooperation should be suspect if it follows full blown after a period of warfare that died down with unresolved issues. The cessation of hostilities is in no way predictive of a couple ready to develop sensible custody arrangements. If the hostilities ended without a corresponding feeling of satisfaction in the participants, the arrangement may well be grossly unresolved and likely to break down somewhere down the line. The therapist must therefore study the way in which the hostilities died down—the way the agreement was obtained and at what price to each of the participants.

The guiding principle for the clinician is to be on the lookout for pseudoclosure. When overt hostilities end, leaving what appears to be an adequate balance between the participants, the precariousness of that balance can be revealed by introducing at the imaginal level every conceivable "minor" change that could disturb the balance, compelling the participants to test it.

An example of pseudoclosure can be seen with a man whose wife becomes involved in a lesbian affair. He may prefer to think "it is only an affair," and agree to joint custody in an effort to stay close to his wife. He hopes to avoid a battle in order to keep her happy and ready to return to the marriage later. The custodial decision is at the service of his need to retain his wife, to deny the separation and build upon his fantasy that she is just experimenting. He moves into an apartment, and she and her friend move into the house. They live in this arrangement for a year. It is all very democratic and child-centered. Later on, the affair crystallizes, and it is clear that his wife plans to live with her partner permanently. The husband now belatedly goes into battle for sole custody. He calls on a lawyer to fight the joint custody arrangement that he was a part of constructing. Everyone suffers in the process. The therapist's task is to bring these undeveloped fights forward—to have the fight now instead of allowing it to occur somewhere down the line, after the children become safe and secure in an arrangement they then have to leave.

A guiding analogue for understanding these couples who deceive each other with arrangements that were doomed to be dismantled down the line might be found in the phenomena that produced the tragic Flight 90 airline crash into the Potomac a few years ago. The co-pilot, though capable of perceiving some major reality obstacles (ice on the wings), suppressed his knowledge in order to accommodate to the pilot's confident attitude and risk-taking stance. The pilot's self-deception, that everything could be handled, made more likely the deception of the co-pilot. The control tower thought *they* had it under control and didn't act. Similarly, the therapist can think that the couple has it under control, and the couple crashes.

TESTING THE LIMITS IN A CHRONIC CASE

A more extensive vignette will clarify the kind of work that must be done and the issues that must be considered in a family-based evaluation. The court referred a family in which the parents had been separated for seven years and divorced for five. The son, thirteen at the time of the evaluation, had stayed with his mother and had had only sporadic contact with his father during the intervening years. During the course of those seven years, a battle raged. There were no less than thirty court hearings, including petitions of spouse abuse, requests to change custody and visitation, and demands for payment of child support. The ex-husband felt that his ex-wife had repeatedly curtailed his access to his son. He took the boy's lack of interest in seeing him to be the result of pressure from his former spouse and nothing else. By the time he came to the clinic, his life was dominated by the very vivid fantasy of murdering his ex-wife's lover, who had been living with her and the boy for the last several years. For her part, the ex-wife felt that she had sustained considerable abuse from her former husband, was furious that he sent her child support payments only sporadically, and would have liked him to disappear altogether. The nature of her multilevel messages to her son was obvious. She claimed to want her ex-husband to have contact with her son, offering lamely that "a boy should have a father." But she worried about whether it was detrimental to her son to be "forced" to see his father, when he kept protesting loudly that he did not want to. (The courts had been insisting that the boy visit his father.) She would have liked to get a recommendation from us stating that "forced contact" was against her son's best interests. She would finally be done with her ex-husband, while doing him in.

We had been asked to evaluate visitation for this boy, but no assessment of visitation could take place until we looked at how the relationship between the boy's warring parents was influencing his feelings about seeing his father. The situation that called for change was the unmitigated hostility between the parents and the pressure the mother placed on her son to limit his contacts with his father. How the father handled himself during visits with his son and whether that could be altered, if necessary, also had to be evaluated. The situation was malignant for the boy, who on the one hand shunned his father but on the other hand hoped that his father really did care for him. He said to the evaluator, when asked why he thought his father wanted to see him: "Well, mostly he can find out a lot of things about what my mom and Roger are doing from me, 'cause he can trick me very easily. I think that's the first reason. And then, the second reason, I'm his son. That's the second reason, not the first." The boy wanted his father to stop pumping him on every visit and wanted reassurance that his father's love for him was his primary, and not secondary, concern.

Some chronic cases require more aggressive testing of limits, sometimes through brief therapy during which the family's response to the possibility of change can be examined while the family is supported by the therapy. Here, the relationship between father and son could not be fairly evaluated on the basis of what had existed up to that point. By "fairly" we mean fair and just to the boy; on the basis of past history alone one could predict little potential of his achieving with his father the kind of relationship for which he secretly yearned. Visits had to be sponsored, and the father had to be helped to see that it was not only what his son did but what *he* did during the visits that made his son feel unwanted and unloved. It entailed telling the father very specifically that if he wanted to have a relationship with his son, he had to stop pumping the boy about his ex-wife and her lover. A direct conversation with the father focused on his priorities. His fantasy of murdering his ex-wife's lover had to be firmly rerouted. He was forcefully reminded of what the violent death of a man with whom his ex-wife was close would mean to his son and what it would mean for the boy to suspect (and perhaps find out) that his father had been responsible for it. He was pushed to think about what it meant for his own life to remain so angry with his ex-wife that in effect he remained married to her, unable to move ahead in his own life. If the fantasy of murder remained his first concern, he was warned that our work could not be successful and he would never have a relationship with his son.

The mother had to be shaken as well. The therapist started by not buying her story of her interest in the boy's having a relationship with his father. The therapist told her that her son was clearly getting a different message from her—that she wanted him to have no interest in his father—through her morbid and exclusive interest in anything negative the boy might have to say after visiting with his father and also through her haranguing complaints about not receiving support payments. It would be clear that she had changed all that and was truly encouraging him to see his father when the boy himself stopped opposing the visits. It was unlikely that she wanted to change, but if she did, it would show in her son's behavior.

The therapist's work involved helping the youngster both to understand his own relationship with his father and to specify what needed to be different in the visits for him to want to go. He offered that his father would have to pay child support and would have to stop asking him questions to trick him into giving out information about his mother. Pathetically, he was sure his father could not change.

In evaluating visitation for this adolescent, the clinician clearly could only *begin* the evaluation at the point of the boy's stated desires. The gains and losses for each family member had to be considered, along with the role each family member was playing in sabotaging the relationship between the boy and his father. In order for the boy to start having the kind of relationship he did not dare hope for, change in both parents would be required.

The evaluation entailed reading broad patterns of interaction between the key participants, but it also involved a concern with each member's wishes when working under some request for change. This meant viewing the people in the family not only as part of a compelling broader system but as individuals with a certain margin of freedom within the system, freedom to hinder or to facilitate movement. An individually based evaluation alone or a rigidly systemic evaluation would have each ignored much pertinent and practical information and would likely have forestalled any possibility of change.

Although initially the mother had looked very flexible, committed, and concerned only for her son, while the father felt murderous and seemed out of control, at the close of the extended evaluation the situation appeared very different. The father had in fact altered his behavior during visits with his son and felt less obsessed with his ex-wife's lover. He became more concerned with the reality of visitation with his son. He curbed his efforts at tricking the son into divulging information about his ex-wife. She, however, dropped her collaborative stance once she realized that she would not get support in severing the ties between her son and his father. She withdrew from the evaluation. The raw and unchangeable quality of the rift between the two could no longer be disguised in a typical formula of a crazy father unwilling to pay child support. The son was probably left confused but more optimistic about a future relationship with his father. Most important, he was under far less pressure from his father to betray his mother.

The remainder of this chapter will describe the process of shaping a court evaluation and some of the pretrial tribulations that face the evaluator.

A Sample Evaluation: The Perron Family

ORIGIN OF THE EVALUATION REQUEST

The actual evaluation starts with the request for the assessment, which cues the evaluator in to key issues. It reveals how the participants, including the judge, see the situation at the moment as well as the overall direction in which the situation is headed.

The request for the assessment of the Perron family originated with a call from the child advocate assigned to the case. According to the advocate, the judge had requested a "psychological evaluation on both parents and the child, with an eye toward shared custody if possible." He went on to describe the family. Carl was a ten-year-old boy who was presently living with his mother. His parents had lived together until the divorce was finalized. After that, Carl lived with his mother for twelve weeks and then asked his father, who lived in Texas, to take him there. The father agreed. The mother thought that her child had been snatched, and after several weeks managed to get him back to Delaware, with the help of an order from the judge. According to the advocate, the judge in this case felt that "neither party is a saint."

The boy had clearly stated that he preferred to live with his father. The boy and his mother were living with her parents, and the judge thought that the boy feared his grandfather, who was "domineering." The judge was leaning toward "shared custody," which would mean scheduling maximum visitation, including summers. The boy, according to the advocate, thought that spending summers with his mother and the school year with his father would be fine. The advocate added that the mother thought the father was "crazy," that he had a bad temper and was very emotional. The boy and his father had already had a previous evaluation by a psychiatrist, who recommended that the boy live with his father. The advocate said that he had spoken at length with the child and confirmed that the child preferred to be with his father.

From this initial phone call, we already knew a great deal about the case. For one, this was no ordinary custody battle. The child had already been snatched, and the judge was sufficiently concerned about the child's welfare to have assigned him his own attorney. We also knew that the child advocate was accepting at face value what his client, the child, was saying, and that he wanted the recommendation to be in tune with the boy's stated wish to go with his father. And we knew that the judge was predisposed toward a decision in favor of shared custody.

AN INITIAL FIX ON THE OVERALL SITUATION

The job of the evaluator is not simply to make a conventional personality assessment, although that is what has been ordered and must be part of the evaluation. The main objective is to get to know all of the participants, in order to advise the judge as to which kind of custody arrangement is in the child's best interest. In this case, it was necessary to see both parents and child. We also felt it necessary to see the maternal grandparents, with whom the mother and child were presently living. The judge already felt that they were having a negative influence on the child. A meeting with the father would have to determine if there were any outstanding others with whom he was connected who would be affecting the child, were the child to live with him.

The evaluator begins by seeing the parents and children jointly. This meeting allows for an early assessment of family functioning, for testing the possibility of parental collaboration, for observing how the children position themselves in the room vis-à-vis their parents, and for observing how the parents respond to the children when they are together as a family. It allows us to make the pivotal diagnosis about whether the couple can work together. We then promote or curtail this kind of working together, on the basis of what happens at that session.

In this initial meeting, the evaluator develops hunches about the participants' overall situation and gets an idea of the extent to which they perceive themselves as helpless actors in a drama that is too far gone and seems to carry them. This is a kind of global assessment of the total situation and of the power to steer it conveyed by the participants. The initial meeting with Carl and his parents, which is described in detail in the court report that follows, was characterized by angry accusations and admonitions that left Carl badly frightened and upset. It revealed that the situation was clearly out of control and that this couple could not work together, even to protect their child.

ASSESSING THE COUPLE'S HOSTILITY CONTROL

The initial meeting gave the evaluator some grounds on which to judge whether this couple could moderate their anger at each other enough to collaborate minimally, or whether such an attempt at modulation would in fact disrupt the process of disengagement and reescalate hostilities to a more dangerous level. The outstanding observation was that both adults were unrelentingly angry at one another, that the hostilities were sufficiently high that no working out of differences between them seemed possible at that time. It seemed important that any contact between the parents should be avoided, in order to spare the boy scenes such as he endured in the first meeting and, more important, to avert further violence.

The evaluation continued with a total of nine hours of contact with the family on five separate occasions. There were individual as well as conjoint sessions, and family members were seen in varying combinations. These prolonged sessions provided the participants with opportunities to exercise recovery of self-control and to muster efforts at collaboration. The evaluator remained open to the possibility that the parents might be seen together again. However, there were no signs that the participants were willing to risk being together again with any sense of responsibility for their impact on each other and on their child. We concluded that this couple was not able to contain its disputes in order to salvage their caretaking responsibilities. They were unable to keep these two tracks separate.

THE COURT REPORT

The actual document prepared for the judge in this case follows. In crafting such a report, the evaluator should keep in mind the primary goal: to be of service to the person who must make the decision for the family. When the clinician does an extended evaluation, it is important that the agencies involved understand the need for some testing of the limits in the patterns of interactions. But this "testing the limits" evaluation, which goes beyond what is generally obtained from psychological testing alone, will not in itself suffice. The evaluator cannot abrogate responsibility for having total command of the history of the participants. Thus, a careful history is required. Let us now turn to our report.

Psychological Evaluation of the Perron Family

Carl Perron, father, age 42
Andrea Perron, mother, age 37
Carl Perron, Jr., age 10 (birthdate: September 5, 1974)
Ralph Crosson, maternal grandfather
Arlene Crosson, maternal grandmother
Michelle McGuffin, Mr. Perron's fiancée

REASON FOR REFERRAL

A psychological evaluation of both parents and their child was requested by Family Court to help determine custody for Carl Perron, Jr.

BACKGROUND INFORMATION

Carl is presently living with his mother in the home of her parents and sees his father two afternoons and on Sunday each week. Mr. Perron filed for divorce in September and continued to live with his wife and child until shortly before the divorce was finalized in December. He then moved to Texas with his fiancée. He returned briefly in January and took his son with him to Texas. Mrs. Perron feels that her child was spirited off without her consent or knowledge. Mr. Perron claims that Carl had asked him to take him to Texas and that he had informed Mrs. Perron that he planned to do just that.

Mrs. Perron went to Texas twice to try to get her son. The second time, one-and-a-half months after her son's departure, Mrs. Perron and her father executed in Texas an order from Delaware granting her temporary custody. She brought her son back to Delaware, where a hearing followed on her petition for custody. At that hearing, this evaluation was ordered. Mr. Perron is staying in Delaware until the next hearing.

COURSE OF EVALUATION

The evaluation lasted a total of nine hours, spread over five separate occasions. On February 28, Mr. Perron, Mrs. Perron, and Carl were seen first as a family. The parents were then seen together, and subsequently each participant was seen individually. On March 7, Mr. Perron was seen for a history-taking and evaluation. On March 17, the same was done with Mrs. Perron, and a psychological evaluation was done on Carl. Projective tests administered to Carl include the Rorschach Inkblot Test, the Thematic Apperception Test, the Draw-A-Person Test, the Draw-A-Family Test, and a sentence completion test. Mother and child were seen together briefly on that day. On March 22, Mrs. Perron, her parents, and Carl were present. The grandparents were seen together, then with Mrs. Perron, and finally all were joined by Carl. Mrs. Perron and Carl were briefly seen individually. On March 23, Mr. Perron and his fiancée were interviewed.

THE NUCLEAR FAMILY

Both Mr. Perron and Mrs. Perron seem to feel positively about their son and want to do what is best for him. Despite their best intentions, however, they have each been making Carl's life more distressing than it need be. Any contact between them quickly turns into an upsetting situation for their son. The initial (and for that reason the only) interview in which mother, father, and child were seen together best illustrates what happens. Before the interview began, Mr. Perron reportedly harassed his ex-wife in the lobby by telling Carl in her presence that his mother does not love him because she is taking him to court and by reminding the child to hate his grandfather. Mrs. Perron's way of dealing with him was to ask for help from the receptionist, who told the father to sit in one part of the lobby and the mother to sit in another part.

In the first sixty seconds of our interview, Mr. Perron accused Mrs. Perron of "using" Carl, of not talking to him, of not explaining any of what is happening to him, and of not being truthful to him. He continued to accuse her of never having done anything on her own, and his way of encouraging his son to talk was by saying to him, "You're allowed to speak up. You're not at your grandfather's house now." Carl sat with both parents, motionless and speechless, quite clearly very much afraid. When asked a question by the evaluator, he hesitated to respond and finally began to cry. Mr.

Perron responded initially by holding the child's hands and then by allowing, almost encouraging, the boy to cling to him as they then both cried in each other's arms. Though certainly responding with warmth and affection, perhaps overresponding, and though clearly in tune with his son's distress, Mr. Perron was exacerbating and prolonging the situation for Carl with his own emotionality. He did not help the boy pull himself together. Mrs. Perron's response was different but no better in terms of being helpful to Carl. She sat there motionless, saying nothing, and made no move to extricate her son from exposure to yet another upsetting episode between his parents.

The evaluator took Carl out of the room at that point, and Carl expressed a preference not to be in there with both of his parents. The initial session then continued with the parents together, and they did no better in terms of any ability to collaborate with each other. Mr. Perron stated that what he wants is to not have his son used against him. He feels that his ex-wife is in court for custody and to prevent him from ever seeing his son again. He accused her of telling Carl that he is crazy. As he related the story of his taking Carl to Texas with him, he claimed that he had returned to Delaware only to get his record albums, when his ex-wife gave him an ultimatum that unless he returned to the state of Delaware, he would never see his son again. It was then that he told Carl that he was going back to Texas and asked Carl if he wanted to go with him. The boy said "yes." Mr. Perron described the boy's mother crying on the floor while he and his son left. Mrs. Perron denied having any knowledge that they were going to Texas and insisted that Mr. Perron said that he would bring Carl back on Sunday. She claimed that his appeal to her son was "Nobody loves your daddy. I want you to be with me. Nobody cares about me." The accusations and counteraccusations continued. Mrs. Perron accused her husband of telling Carl, in front of her and other people, to beat her up and to refuse to go to school for her. Not only could this couple not agree on any aspect of planning for their son, but they could not even agree on any one piece of reality.

Regardless of what parts of each of their stories might be an exaggeration, what is clear is that both adults are extremely angry at one another and that the hostility is sufficiently high that no working out of differences between the couple is possible. Mrs. Perron reports threats of violence as well as actual violence from her ex-husband, and Mr. Perron reports provocative statements from his former father-in-law, whom Mrs. Perron has not controlled. Shared parenting, to the extent that the couple would negotiate with each other around the needs of the child, is completely out of the question at this time and would only become an excuse for further provocation and threats. In fact, any overlap between the parents should be strictly controlled at this time and if possible should be completely eliminated with the use of attorneys as go-betweens.

THE EXTENDED FAMILY

An interview with the extended family was conducted in which the maternal grandparents were seen first alone, then with Carl's mother, and finally with Carl. The grandparents were understandably distressed by the transformation in their grandchild and by the entire situation unfolding before them. Mr. Crosson, Carl's grandfather, could not understand why Carl will no longer talk to him and is convinced that this marked change of behavior is a result of directives from Carl's father. He reported a recent incident in which Mr. Perron told Carl in his presence that Mr. Crosson is not his grandfather and that he does not have to listen to him. Mr. Crosson spoke fondly of activities that he and the boy had shared in the past.

When questioned about saying negative things to Carl about Mr. Perron, Mr. Crosson said that he rarely does this but that he has at times been sufficiently provoked that he has not kept quiet. When asked directly about the time he was reported to have said to the boy: "I wish your father *would* kill me, so that he would never see you again," Mr. Crosson said that this statement had come after a threat to his life by Mr. Perron. What he claimed to have meant was "If he does, *that* will take care of him." Mr. Crosson was able to see that it would be important to his grandson that he not make negative statements about the boy's father and he said he had already stopped doing so. The fact that he had stopped in the last week or so was corroborated in an individual interview with Carl, who also affirmed that he would like it if his grandfather would not say bad things to him about his father.

When the evaluator questioned them, in the presence of Mrs. Perron, about their ideas about child rearing, Carl's grandparents shared their feelings that their daughter's biggest fault as a mother was her leniency. They claimed, however, to keep their opinions to themselves about these matters. Judging from Mrs. Perron's surprise at their criticism, it does in fact seem likely that they are allowing her to do the mothering and disciplining of her son, even under their roof. Mrs. Perron was able to disagree with them face-to-face and has clearly been using a counselor from a local mental health clinic to gain help and support for herself in dealing with her son, rather than relying on her parents for this.

MR. PERRON AND HIS FIANCÉE

Mr. Perron was seen on one occasion with his fiancée, in order to assess both the stability of that relationship and the extent to which Ms. McGuffin could act as a support to Mr. Perron by helping him to reorient his behavior toward his ex-spouse and his son. Ms. McGuffin was very interested in being helpful and appeared to have the capacity to do so. The relationship appeared to be a stable one, and both she and Mr. Perron noted that her relationship with Carl was a positive one.

PSYCHOLOGICAL EVALUATION OF CARL PERRON, JR.

Carl was seen on four different occasions. He was interviewed both individually as well as with different constellations of his nuclear and extended families. Psychological testing was also performed. Projective testing confirms interview material indicating that Carl is a child at high risk for becoming chronically depressed and anxious. He is very depressed, afraid, and constricted. On the Rorschach test, his depression was evident in his inability to muster the energy to respond to the task. He lacked flexibility to respond spontaneously and freely. On the Thematic Apperception Test, which requires telling stories about particular pictures, five out of the ten stories that Carl told had themes of sadness or crying, and four had themes of someone being killed or of someone dying. He is very unhappy about the situation in which he finds himself—being in the middle between his mother and his father—and his fears of violence relate directly to his fears of what might happen to his father or his mother if the situation continues. Projective material indicates that unconsciously he fears a murder. Reports from both his mother and his father indicate that he has witnessed physical threats and that adults in his environment have talked about the possibility of someone being killed.

Carl needs, and has clearly stated his need for, both of his parents. He accurately perceives that his parents are in a war with each other, and although trying to figure out which parent is at fault, he does understand that both parents love him. He is trying to be loyal to both parents while remaining protective of his father. He urgently stated a preference for living with his father but could not give many reasons for this preference. He said that he wants to be with his father because his father can help him build things and help him with his art and other things. He stated that he likes Texas. When asked if there were other reasons, he could not provide any, but the evaluator had the impression that there was a great deal that he felt he could not say. His statements probably do reflect the enjoyment that he certainly derives from activities with his father. The concern of this evaluator has to do with checking the extent to which his wishes reflect a self-appointed mission to take care of his father. Upon checking, it is clear that the boy does not feel that his father could manage without him, while he does feel that his mother could manage without him. He agreed that if he were with his dad in Texas, he would not have to worry about him as much because he could see what his father was doing. He felt that his father would be really miserable without him. The question then becomes, to what extent is his wish to be with his father his way of protecting his father and perhaps, in his own mind, even preventing any incidence of violence in his family. I see in Carl a child who is sacrificing childhood. Although his grades have apparently held up, he is overstrained, closed, and fearful lest he do something disloyal to either parent.

In terms of his behavior since his return from Texas, his mother reported in the first session that he returned a different child. Whereas before he went to Texas he would occasionally call her at work to tell her that he loved her, Mrs. Perron felt that when he returned, he hated her. He hit her, and when she first brought him to school, it took her two hours to get him into the school. He would walk about with his head down and wouldn't talk to her, and he was drawing pictures of people crying. He is particularly troublesome after visits with his father, when he is fresh and will not answer his mother. When asked what makes him feel better, his mother reported that being with friends seems to help him and that she has facilitated this contact.

By the second interview with Mrs. Perron, two-and-a-half weeks after the first one, Mrs. Perron reported that the situation with her son had improved considerably. This sense of relief is expected in these crisis situations, as the son, by virtue of the evaluator's involvement, comes to feel that someone will finally take charge and unburden him by helping his parents. But even when this is taken into account, one is impressed by the mother's reported changes in their relationship. There were times when he was able to relax with her, and he was willing to sit with her in the front seat of the car rather than in the rear. Contact with the teacher revealed that he had improved in school during this period.

His behavior after visits with his father, however, has remained problematic. Carl tells his mother that he doesn't have to listen to her, and she was disturbed to report one occasion during the previous week in which Carl "beat her up." She let him hit her, thinking that it would help him get the feelings out, and although he bruised her legs, he did not continue hitting her for more than two minutes. Her own mother wanted to intervene, but Mrs. Perron told her that she would handle the situation on her own. In talking about the incident, Mrs. Perron said that she has been in constant contact with a counselor from a local mental health clinic since Carl's return, because she has been troubled by his behavior and has needed help in learning to deal with him. She initially responded to his demands and his anger by being indulgent and lax. In talking with the counselor, she understood that it was not helpful to Carl to allow him to hit her.

It seems that Mrs. Perron is learning to control her son but that she feels dependent and under scrutiny in relation to the agencies involved—the mental health clinic and the court. She reported two instances that occurred after the "beating," in which Carl ran away from her and she had to "drag him back to the car." What is important in this is that she did not shirk her parental responsibilities and did set limits for Carl, something that he needs to know she is able to do.

It must be emphasized that although Carl is angry with his mother for taking him from his father, he also loves her and does not wish to speak poorly of her. When asked about what he did not like about living with his mother, he could not or would not answer. He told the interviewer that he would like it if his mother spoke more to him, rather than allowing him to go off and be alone. When asked if he would like his mother to know that he felt that way, he said that he would, and he further agreed to tell her this during the interview, with the help of the interviewer. Such behavior is not the behavior of a child who wishes to have nothing to do with a parent.

SUMMARY AND RECOMMENDATIONS

Carl's father is a man who is extremely agitated with the fear that he may lose his son, whom he desperately needs, and Carl's mother is a woman who has demonstrated an inability to control her son and is perhaps only now learning to do this effectively. Both parents are extremely angry at one another and wittingly or unwittingly let the child know things like, "you don't have to listen to her," or "he's crazy." There have been threats and counterthreats, and the potential for violence is there. The child is caught in the middle between his parents and is very depressed and afraid. His needs are for them to stop fighting with each other and to allow him access to both of them. He does not expect that the fighting will stop soon, and he is probably correct. Who the child ultimately stays with is less important to his well-being than is the situation existing between the parents. In terms of the physical circumstances of providing adequate schooling, housing, neighborhood, and so forth, both parents will be able to provide adequately for Carl. However, both parents are presently harming their child psychologically with their unmitigated hostility toward each other and with their insistence on pulling him into their battles. The situation is extremely volatile, and not only the child but the mother and father need to be protected. In light of this situation, the following recommendations are made:

1. The court should demonstrate its interest that all threats and coun-

terthreats between the parents (and the relatives) cease. It should further insist that neither parent continue to mobilize the child against the other parent. That means that the parents must not denigrate each other in front of the child, even in an attempt to defend themselves or their actions, and must not give directives to Carl or even imply that he misbehave with the other parent. When Carl is with his father, his father should not say negative things to him about the boy's mother or grandparents; likewise, when he is with his mother, his mother and her parents should not say negative things to Carl about the boy's father. This is a way for the court to install itself as an external mechanism that puts pressure on the parents.

Let the court be advised that neither parent was very receptive to the importance of the above message. The court therefore should operate as an open agent of social control, assessing periodically if over the coming years the parents can be civil with one another, to reduce the level of hostility to which their child is exposed. Thus, for example, it would be important for the court to request each of them to encourage their son explicitly to behave himself when with the other parent.

2.   I am recommending that Carl live with his father during the school year and with his mother during the summer months and Christmas vacation. I recommend that this arrangement begin *after* his father has had ample time to prepare himself adequately to have his son. This will require at least a year. The boy should therefore spend the summer of 1985 with his father and the school year of 1985–86 with his mother. I realize that recommending such a time lag is unusual, but in this case it is a significant part of the recommendation. An option that has to be resisted is simply to grant custody to the mother with a review in one year's time. It is crucial to the child's adjustment to know that in one year's time, if he so desires and if the father's situation improves, he will be with his father.

The court should convey to Mr. Perron that he should use this time constructively to obtain stable employment, to calm himself down, and to develop his relationship with his fiancée. It must be remembered that Mr. Perron is presently in the midst of a radical career shift, which could explain much of his intense anxiety, although his escalating agitation and anxiety are also triggered by his fear of separating from his son and leaving him in what he considers to be an unfit situation. A year's time to prepare will allow Mr. Perron the chance to secure employment and feel fairly safe and at ease in a new job, which should help to stabilize him emotionally. By that time, too, his defensive stance and bitterness toward his ex-wife and her family should have lessened, evidenced by a cessation of the threats and counterthreats now rampant. A positive aspect of Mr. Perron's interpersonal context is his relationship with his fiancée, who so far seems to help stabilize him, who has a good relationship with Carl, and who presents a responsible image to him.

This recommendation grows out of Carl's repeated requests to live with his father. The recommended delay is aimed at insuring that Carl has a father who is well prepared to make a home for him and at providing additional clarity regarding Carl's stated desire. The confusing and hostile situation existing between his parents and the upset experienced by his father do not allow Carl at this time the freedom to make a decision in his own best interests. Carl has said that although he would not like to remain with his mother, he could live with that decision for now if he had an extended summer with his father and if he felt that his father would be all right. The additional year with his mother would give his father the opportunity to show Carl that he will not fall apart without his son. In the meantime, Carl could maintain the stability of his home environment, where most of his friends are, and would not feel that his wishes to be with his father were being completely ignored. He could look forward to a long summer and to Christmas vacation with his father. With a cessation of hostilities, a continued expressed desire on Carl's part to be with his father could be understood in a more straightforward way.

The court should be most concerned with how the parents react to the court's decision. Their response should not leave Carl with the feeling that *he* has lost. The chronic hostility that characterizes the present situation could lead to an endless number of appeals, which would further upset everyone. The court should make the parents aware that by responding well to the decision they can help shape a new family atmosphere that will *support* their child's well-being.

3. If the court implements the second recommendation, leaving Carl with his mother during the next school year, certain requirements should be built in. Mrs. Perron should have family counseling to help her with the behavior problems that Carl has demonstrated and also to help her communicate more effectively with him. Mrs. Perron has shown an interest in obtaining this kind of help on her own. The counselor or therapist should understand the need for a child to have contact with both parents. In addition, both parents would benefit from some counseling that would help them contain their hostility toward each other and to allow their son appropriate access to the visiting parent.

4. If the court awards immediate custody to Mr. Perron, it would be crucial for him also to be in similar counseling to help him in the ways mentioned earlier in relation to Mrs. Perron.

5. Whichever parent is awarded custody, a reevaluation by the end of the next school year is very strongly urged. The evaluation should look for a change in mood in Carl; one hopes that it will see a boy who is less scared, less constricted, and less closed, as well as less depressed and less concerned about his parents. It is unlikely that this change will take place unless Carl's parents are able to contain their hostility and provide him

access to the visiting parent. Evaluation of the parents should look for this change. Similarly, threats and counterthreats of violence, of disappearing with Carl, and so on, must have stopped. This is a necessary step to prevent the consideration of a most painful possibility, which is removal of the child from both parents. If the parents continue their raging battle with no sparing of the boy, boarding school (where he would be less at the mercy of his parents' fighting) might have to be considered.

6.   Whichever parent is awarded custody, there should be no overlap between the parents (at least initially) in terms of decision making for Carl, which should be done through the lawyers.

7.   Whichever parent is awarded custody, the court should use every safeguard to protect the access of the noncustodial parent to the child. Carl wants and should have unlimited access through such channels as phone calls and letters. The parent with custody must understand that Carl needs to be allowed private phone contact with the other parent. That means that he should be alone in the room when speaking on the phone with the other parent and that there should not be another person on the extension. Phones must not be disconnected to curtail access, and letters must be delivered. The parent who is not living with Carl must understand that the phone calls must not be used to denigrate the other parent or to encourage misbehavior with that parent. Carl's access to both parents and his right to a guilt-free relationship with each parent should be explained to him by the court in the presence of both parents, so that he knows what the court insists he is entitled to.

BEFORE THE HEARING: VYING FOR INFLUENCE

Right before the hearing is the key time for interactions that will influence the nature of the cross-examination from each attorney. Most or all of these interactions may be of questionable propriety, since they do not usually occur in the presence of all interested parties and/or their lawyers. Yet they happen. Attorneys use this time to size up the expert witness and to try out lines of argument as well as patterns of intimidation, all in the name of "checking on findings." It behooves the witness, then, to use that time to serve the purposes of the child.

The attorneys for the mother, the father, and the child all hover around the witness, hoping for last-minute influence before the judge appears. They make thinly veiled attempts to find holes or insufficiencies in the witness's observations in order to shatter the recommendations they don't like, and they attempt to form coalitions with the expert in the hope of swaying the material to their side. To master the social dynamics of this situation, the expert witness must understand each player's objectives.

In the case of the Perrons, a hearing was held following the submission of the report, by which time all parties knew of the recommendations. None of the participants was pleased. The mother was upset that there was no clear recommendation that custody go to her; the father was upset about the same; and the child was upset that it was not recommended that he go immediately to live with his father. One by one, the advocates confronted the evaluator.

Child Advocate. The evaluator was first approached by the child advocate, who announced that his client was not pleased with the recommendation. Dealing with him was relatively easy, since he was on the child's side and more willing than the adults' attorneys to listen to recommendations made in the child's best interests. The evaluator stressed to the advocate that it was her hope as well that the boy would eventually go with the father, but that if she were to expand on the reported extent of the father's psychopathology, the judge would not be likely to grant custody to the father. She reminded the advocate of the material in the report pertaining to the father's threats to the mother and his potential for violence, and she conveyed her concern that unless the father had time for self-restoration, he might defeat his own purposes. She told the advocate of the father's determination to build up a so-called "child abuse" incident between the boy and his grandfather. The boy had not even been struck, yet the father marched him, unannounced, into the evaluator's office days after the evaluation had been completed. The father was not likely to help his own case by overplaying the episode.

The child advocate could easily see that the evaluator had done all that was possible to set up the machinery whereby the father could eventually have his son, and he heard the evaluator's concern that the father, through his own inappropriate behavior, might destroy his chances if he pushed for custody now. The child advocate's position shifted, as he sensed a selecting, almost a withholding, of potentially decisive information.

Is information withheld if it is documented and put into perspective? Would the evaluator have some liability for not having more fully articulated a psychopathologic possibility, even though it had been clearly stated in the report? How fully does one have to articulate a psychopathologic possibility, if the report has already stated that the potential for violence is there and that the situation is a volatile one in which all family members need protection?

Regardless of what may be the ultimate answers to those very real and troubling questions, the evaluator's reactions did get across to the child advocate that the father should not press his point at this time. The advocate's job was now clear. Since he wanted his client to go to the father eventually, he had to talk to the father immediately and help calm him down, reassuring him that it would not be long before he could have his son.

The child advocate finds himself in a very special position, since often he is the only legal representative whom both sides will talk to. That was certainly the case here. And although both parents and child talked to the evaluator during the assessment, the father would not even say hello to her at the hearing, once he had read the report. A pitfall of being in the position of expert witness is that any power as a direct intervener can cease abruptly.

Father's Advocate. The next attorney to approach the evaluator was the father's lawyer. The line of argument he was testing was, "Why the delay?" His point was that the boy wanted to be with his father. The father was understandably agitated, since the boy had been taken from him against the boy's own wishes. Moreover, having his son with him would certainly end all of the hostilities about which the evaluator was so concerned.

Using the father's history, the evaluator was able to explain to the attorney that all hostilities would not be over if the father got the boy. The father had had no contact with his own mother during adolescence, and it was important that Carl not have the same experience. The father's parents had separated when he was thirteen years old, and he had gone to live with his father. He had not seen his mother for many years, and had felt extremely angry toward her during that period. In adulthood, after his father had died, he had mysteriously reunited with his mother. In the last interview with the evaluator, the father had admitted that he could see this very same thing happening with his son, but this posed no problem for him whatsoever.

As the lawyer persisted, the psychologist reminded him that the father was extremely agitated and that if the full extent of his agitation were detailed, she doubted that the judge would allow the father to have custody.

In this exchange of subtle intimidations, the witness did not allude to material that was not clearly implied in the report, though some discretion on matters of emphasis and interpretation is unavoidable. The lawyer uses the report to try to change the overall balance of its content, by minimizing some problems and maximizing others. The psychologist then uses the report to restore the balance, not by bringing in new material about the client but by highlighting what already is in the report.

After being interrogated by the father's attorney, the evaluator recommended that he go outside the courtroom and calm down his client. She reiterated what was in the report: that if the father wanted to have his son, he had to calm down, stop threatening the mother, and stop denigrating the mother and her family in front of the boy. She reminded the attorney of the advantages that the recommendation held for his client: he would soon have his son for the entire summer, and then it would be a matter of just nine months until he had his son with him permanently— if he could accomplish the necessary changes.

Mother's Advocate. The evaluator was also approached by the mother's attorney, who began by telling her just how concerned he was for the boy. Since this did not move her, he went to his next gambit, which was to delve into the father's problems, pointing out how disturbed the father was. The evaluator told—almost warned—the lawyer that if he followed that route, his opponent would be likely to counter by delving more fully into the mother's psychopathology, and that the mother would not look too good, either.

Convinced that the father was worse, he persisted. The psychologist then took details from the report and laid it out for him: it would not be difficult to make an issue of the fact that the mother was unable to control her son, who was entering adolescence, to the extent that she allowed him to beat her up. Further, his opponent could easily make the case that living with a parent who could not control him would be extremely detrimental to the child. The lawyer quickly countered that the boy had never been a behavior problem or difficult to control in any way until this custody battle began. He was told that that mattered little, since the boy was an outstand- ing behavior problem now. Were the mother given custody, he might well become more of a behavior problem, since that decision would go against the child's wishes.

The lawyer persisted in what he felt was in the child's best interests, stressing the child's inability to make the best choice at such a young age. He then movingly and sincerely recounted an important piece of his own history. When he was eleven, his parents divorced and he wanted to live with his father, whom he adored. He thought most boys at that age would prefer that. His father then died, so he did not have the opportunity to live with him. He realized when he was older that his mother was clearly in a better position to raise him appropriately. But had he gotten his way, he would have been with his father, and the choice would have been a wrong one. What became clear was how skillful this attorney was and how emotionally invested he was in getting his client what she wanted. And he had employed means of persuasion that he considered would have the greatest impact on a psychologist.

Some lessons emerge from this unstructured prehearing drama. The actors in this common practice, including the judge, may know very well what is happening. The judge was a full forty minutes late to the hearing. Maybe

THE DIFFICULT DIVORCE

he was just busy, but maybe he was colluding with the rest of the actors to allow these events to take place. In this situation, if the attorneys find the expert witness a pushover, the cross-examination is likely to be a difficult one. In this case, the father's lawyer did not cross-examine the evaluator at all, and the mother's lawyer did so only minimally, without much force. The judge accepted the recommendations. The outstanding lesson is that it would have been useful, from the standpoint of the court's utilization of expert testimony, to have had direction from the court as to what communication, if any, is permissible between the evaluator and the various participants before the testimony of the evaluator is heard—and afterwards, too.

AFTER THE HEARING: RECONCILING THE PARTICIPANTS

Lawyers are often a significant resource for emotional support after the hearing. The child advocate can be particularly helpful, generally having had a successful relationship with the entire family. Such was the case in the Perron family. The child advocate spoke with his client and got a statement from the boy that he was glad it was finally over. When the father talked about appealing, the child advocate told the father that it would be the worst thing for his son and reported the boy's relief that it was over. He again reassured the father that he would have the entire summer with his son, and that if he complied with the judge's orders he would probably have custody after only nine more months.

He then talked to the mother's side of the family. The grandmother was livid at the outcome, expressing her disbelief that a judge could give custody to a man like the boy's father. The child advocate pointed out to the grandmother that this was precisely the kind of talk that she had to stop, that it was not good for her grandson and would not help resolve the situation. He then went to the boy and talked to him about his behavior with his mother. He told the boy that if he did not behave himself when with his mother, everyone would say that his father had put him up to it, so that the best way to be with his father in the end was to calm down during the time with his mother. The boy agreed to do so.

REFLECTIONS ON THE FINAL RECOMMENDATION: THE ART
OF CONSIDERING UNCERTAIN SCENARIOS

The recommendation that the child spend the first year with his mother was not a matter of sending the youngster to live with the "hated" parent. Nor was it a matter of exposing one parent's opinion of the other as a lie when the youngster improved his relationship with the one who had been hated. That recommendation could be useful when the poisoning of the child is clearly coming from one parent only, and when the case made about the hated parent is illusory, mostly a self-serving exaggeration of negative attitudes. In most situations faced by the court evaluator, however, both parents are engaged in poisoning the youngster's thoughts about the other. Carl had implicit loving coalitions with both parents, and both were attempting to brainwash him against the other. The main thrust of the recommendation was to protect each parent's right of access to the child while making the child's living situation contingent on the parents' demonstrated emotional stability, restraint of bitterness and hostility, and efforts to keep the child out of the middle of their battle.

It might be argued that custody should have been recommended for the mother. She was obviously the more stable parent, as well as the parent with a job and a support network (her parents and sister). Moreover, the boy would have had continued stability living with her, since he could continue in the same school and be with the same friends. Had custody gone to the mother, what might have happened in the family?

Very likely, the father would have become considerably more agitated, perhaps convinced that there was a conspiracy against him. He certainly would have continued to agitate his son and to poison the boy against the mother and her family. He also might have deteriorated psychologically to such an extent that Carl would have worried excessively about his father. The boy would then have likely become even more unmanageable with his mother, so that he might be sent to his father.

This was the scenario predicted by the father in the event that the mother was awarded custody, and we have reason to believe that the father would have done all he could to encourage it. At the very worst, the father would have escalated his attacks on the boy's mother, she would in turn have curtailed access, and the father would have been provoked into an act of violence against his ex-wife or his father-in-law. He had already made such threats. In the past, he had pulled both knives and guns on his wife. Thus, the luxury of simply recommending custody to the one who might appear to be the "better parent" is no longer a simple, straightforward choice.

If, on the other hand, custody had been awarded immediately to the father, what might have ensued? It is unlikely that he would have stopped denigrating his ex-wife. His own history revealed that his model for growing up was: hate your mother and have no contact with her. The boy, then, would have had the burden of growing up much like his father, without a relationship with his own mother.

And what about a recommendation for joint custody? This form of custody necessitates sharing and communication on the part of the parents.

They must be able to communicate directly with each other about their child on an ongoing basis, and they must be able to share in major decisions concerning the child, such as schooling and medical care. The advantages of this arrangement need not be explicated here; its dangers with warring couples warrant discussion. In a volatile situation, the least favored alternative is to create proximity between the couple. Joint custody would do just that. It would force them to discuss child care issues and to try to reach a consensus about the very thing on which they have been most unable to agree. At best it creates an impossible situation for the child, who is at all times caught between his parents in a continuing battle. At worst, where one of the participants owns and has used a gun, imposing such an arrangement is courting death.

We made the case that keeping the child with his mother *initially* was in the child's best interests. He would be in the same situation that he had been in for most of his life, not shifted for one year with a chance of having to shift back the following year. The change that might take place—to go to his father in Texas—would be a one-time change, but if it were decided that he would stay with his mother he would lose no continuity in his environment. If at the end of a one-year period the father had not changed, we would agree that there should be a final decision in favor of the mother having custody. Before we took that route, however, we felt we had to be quite certain that the situation between the parents and their emotional status had proved intractable.

A worst-case scenario, that the father would fall apart without his son, was considered unlikely. The father's fiancée had been made part of the therapeutic aspects of the evaluation process. Her cooperation and understanding were elicited, and she was helped to serve as a continuing prop for the father. She would remind him, as would his lawyer, of the short-term nature of the ruling (and indeed it was just one month until the father was to have the boy for the entire summer). If the father was unable to restore himself, despite all the props offered to him, then it would be clear that he should not be the parent to gain custody. Our recommendation assumed that the father's condition might not be final and unchangeable, and that it was in the child's best interest to test that assumption.

Finally, a decision to go immediately with one parent would have settled the matter early, but it would have precluded the possibility of change in the parental relationship, which would not have been in the best interests of the child. One parent would have felt the total loser, the hostility would have continued, and any assumption that the child would be insulated from the battle would prove false. Our clinical work and research have taught us that although hostilities certainly can remain at a very high level, parental anger can also be a time-bound, fluctuating phenomena that tends to diminish after the initial period of separation. Our view does not take as a given that all family dynamics are static. Though we have certainly seen families that do not change and where hostility between the parents remains high for years, we have also seen families that do change. Our recommendation for custody is based simply on the premise that change is possible for some families and that time becomes the measure of this potential.

We do not presume that simply because the court orders a particular behavior, the participants will produce it. In fact, this family may well have deteriorated because of the nature of the forces at work—the vindictiveness, the psychopathology. We hoped that the fiancée would stand by as a support for the father, but we knew that if he lost that relationship, things would get worse. On the other hand, imagine this set of circumstances: The court orders you to do something, and your lawyer, whom you trust and who has been fighting for your best interests, urges you to comply, telling you that the only way for you to get what you have been fighting for is to comply with that order for a set amount of time. A convergence of network forces occurs that creates a chance that you will be able to change. You are also told that at a certain date there will be a reevaluation. You will have to think twice before acting against the order, because any inappropriate behavior will come to light at the time of reevaluation and cause the court to view you negatively. We certainly agree with Goldstein, Freud, and Solnit,[1] that the legal system does not have "magical power" to compel human relationships to develop. Nor can it supervise everyday happenings between parent and child. However, the court in the circumstances described in this chapter might become, in some small measure, part of the process of facilitating positive change by acting as a controlling agent that will not disappear.

1. J. Goldstein, A. Freud, and A. Solnit, *Beyond the Best Interests of the Child* (New York: The Free Press, 1973).

10

Assisting with Blending

Emily (age eight): I don't think I'll ever get used to it (*referring to the mother kissing her boyfriend*).
Mother: Do you know why it bothers you?
Emily: I just wouldn't want another father, like I told you before.
Mother: But even if I got married again, whoever I marry would be my *husband*, but not your father, maybe your friend. Daddy would *always* be your father, *always*, no matter what.
Emily: Wouldn't he be my *part* father? My stepfather?
Mother: Yeah.
Therapist: What's a stepfather?
Susan (age ten): Someone who's not *really* your father. Somebody who marries your mother.

At some point in most divorces, at least one parent becomes involved in a new relationship and considers remarrying. The term "blending" is used to describe the formation of the second, reconstituted, or stepfamily. It is the parent's hope that the children will accept and like the new person, and in some families this occurs with little trouble. In other families, however, the children's linkage to the new person is thwarted from the start. This chapter focuses on problems and dilemmas of blending by presenting brief vignettes as well as an extensive case study detailing how the therapist works to facilitate the links between the "original" and the "blending" family.

Blending involves the rearrangement of the structure of the family, and like any such process it requires time. Failing to recognize that fact, adults sometimes try to create instant blended families. Occasionally the motive behind rushing the transition is to send a message to the former spouse, continuing the fight, or demonstrating forcefully the end of the marriage. In some problems of blending, however, the adults appear to have successfully moved through the stages of their own disengagement from their spouse and reengagement to the new person, but have failed to realize that children also have to adjust to the divorce.

Problems in blending are generally revealed in two specific areas. The first actually does not involve the children directly but instead is seen in the interchange between the adults. The parent uses the issue of blending to encourage or discourage the new partner's commitment, thus strengthening or weakening the foundations of that partnership. For example, a man is having an affair and in the process of separation from his wife casually tells his girlfriend how his daughters are reacting to their knowledge of her. He emphasizes their curiosity and flexibility but is sure to mention briefly, as a kind of reluctant afterthought, that the daughters are angry. His girlfriend, who was initially pleased to be the source of wholesome curiosity, soon begins to imagine the girls' resistance and how she would fare as a stepmother. She concludes she would probably fail if she attempted to blend her life more fully with his. Soon her enthusiasm for a future with this man begins to fade. The man, of course, feels that she has spontaneously and independently closed the door on him; he thinks he has had nothing to do with organizing the new scenario. It was his girlfriend's decision to begin the end of the experiment at blending.

The second problem area in blending involves the transposition of caretaking rituals from the absent parent to the new partner. The routine activities that bind parents and children—a bedtime story from Dad told in a certain chair, or making a special recipe with Mom—represent for the child the stability of the parent-child relationship. Such rituals come to express the special prerogatives and claims of the child on the parent; to move them from the absent parent to the new partner risks insecurity. Such moves change interpersonal boundaries and are experienced by the child as unmanageable, uncontrollable invasions.

Reactions to changes in the ritualized activity need not even entail the child's direct interaction with the adults. Changes in the adult-adult interactions are often the source:

Mother to eight-year-old daughter: You
said something to me when I was giving
Harvey a backrub in the living room. Do
you remember what that was, that you
said?
Eight-year-old: I remember, but it would
be weird to say except in front of any of
my relatives.
Mother: Is it okay if I tell Dr. I?
Eight-year-old: I suppose.
Therapist: Wait a minute, can I be
considered a relative for tonight?
Eight-year-old: Yeah, I said, "Don't get
personal on the couch."
Therapist: Why did that bother you?
Can you tell your mother?
Eight-year-old (*to her mother*):   Because
you *used* to do that to *Daddy*.

For this child, the physical and emotional space that once belonged to
the absent parent had been violated. During the marriage, the mother had
given the father backrubs on that same living room couch. While the child
was able to tolerate behavior of a more intimate nature between her mother
and her mother's new partner, the backrub became intolerable for her to
watch because of its particular history and locale. The concreteness of her
thinking had to be respected. "Don't get personal on the couch" meant
just that.

A Do-Not-Blend Approach

In their anxiety over whether the children and new partner will work as a
family, parents often push the new partner into the absent parent's role,
thereby rushing a process that, by definition, takes time. The job of the
therapist in that case is to emphasize the importance of respecting the
absent parent's role. In the case just mentioned, the therapist advised the
mother to stop the backrubs because at this time her daughter could not
tolerate them. A more appropriate public display of her relationship in
front of her children soon followed.

The child who cannot tolerate watching the backrub or the kissing between mother and boyfriend has a valid complaint that must be taken into account. The complaint, which the therapist treats as a significant communication, is precisely what can help the mother regulate and accommodate her behavior. Healthy blending depends on reciprocal, though not necessarily unerring, accommodations by the parent and the child.

To facilitate a relationship between the child and the new partner, it is of paramount importance that the custodial parent protect the space of the absent parent. That space might be represented in many ways: a particular game that the absent parent and the child played together, the reading of a particular bedtime story, going to church as a family, or even the backrub that the child used to witness. If the new partner is respectful of that space and does not enter until invited by the child—who in turn must have the mother's sanction—the possibilities of linkage occur without requiring forceful accommodations or confrontations.

A mother with two daughters, five-year-old Amy and nine-year-old Harriet, remarried. The children saw their biological father weekly, but the mother gave her daughters a directive that her new husband was also to be their new father and that they were to call him "Dad." The new man, who was loving toward the children, was happy to be elevated to this role, all the more because he had stopped visiting his own two daughters, who lived with his first wife on the opposite coast. A year and a half into the marriage, this family came to treatment after the younger child had become hyperactive in kindergarten and the mother had discovered the diary of the older child, in which she wrote about her unhappiness.

The mother's directive had had a differential impact on her two daughters. Harriet complained to the therapist that she could not stand to call her stepfather "Dad." She said that he could never be her father, that she already had a father, but that she was afraid that if she called him anything else she would get in trouble with her mother. On the other hand, Amy, who was just two and a half when the marriage ended, felt as though her stepfather were her real father and was comfortable calling him "Dad." When they visited their biological father, however, if Amy accidentally referred to her stepfather as "Dad," her father would become furious and would order them never to call the stepfather that.

The mother's directive was experienced by the older girl as an invasion of her father's turf. The younger child also experienced an invasion of turf, but reversed: she felt that her father was trying to take away her new dad. She had grown to love this new man, who acted like a father. Thus she became confused and guilty each time her biological father became angry at her for referring to her stepfather as "Dad," the only name that was natural for her. By attempting to hasten the process of blending, the mother had invaded what for Harriet was the father's space. By not allowing Amy to call the stepfather "Dad," the biological father was not respecting and protecting the genuine blending that had developed between the five-year-old and the mother's new husband.

Each parent had operated with good intentions but under an abstract conception of how children in a family ought to feel, and they tried to impose their rules on their children. The mother was driven by her wish to skip the ambiguity of working her way into a new situation. Propelled by acknowledged anger at her previous husband, who had left her, she was rushing the forming of a new family, to show him that in leaving her and the children he could no longer "have it all." Each time the father heard his little girl call this stranger "Dad," he was injured. The word reminded him of just what he was missing out on by having left. His whole behavior became oriented toward blocking what he considered to be an unwarranted and premature blending, one in which he was not only unacknowledged but replaced.

In this family, the urgency of the directive to call the stepfather "Dad" had to be clinically removed, for it was preventing the emergence of any true closeness between the stepfather and the older girl. Simultaneously, it was important to emphasize that the new husband was not just any other person to the children. He was accepted by the therapist as an important person and one whom the girls regarded as important. The mother was asked to tell the children that they could call him anything they wished, and that she no longer required that they call him "Dad." An entire session was devoted to the children's playfully deciding on a special name for him, one that would connote the unique place that he had in their lives. The children took to this task enthusiastically in collaboration with their stepfather. What up until then had been a heavy issue in this way obtained lightness and closure.

The biological father could not be left out, since he was clearly part of the system that was making the blending difficult for the children. The therapist agreed with him that the children should not be required to call anyone but him "Dad" and that in fact his older daughter would probably never be comfortable calling anyone else that. After he felt reassured, however, he was reminded that his younger daughter was only two and a half years old when he left the marriage, and that it was appropriate for her to feel close to her stepfather. He accepted a suggestion that he take credit for his younger daughter's ability to form intimate relationships, despite the divorce. Soon he came to see her calling the stepfather "Dad" as a good sign of adjustment and a good prognosis for her future development.

Therapists can be alerted to the early stages of forced blending and can intervene so that the difficult situation of the family just described can be avoided. Forced blending usually implies an assumption on the part of the parent that his or her children will fully accept the new partner as quickly as the parent had. That assumption, in turn, can be based on and complicated by issues of incomplete emotional separation from the former spouse. Yet that feature is not always the most conspicuous when dealing with difficult blending.

The easiest feature to perceive with forced blending remains the youngster's feeling that he or she is not being given sufficient time to accommodate to the new adult. A ten-year-old girl complained to the therapist about the mother's boyfriend: "She's always telling us how much she loves him, and that makes us feel that we have to love him too. But we don't see as much of him as she does." This mother was indeed pushing her boyfriend onto her children by imposing her own excitement about him in the early phases of the relationship. Behind her insistence that they love him were ill-concealed problems in severing the relationship with the children's biological father. Pushing the children to love her new boyfriend represented her wish to "put a final nail in that coffin."

A very common problem of blending occurs when one of the participants becomes the dominant organizing force in the blending, by trying to recreate patterns of the old marriage. A forty-five-year-old father of two early adolescent children was living with a thirty-year-old woman who had no children of her own. Five or six times a year, the children would visit him for a week or two at a time. The father, a surgeon, had an inflexible schedule, but the woman was able to return home at 3:00 P.M. daily. During his children's visits, the father continued his normal routine and on occasion even flew out of town to give talks. The young woman was given the role of caretaker, cook, and entertainer. Then the eleven-year-old boy, who was having problems with his mother, came to live permanently with his father. The father, however, was even less able to free up his schedule at this time. Instead, his new partner gave up her social contacts to be home by 3:00 P.M. because she was worried about the boy's hanging out in the neighborhood. A woman of strict standards of cleanliness, she also became the boy's disciplinarian. The father and the boy were able to maintain a conflict-free relationship, while tension grew in the relationship between the new partner and the boy. She felt overburdened, and the boy missed time with his father and resented the young woman's telling him what to do, since she was not his mother.

Therapy with the family involved first helping the father to see the way his abdication of responsibility was affecting both his son and his new partner. This man had established a pattern of denial that protected him from seeing the extent to which his partner was burdened with the new task of mothering his son and the extent to which his son was upset about seeing so very little of him. Breaking through his denial was not simply an intrapersonal task to be accomplished on his own. It was accomplished interpersonally, when both his son and his partner were encouraged to begin actively complaining to him in the therapy session. The father offered some resistance but moved on to reset his priorities. He had hoped to form an instant family, so that he could have his son, his work, and his woman, and he thought that he had been managing successfully in all three areas. He was now forced to reexamine his commitments and to face, with his partner, the ways in which he was recreating his first marriage by giving the full job of child care, with its inherent headaches and problems, to his partner. Pretending that everything was the same and that people were replaceable had been a way of not acknowledging that the divorce had created a trauma for himself and for his son. He could not continue to act as though it were a simple matter, like changing clothing or putting on a different mask.

Stress can come not only from forced blending but from understandable attempts to obstruct it or slow it down. One mother, unable to accept her ex-husband's new relationship, burdened her son with her intrusive curiosity about the new woman. The youngster accepted the father's new relationship and wished to blend, and on one level his relationship with his mother permitted it. Yet he was stressed by his mother's jealousy and wished that the mother, if not able to show some acceptance, would at least not impose her difficulties on him. In order to protect his mother and, self-protectively, not betray his father, he would prefer that she not dwell at all on the new woman:

Sixteen-year-old (*referring to his mother*):
I wish she would just act like it was just
Dad we were visiting. Like she wouldn't
even mention anything about *her* and
wouldn't ask us about her.
Therapist: Do you think your mom could
do that?
Sixteen-year-old: No, it's like a
birthmark, it just won't go away.

The relationship between the new partner and the ex-spouse is often the most difficult one in which to intervene. A marriage partner who has been left behind is especially likely to find a natural target of anger and jealousy in the ex-spouse's new partner. When the new partner is seen as having contributed to the dissolution of the marriage, the adversarial relationship is on its way. If that conflict develops and becomes chronic, it can have lasting effects on the children and on the relationships between the children and their parents. Loyalty battles become exacerbated. Some children feel the need to protect the parent who does not have a new relationship. Others wish to be close to the new partner, but the hostility of the other parent makes them feel guilty.

Friendships between the spouse left behind and the new spouse remain rare, despite the chic belief that this is a very civilized and prevailing model. Generally, blending occurs through the maintenance of fairly clear boundaries and "no trespassing" rules between the ex-spouses and their respective families. For many couples, blending difficulties are revealed in the way one of the participants unwittingly allows the child to feel in charge or to take precedence over the new partner. One such reversed hierarchy of a difficult blending will be illustrated in the case that follows. The therapist found in the ex-wife a workable ally, rather than an obstacle, to the fiancée. The resolution of the case involved the development of sensible, indirect collaboration between the child's mother and the father's fiancée.

Facilitating Relinkage: A Case Study

Nine-year-old Rachel was brought to therapy by her separated parents because she was phobic. She had difficulty being without her mother, would wait up fearfully at night whenever her mother left the house, needed to sleep with whichever parent she was with, and generally created much agitated interaction between her separated parents. The separation had taken place when she was seven-and-a-half years old, and since that time she had been living with her mother in her grandmother's home and visiting her father every other weekend. During the last year her father had become involved with a woman named Lynn Cox, whom he planned to marry shortly. They did not live together, but in the last six months Miss Cox had stayed at his home, with the exception of those nights when the child was visiting her father.

In the session to be described, which occurred after the child's phobic symptoms had abated considerably, the father had for the first time appeared with his fiancée. He had given neither his daughter nor the therapist any warning that she would be coming along, though he had on previous occasions brought up his desire to have her accompany him to the sessions. This expressed desire on his part had allowed the therapist to respect boundaries and protocol, by checking with the mother. When the two showed up together, the therapist was able to clarify for the child that the mother knew that Miss Cox would be coming to one of the sessions and that it was fine with her.

The therapist then began this new phase of therapy by asking the father for a statement of the problem. He brought up three points: (1) his daughter had not accepted the divorce or his plans to marry Miss Cox; (2) he felt torn between what he wanted in his new life with his future wife and what he wanted with his daughter; and (3) Miss Cox had problems adjusting to having an instant family.

The therapist immediately went in search of Miss Cox's opinion. Miss Cox thought that the child had not adjusted because her parents had failed to explain to her adequately that their separation was to be a permanent one. She added:

Miss Cox: I think that there's a lot of strong loyalty to her mother that she's afraid that she's going to have to give up because of me. Or that I might ask her or her father might ask her to have loyalties to me that she can't bring herself to have because she has them for her mother, which is the most natural thing.

Miss Cox is talking about Rachel's fear of being asked to cross boundaries by instantly having a very special relationship to her father's wife-to-be. She is also presenting how the conduct of her fiancé and his ex-wife are setting her up to be the one who Rachel will blame.

Therapist: Do you think Rachel could ever feel about you the way she feels about her mother?
Miss Cox: No.
Therapist: Do you think she should?
Miss Cox: No.

The therapist indirectly reassures Rachel that her father's new partner does not have special expectations of her. Miss Cox conveys to Rachel, who is listening intently, "I don't want to take over your mother's job."

The father, through his clever passivity, has supported Miss Cox's taking over with the child. This helps foster Rachel's fears and expectations. In the next segment, the therapist works on turf reorganization:

Miss Cox: I think she is not sure of what her role should be. I think that's the problem. So as a result I guess it's difficult to put another adult who's going to marry her father into perspective, like "where does that person fit into my life?"

Miss Cox's uncertainty about where she fits into the child's life is also an expression of uncertainty about where she stands with the child's father. Talking about such issues lets her discover that as a unit they are not yet a family.

Therapist (*to Miss Cox*): Where do *you* fit?
Miss Cox (*interrupting*): I don't know.
Therapist: In Rachel's life.
Miss Cox: I don't know.

More significant, the talking also begins to dispel the pretense that they are already blended, which has proved troublesome for all involved and has fostered the child's insecurity.

The therapist next turned to the child, affirming that if the grown-ups did not know where Miss Cox fit, a child could not possibly know either. Finally, the therapist focused on the father, taking the pressure off Miss Cox, and worked through him to reorganize the family structure. A seemingly benign situation, recounted by the father once Rachel is out of the room, reveals the father's equivocal siding with his fiancée and his ultimate alliance with his daughter.

Mr. Cain: I can see the value in that, like drying her hair. I can see it. Okay, her hair should be dried instead of sitting around on a chilly night with wet hair. But like even this weekend, we had a discussion about it, and I said, "Hey, get off the kid's back. I really don't like the way you treat her."

The father, in a coalition with his daughter, placed the child higher than his fiancée in the hierarchy of the family-to-be. As a result, the child was disobedient to the fiancée, sensing that her father would support her instead of his fiancée. Additionally, until this point, Miss Cox had done all of the worrying and all of the father's work. In a way, she was accepting her fiancé's invitation to recreate his previous marriage in which the wife had done all the work. This classic problem of blending, in which one of the participants swiftly organizes with a new partner essentially the same pattern that he lived before, helps explain the high incidence of second divorces. It also clarifies the main item on the agenda for working with blending families: to prevent, if possible, the start of a new divorce.

In families that are becoming blended, the new couple's problems are often deflected through the outside parent (the former spouse) and through the child. The adults use the powerful presence of the child to suppress questions about how much loyalty and commitment to invest in the new relationship. By declaring the child as the trouble—and the outside parent as the accessory who created that trouble—they protect themselves from looking at any conflict within the new relationship and avoid the frightening prospect of another divorce. In the session presented here, that process shows as Miss Cox, feeling supported by the therapist, begins to talk about how she and the child's father have different expectations of Rachel. She is reluctant to accuse her fiancé but she has a ready target in his former spouse. Yet, to her credit, she does not fully succumb to the temptation to blend with him mainly through declaring his ex-wife a common enemy.

Miss Cox: I think my major problem is I don't know what things are expected of her from her mother and I know what my expectations are, but her father lets a lot of things slide so he doesn't have the same kind of expectations that I do.

Therapist: I think the major problem is not that you don't know what to expect from her mother but that you and her father don't agree on what is expected. . . . How are the two of you going to be able to get together on this (*turning to Miss Cox*)? Because the way it's set up now, you get to be the bad guy.

Holding the couple at hand to examine their relationship must be a focus of the therapy with blending families. The therapist is indirectly asking Miss Cox if her fiancé will support her. The true unknowns for Miss Cox are what her fiancé expects of his daughter and whether he will give her, his future wife, license to intervene in these areas with the child. To resolve these issues the therapist must be ready to explore the penalities on the new partner and how she is set up by him.

Miss Cox: Exactly. An example of me being the bad guy: my car has bucket seats, and Rachel always wants to sit in the front seat, and the way bucket seats go it's not comfortable for her to sit in the middle section between the two seats because the seat belts are there. So she always has to sit in the front seat and what happens is she winds up sitting on my side and I'm squashed; she's comfortable and I'm squashed! She says "Can I sit in the front seat?" and he says "Yeah, okay, sit in the front seat." I don't think that's something she should have a choice . . . it's a matter of three people; that car is not built for having three people sit in the front.

The father would rather make his fiancée uncomfortable than refuse his daughter, thus fashioning a kind of unhierarchic family with three people at the helm. If this process continues, this woman will never be able to find a place with her fiancé and his child. She is contributing to the problem, however, by never giving her fiancé an ultimatum: she will not ride in the car unless the child sits in the back. She is not convinced that she has a right to make that kind of assertion, nor is she certain about how he would react. Still, an element of protest does show in her unconscious metaphor for the emerging blended family—a car that fits two in the front, and where three are squashed.

Therapist (*to Miss Cox*): So what do you think, then?

The therapeutic job is to feed her protest, fostering constructive conflict between them *now* rather than letting it fester until it ruins their possible new family.

Miss Cox: I don't think that's something

she should have a choice, well do you
want to sit in the front or the back, it's a
matter of safety for one thing. . . . I don't
know if I'm being unreasonable to feel that
way.
Therapist: Does he think you are?
Miss Cox: I think so.

The therapist worked on strengthening her efforts to assert her rights, but Miss Cox hesitated because she knew that in the previous marriage the child had come first. If she became demanding, she might lose him.

MAKING ALLIES OF POTENTIAL ADVERSARIES: A YENTA APPROACH

In discussing the issue of seating in the car, Miss Cox questioned whether Rachel's mother let the child sit wherever she wanted. Sensing in this question her consideration for and potential identification with the mother, the therapist decided to capitalize on that process. The therapist assured her that Rachel's mother would not allow the child to do whatever she wanted, and Miss Cox showed clear nonverbal signs of surprise and pleasure. To foster the possibility of forming an alliance between these two women, the therapist went into detail, portraying them as facing similar problems and maybe even sharing the same values.

The therapist worked here by being intrusive, deliberately taking a position between the two women. Each time Miss Cox tried to retreat from the problem by bringing up her lack of knowledge of what happened to the child at home with the mother, the therapist went to the mother and brought back information about that mysterious relationship, conveying it in a way that emphasized what the mother and Miss Cox had in common. The therapist was meeting with the mother as well as with Miss Cox and the father every other week, and therefore she knew what was happening in each camp. Operating openly as a "yenta," a busybody, by shuttling back and forth, she was licensed to soften boundaries in order to foster blending. By operating on the premise that things were not that different at home with Rachel and by getting that message across to Miss Cox, the therapist removed the primary excuse offered by the new couple for not working together to alleviate the tension with the child. That liberated the therapist to center on the new couple.

This yenta approach will not succeed with most families, but under certain conditions it works well. There may be hostility between the two women—the potential rivals—but it must be essentially under control. The separated couple must basically no longer want an intimate relationship with each other, though threads may remain.

In working with Rachel's mother, the therapist used four main appeals. First, she let the mother see that it would be in Rachel's best interests if the father's fiancée were involved with the child. The therapist introduced the idea by questioning Rachel's mother about her former spouse. Was he the kind of man who knew how to take care of a little girl? Would he notice if she were sitting around with a wet head in a cold room? Did he know how to braid her hair so that it looked just right? Would he know to send her to bed at the right time? The mother knew that her former husband was not that kind of person, and she began to see the advantage in having the new woman do some of the nurturing.

The second appeal was to the mother's pride in her competence as a mother: it was a bad reflection on her when Rachel disobeyed Miss Cox. The father's fiancée would begin to think that the mother was a pushover who allowed this kind of behavior at home. The insinuation is, "Your daughter's behavior is creating an offensive image of what you are like at home."

The therapist then pointed out that Rachel's nonacceptance of the separation was creating problems for the mother's own development. The mother had told the therapist, "Rachel sees me as his wife, divorced or not, and she knows that there's a divorce and that it's final and everything is over with, but in the back of her mind she still sees me as married to him." The therapist magnified for the mother how Rachel's view represented not a reconciliation fantasy but a denial of the divorce that would create a real obstruction when the mother wanted to start dating. The appeal was to the mother's enlightened self-interest.

Therapist: You're going to get it from her! If you start dating, with her having these ideas! And why should you get the blame for being the one to break up the marriage?

Mrs. Cain: I don't get blamed.

Therapist: You will if you start dating.

Mrs. Cain: Do you think so?

Therapist: Yes.

Mrs. Cain: Terrific!

Therapist: Why should you get the flak? You see, what Rachel sees is that you're Number One for her father, because that Number One place is being saved for you. Rachel is kind of house-sitting in that place, like when she sleeps with her dad,

This provocative interpretation does not center on changing the daughter. Rather, it centers on the threat that the child's behavior will create it's like your ghost is there. . . . I mean why should she believe that it's over when she knows about intimacies that adults share in long-term relationships and she sees that her dad is somehow saving the Number One spot next to him, not for this woman he is going to marry. She sees that her dad keeps his new lady out in the car when he comes to pick Rachel up. This is a real setup for you. If you start dating, you'll be the one she'll see as breaking the marriage up. Rachel sees reality, so she knows that when her dad picks her up, he has Number One lady in the house so he can't bring Number Two in, he has to keep her out in the car. Quite a stunt they're pulling on you, and it's not doing you a favor actually.

for the mother's own development. This way of motivating helps mothers in this situation to see that it is to their advantage to accept responsibility for the child's nonacceptance of the divorce and then to work on changing that immediately.

Finally, the mother was shown how she contributed to Rachel's reluctance to accept the finality of the separation. The therapist brought up the fact that in two years the mother had not dated, and suggested that Rachel must have the idea that the mother still cared about her ex-husband and did not want him to have another woman. Was her daughter's unwillingness to relinquish the marriage actually the mother's unwillingness to end that part of her life and move on?

At the end of this session, the child was invited into the room.

Therapist: Maybe Rachel has the idea that you don't really want her to listen to Lynn.

Mrs. Cain (*emphatically*): Well, she has the wrong idea! (*To her daughter:*) When you are over at Daddy's house and Lynn tells you something to do, then she's the one you have to listen to.

As the mother sternly tells her daughter that she wants her to obey the father's fiancée, she and the fiancée move toward being allies. The mother begins to let go of the marriage and prepares to move ahead with her own life.

Next the therapist worked with the father and his fiancée, who reported that Rachel had acted differently during her last visit and that things had gone smoothly for the first time in a long while. But they knew they were there to deal with their own relationship.

Therapist: The two of you have a problem, I mean you really do.

Miss Cox: I know.

Therapist: It's much more with each other than with Rachel. Rachel is just a reflection of it.

Miss Cox: I know.

Therapist: It's something that you're going to have to come to terms with and you're going to have to come to terms with it whether you're just living together, married, or whatever. The two of you need to find ways to have Rachel realize that the Number One lady is sitting right there (*pointing to Miss Cox*). (*To Miss Cox:*) Right now she knows that you're the lady that her dad keeps out in the car.

The ability to agree on the demands to be made on Rachel is key to whether or not the child will comply.

The therapist is careful to formulate the need for agreement on what to do with Rachel as apart from their decision to marry. The "whatever" indirectly addresses the participants' prerogative to flee if they so desire. The therapist then moves to maintain support for the fiancée's new position, which marks the completion of the blending.

Miss Cox admitted that she didn't feel very good about that arrangement, and the father was forced to confront his behavior, which was being called into question by both the therapist and his fiancée. To underline the crucial role that the father can play in facilitating the relationship among the three of them, the therapist reminds him how his fiancée becomes the bad guy when she tells Rachel what to do.

Therapist (*to the father*): You have to do something so that Lynn doesn't feel that she's walking on eggs, that every word that she says to Rachel has to be weighed. You're the only one who can change that.

Mr. Cain: By the same token, at some points I felt that every word I had to say to

The father is also clearly feeling the tension built

Rachel or to Lynn, to either of them in   between his daughter and
front of the other, where I worried, oh, if I   Miss Cox.
say this to Rachel, then Lynn will get
upset, or to Lynn, then Rachel will get
upset. Why does that have to be?

It is the father's fiancée who underlines the change that has to take place:
a change in the hierarchy.

Miss Cox: I'm coming to a realization
that if I'm his wife, I'm first. Now that's
hard. And I'm first now. I can understand
how it would really really hurt her.
Because I think that Rachel knew that she
was really first, above her mom when they
were married. So all of a sudden, not is it
only the relationship of mother and father
breaking up, but somebody's usurping her
place.

The fiancée accepted the support and encouragement of the therapist to
take her proper place in the front seat of the car with her future husband.
She was not, however, entirely certain that she wouldn't find herself in
the same position as the first wife, taking second place to the child. She
reported a "secret" intimacy between the father and daughter that pointed
to a pathologic coalition between them: they had been showering together,
a practice that stopped only when Miss Cox objected. Hearing her doubt,
the therapist brought up the father's tendency to let things slide and ended
the session by conjuring up the worst possible outcome: a spoiled brat and
another divorce.

In these sessions, the overlapping family unit made significant gains.
The mother relinquished her hold on her old marriage and made her feelings
clear to her daughter. The forced blending was curtailed with an exploration
of the dynamics of the new family, with special time set aside for father
and child. The fiancée's fears of the reversed hierarchy, in which she was
less important than the child, were heard, and changes were made to correct
it. Finally, steps were taken to create an alliance out of the adversarial
relationship that had been developing between the two women. The child's
phobia and complaints ended. The work that remained was work for the
new couple, to ensure that in his second marriage the father would not
recreate his failed first marriage, but that instead he would allow his fiancée
to take her place beside him, with the child in the back seat.

11

Tracking Divorce Effects: From Therapy to Research

THIS BOOK has been about the difficult divorce—the divorce in which participants find themselves at an impasse, unable to move ahead with their lives. The families we have seen were stuck in different ways and at different points in the divorcing process. The Allens, the Franks, and the Garceaus were deadlocked in the preseparation stage and needed help in order to be able to effect a responsible separation. The Trezanos and the Daleys were warring couples who remained entrenched in combat positions long after the separation. The Franks and the Perrons were especially ensconced in incendiary extended-family networks. And the Jarrets had been unable to maintain their parenting functions after the separation. What these and the other families in this book have in common is their inability to traverse the divorce experience without assistance.

Not all families get stuck, however. Many couples are able to reorganize their relationships after the separation and manage successful ways for both parents to remain involved with the children. Many couples, though not friendly after a separation, develop ways to contain their hostility so that the children are not burdened in the process. While learning to parent their children independently, many couples are able to maintain the necessary links with the ex-spouse where the children are concerned. Not all parents abdicate their responsibilities.

Our clinical experience has provided us with some guidelines toward identifying the factors that are important to the success or failure of a divorce. As a form of research, clinical work provides a richness of detail that is impossible to achieve in survey studies. Surveys, however, allow us to gather information more systematically and are therefore appropriate for substantiating and generalizing our clinical findings. The Families of Divorce Project has been funded to study a population of separated families as well as to develop a divorce therapy service and train professionals working with this population.

The objective of the research component of the Families of Divorce Project is to examine the concomitants of adjustment and maladjustment among members of separated families over a five-year period. On the basis of our clinical findings, we started out with the perspective that divorce can take a number of different paths, some of which will be beneficial and some not beneficial in complex differential ways to children and their parents. We have approached this research with several questions. What factors inhibit or enhance the process of an effective divorce? How do families generally fare at different points in the divorcing process? Can critical time periods be identified when children or adults are most vulnerable? Are children, for example, more affected by their parents' displays of conflict soon after the separation, or by patterns of chronic conflict, as in the case of the Daleys? Can broad trends in adjustment be identified?

The remainder of this chapter will describe our research methodology and report on several of our findings. We will focus on general trends in adjustment during the first three years of the separation, on the post-separation relationship between the parents, on visitation arrangements, and on the role of grandparents. We will also report our findings from a projective test that we used to track changes in the child's perception of the divorcing family over time.

Method

POPULATION OF THE STUDY

The sample consists of 103 families interviewed initially in or around the first year of separation. Ninety-two of the couples had been separated for one year or less, with the remaining eleven ranging from fourteen to twenty months. The median separation period was seven months. For ninety-one of the families, it had been the first marriage for both the husband and wife. The length of the marriages ranged from two to twenty-nine years, with a median of ten years. Three-quarters of the couples had been married twelve or fewer years. Following separation, the mother had custody of the children in ninety-eight of the families, the father in two, and three families had joint custody arrangements. By the third year of separation, divorce was finalized for over half of the couples.

Families were recruited through advertisements in the newspapers and in the community and through our divorce service. Families requesting divorce therapy who also met our research criteria were included in the study. Because we were interested in investigating how "normal" children traverse the divorce experience, we did not accept into our sample children who either had been referred for therapy prior to the separation or had been left back in school. These criteria were employed as a way of screening out children who might have had adjustment problems prior to the separation.

A strength of our sample, we feel, is that it was equally divided between those who requested counseling after the separation and those who did not. This factor allows us to generalize our findings to populations that are not strictly clinical ones. All families in the study first participated in the research interview. Afterward, those families who had requested counseling were seen in our divorce service.

An analysis of the child adjustment scores reveals that those children whose parents had requested therapy were more maladjusted initially than those whose parents had not.[1] By the third year, however, there was no longer a significant difference in pathology between those who had received and those who had not received our therapy. This might be taken to show that our treatment was effective, but it must be noted that our study was not designed to test the efficacy of treatment and that any conclusions along those lines must be considered tentative.

Since the unit of analysis was the family, we chose one child per family as the target child, selecting the child who the custodial parent felt was most affected by the separation. The target children ranged in age from two through seventeen at the time of the initial interview. Half of the sample were between the ages of five and ten, with a median age of eight. The sample was evenly split between boys and girls. Data were also col-

1. M. B. Isaacs, G. H. Leon, and A. M. Donohue, "Who Are the 'Normal' Children of Divorce? On the Need to Specify Populations," *Journal of Divorce* (Forthcoming).

lected for "nontarget" children, enabling us to examine the total family for some of our analyses.

The families represented a broad spectrum of social classes, clustering in the middle and working classes. Of the mothers, seventy-seven were white and twenty-six were black. These figures were the same for the fathers, but in two of the couples one partner was black and the other white. The mothers' educational levels covered a wide range: less than high school (4 percent), high school graduate (31 percent), some college (26 percent), college graduate (20 percent), and professional training (18 percent). Thirty-five percent of the mothers were Catholic, 26 percent Protestant, 22 percent Jewish, and the remaining 17 percent "other" or "none."

Among the fathers who were interviewed, 5 percent had less than a high school education, 24 percent were high school graduates, 18 percent had some college, 23 percent had graduated from college, and 30 percent had graduate or professional training. Forty-one percent of the fathers were Catholic, 15 percent were Protestant, 25 percent were Jewish, and the remaining 19 percent "other" or "none." The apparent differences between the mothers' and fathers' distributions of religion and education is due in part to the fact that not as many fathers as mothers were interviewed.

At present, data is being analyzed for the fifth year of separation. The findings reported here are from the first and third years of separation and do not include the siblings of the target children, with the exception of our discussion of the projective material, which was collected in the first and second year of the separation and includes both target children and siblings between the ages of five and eleven.

Because we value a family approach, whenever one parent agreed to participate in the research we tried to get the other parent to participate as well. However, we did not restrict our sample to families in which both parents agreed to participate because such a sample would represent a skewed divorce population. Some divorcing adults could be expected to refuse to participate in research or in fact in anything suggested by the ex-spouse. We conducted individual interviews with each family member and were able to obtain interviews from the fathers in over half of the families.

INSTRUMENTS

The interview schedules consisted of structured and semistructured questions concerning various aspects of the divorce experience. Some projective material, such as the Draw-A-Family Test, was included in the children's interview. The interviews lasted an average of two and a half hours for the adults and under one hour for the children. The emotional adjustment of the parents and children was ascertained through the use of standardized tests. The Hopkins Symptom Checklist[2] gave us a measure of adjustment in the adults. The Child Behavior Checklist[3] gave us two broad measures of adjustment—behavior problems and social competence. Behavior problems included both negatively valued acts against persons or objects and inner discomfort experienced by the child. Social competence tapped adaptive functioning in terms of participation in a variety of typical childhood activities, such as chores, sports, and hobbies, as well as social relationships and academic performance. A separate measure of school performance was derived as part of the social competence score and appears as such in our findings.

General Trends in Adjustment

Our clinical work suggested that the early postseparation period is crucial in setting the stage for later outcome. It appeared that if individual maladjustment and dysfunctional postseparation arrangements are rigidly established early on, this pathology and their arrangements would be likely to endure and jeopardize later family and individual success. We were interested in testing this assumption in a more systematic and quantitative manner. Our goal, therefore, was to investigate the longitudinal aspects of postseparation adjustment, specifically whether problems in adjustment for the youngster and the custodial parent persist over time.

We found that both mothers and children improved from the first to the third year of separation.[4] Eighty-one percent of the mothers showed improvement by the third year, as did close to 70 percent of the children. But while the majority of children showed improvement by the third year and in fact resembled a normal population, those children who were initially more disturbed remained relatively more disturbed than those children who were better off early on. This was also true for the mothers, but to a far lesser degree. Thus, child outcome levels are far more persistent over time than are the mothers', suggesting that the mothers may be recovering more fully than the children over this initial three-year separation period.

2. L. Derogatis et al., "The Hopkins Symptom Checklist (HSCL): A Self-Report Symptom Inventory," *Behavior Science* 19(1974):1–15.

3. T. Achenbach and D. Edelbrock, *Manual for the Child Behavior Checklist and Revised Child Behavior Profile* (United States: Queen City Printers, 1983).

4. M. B. Isaacs and G. H. Leon, "Mother and Child Adjustment After Parental Separation: A Three-Year Study" (Manuscript, 1986).

Moreover, the levels of adjustment of mother and child were closely related to each other at both the first and the third year of separation, suggesting that maladjusted children are more likely to be with maladjusted mothers. These levels of adjustment were more highly correlated, however, in the first year.

We did not find differences in adjustment based on the sex of the child, but we did find differences based on age when we looked at improvement over time. The older children improved more with respect to behavior problems than did the younger children; the younger children improved more with respect to social competence. Social competence measures the involvement of youngsters with activities and with peers. Our finding suggests that the younger children are able to reconnect more quickly in this realm and can continue their social development unhampered. Although older children more quickly cease demonstrating overt behavior problems, the divorce experience may have a more subtle effect that influences their relationships with other people. Perhaps these subtle effects are the beginnings of what Wallerstein[5] describes in her ten-year follow-up on children of divorce. She raises the possibility that children who are older at the time of the divorce become considerably more burdened, apprehensive, and pessimistic about the future than do children who are very young when their parents separated.

In summary, in our work we see that despite overall improvements from the first to the third year, the mother's and the child's adjustments are strongly intertwined, and that child maladjustment that is manifest early on persists over time. This latter finding underlines the importance of a clinical intervention as early as possible after the separation, in order to prevent a pattern of pathology from emerging.

The Relationship Between Separated Spouses

The relationship between separated spouses has been important to consider and evaluate in our therapy with divorcing families. A key component of their relationship is the communicational features—specifically, what they talk about and argue about and how that affects the child. We found that talking about the children early in the separation was important and that the more often parents did, the more socially competent the children tended to be in that first year. It may well be that not talking during that period

5. J. Wallerstein, "Children of Divorce: Preliminary Report of a Ten-Year Follow-Up of Young Children," *American Journal of Orthopsychiatry* 54(July 1984):444–58.

is characteristic of families that are undergoing severe atomization and fragmentation, illustrated in chapter 8 by the case of the Jarrets. This finding has powerful implications for family therapy practice. Too often family therapy tends to curtail discussion about the children, tending to perceive it as an escape from the couple discussing its own problems. But this finding implies that discussing the children is a most natural process which the therapist should not curtail or block while examining it for detouring maneuvers or its possible metaphoric messages about the couple. Discussing the children is essential business for recovery from the divorce and for assembly of a good adjustment in the postdivorce stage.

We also found that *what* parents fought about made a difference. Children whose parents disputed about visitation were more likely to have behavior problems than children whose parents did not dispute in this area. Other kinds of arguments did not produce a similar effect. Visitation—the amount of time the child spends with the noncustodial parent and where he or she spends it—affects the child deeply. When parents fight about visitation, the child is not merely a metaphor for or the indirect expression of general conflicts between participants elsewhere in the system. The child *is* what is being fought about. Therefore, being able to resolve or at least to deflect this area of dispute can have clear preventive import for the child's mental health.

Are couples who are talking about one thing more likely to be talking about other things? Are couples who are fighting in one area more likely to be fighting in other areas? In order to answer these questions, we identified broader patterns of disputing and discussing—patterns that were found to influence adjustment over and above the effects of the specific content areas noted earlier.[6] The analysis provided here is of the data reported by the mothers. The findings were substantiated by the fathers' data.

Disputing in the first year encompasses a variety of themes, including finances, property, child support, visitation, and custody. Visits tend to be occasions for arguments. The relationship is a hostile one, and the parents do not talk as friends or do things together with the children. The mothers tend to be highly anxious. Couples who fit this picture in the first year of their separation tend, not surprisingly, to have children with behavior problems two years down the line.

Discussing, on the other hand, is associated with a friendly or at least a neutral relationship. They are likely to talk as friends. The father may visit the child in the house and even have meals with his wife and the children

---

6. M. B. Isaacs and G. H. Leon, "Child Outcome and the Relationship between Separated Spouses: A Three-Year Study" (Manuscript, 1986).

on occasion. We find two kinds of discussing—practical and personal—
and the former seems to bode especially well for all family members. The
couple tends not to get overly personal; they talk more about practical
matters and the children than about their own personal problems or their
relationship as spouses. A kind of affective control is implied. When this
kind of parental communication characterized the first year, a clear relationship with adjustment was found in both the first and the third year of
separation. Not only did the mothers themselves tend to be well adjusted,
but their children were socially competent in the first year of the separation
and had few behavior problems by the third year.

Thus, a clear pattern emerges. Disputing behavior hinders the child's
adjustment, a less personal kind of discussing facilitates it, and the impact
of an overly personal kind of discussing falls between the two.

Further, we found these styles of communication to be embedded in a
history of behavioral shifts in the last year of the marriage. Discussion was
not associated with a tense atmosphere during the marriage or elevated
tension near the end, but disputation after the separation was preceded by
increasing arguments and a tense atmosphere in the home during the marriage. Thus, there is evidence that these patterns of disputation and discussion arise not from the divorce process per se but rather from antecedents
in the marriage. The apparently chronic pattern of postseparation disputation is a continuation of argumentation and hostility rooted in the marriage
and not merely the result of the separation process itself. Different kinds
of marriages result in different kinds of divorces.

By the third year, couples tended in general to discuss and dispute less,
showing that they had disengaged from each other. While patterns of disputation and discussion can still be identified, the patterns looked somewhat
different in the third year. By the third year, the nature of the disputes has
become differentiated, with on the one hand generalized disputation, in
which everything but custody is disputed, and on the other hand child-
centered disputation, involving custody and visitation disputes.

Discussion also persisted, but by the third year there is only one kind of
discussing, which includes all of the subject areas—personal, practical, and
issues relating to the children. This pattern contrasts with that of the first
year, when practical discussion appeared distinct from more personal discussion. These changes suggest that, with time, some of the more personal
topics are no longer so dangerous, and the separated couple no longer
needs the discipline of segregating the tracks of acceptable conversation.
Talking occasionally about more personal things three years down the road
is different from doing so from the beginning of the separation. Earlier, it
was part of the job of setting boundaries in the relationship. But once these

boundaries are established, it is possible to exhibit a wider range of behaviors without negatively affecting adjustment.

Unlike the findings in the first year of separation, there was no correlation between the third-year patterns of discussion and disputation and the adjustment of the child or the mother. These results suggest two key aspects of separation. First, the nature of the postseparation relationship with respect to discussion and disputation changes over time. Second, it appears that the relationship in the first year of separation is critical in influencing the adjustment of children, while the relationship in the third year has less influence.

Finally, the broad patterns of arguing and talking that we have identified call into question assumptions concerning the inevitability of disputation in the divorce process. While some couples seem to be continually embroiled in conflict, as were the Perrons, others are able to resolve disagreements without an ever-escalating process of conflict. Not all divorces, therefore, display the same pattern of conflict or manage conflict in the same fashion.

The Visitation Arrangement

The establishment of a pattern of visitation constitutes for the child tangible evidence that the family will endure, despite the many changes brought about by the divorce. Setting up visitation often reflects an underlying collaborative arrangement between parents who want to uphold, not abdicate, their responsibility for shared caretaking. Regular, predictable visitation implies stability in the child's relationship with the noncustodial parent. We hypothesized that such stability would be more predictive of the child's well-being than frequency of visits alone. Our data substantiated this view.[7]

Our population consisted of families that had a regular visitation arrangement and those that did not. Initially the child was not affected one way or another. That is, there were no differences in pathology in the first year between children with and without such an arrangement. However, differences did emerge in the third year. Children who then had a regular schedule for seeing the father were more socially competent than children who did not have a set schedule for visitation. This finding held true regardless of the frequency of the visits. What seems to have actually been

7. M. B. Isaacs, "The Visitation Schedule and Child Adjustment: A Three-Year Study" (Manuscript, 1986).

evaluated, then, in this third year, was a sustained regularity, a continuity, since those with a schedule in the third year were likely to have had one early on. In fact, in terms of social competence, children with a regular visitation schedule in the first year and thereafter fared the best, followed by those who did not have one initially but acquired one. Next came those who had a schedule in the first year but had lost it by the third. The least well adjusted were those who never had a schedule.

What differentiated those children who had had a regular schedule but lost it? Were they the children whose fathers had been visiting only infrequently and who with time just gave up any schedule? Investigation revealed the opposite. Those fathers who dropped the schedule had been particularly frequent visitors at first, then had visited less often and in some cases never visited again. The ones who acquired a schedule were fathers who had kept up a fairly high level of contact with their children and simply confirmed it with the schedule.

In trying to understand what may have caused the shifts, we turned to the affective states characterizing the relationship between the parents. We found that those couples who discontinued the schedule were those who had a hostile relationship in the first year, whereas those who described their relationship as being more neutral were more likely to have acquired a schedule by the third year. The affective states of couples during the first year after the separation seem to suggest an especially critical period for clinical intervention, since the couple can either impair or uphold the visitation schedule, which in turn is fundamental to children's emotional stability during this period of greatest flux and reorganization.

Further evidence corroborating the importance of a visitation schedule emerges when we look at the effect of the parents' arguing about the visits. In our sample as a whole, including families with and those without a schedule for visitation, the more the parents argued about visitation in the first year of the separation, the more the child was likely to have behavior problems that persisted into the third year. When we look separately at those children whose fathers had an arrangement and kept to it, however, we do not see a higher incidence of behavior problems even when the arguments are frequent. Furthermore, the best predictor of social competence in the third year is whether the father kept to a visitation schedule in the third year. This finding holds true when we take into account the extent of the arguments about the visits and the level of the mother's adjustment.

The unavoidable conclusion is that the scheduling of visits compensates children whose parents argue more and whose mothers are less well adjusted. One might speculate that in families that argue about visits and have no set schedule, each argument is taxed with the fears that the visits themselves might stop, threatening the very foundations of interpersonal order. This finding also raises questions about the overriding significance many clinicians give to fighting among divorcing couples and its deleterious effects on the children. Those effects, it turns out, are modifiable by other significant influences creating stability. This finding may be reassuring to parents and to clinicians in cases where the couple is unable to stop fighting but is able to maintain parental responsibility for structuring the children's lives.

Exploring Network Patterns

The clinical importance of different kinds of social networks alerted us to the importance of studying their effects. Here we will look at adult daughters—that is, the relationship between the mothers in our study and their own parents. In order to explore for patterns of family network support, we asked about the types of support that the divorcing mother received from her parents and about her feelings about the relationship. We asked specifically if the parents offered to help, offered to let her live with them, gave her financial help, gave her advice, babysat for her, gave emotional support, or helped in other ways. Additionally, we looked at certain structural aspects of the daughter's relationship with her parents, including residential proximity, frequency of interaction both before and after the separation, and the degree to which the parents were critical or accepting of the separation.

We examined these characteristics with an eye toward discerning distinctive parental "network support" types. It was our expectation that the daughter's feelings about interaction with her parents and their degree of helpfulness would vary with network type. Based on the responses from these separate items, we found in the first year of separation four network patterns, which we called *local, helpful, directing,* and *detached.*[8]

The local network was characterized by the adult daughter living close to her parents, seeing them often in the first year after the separation as well as having seen them often in the last year of the marriage. The high

8. M. B. Isaacs and G. H. Leon, "Social Networks, Divorce and Adjustment: A Tale of Three Generations," *Journal of Divorce* 9(Fall 1986).

frequency of interaction both before and after the separation reveals the close-knit nature of the family network. The grandparents offered a lot of help, but were most helpful with babysitting. The divorcing mothers, however, felt that their contact with their parents was too frequent, and they viewed their parents as being neither helpful nor unhelpful in an overall sense. It is possible that these women may have felt overwhelmed by the grandparents' active role in the daily management of the postseparation family. Albeit with all good intentions, the local grandparents may have infringed upon the mother's independence.

The helpful network was characterized by a strong degree of acceptance of the separation by the grandparents. These grandparents also tended to provide a high degree of financial and emotional support, and were viewed as being very helpful in an overall sense. The divorcing mothers felt that the amount of contact they had was "just right." While these mothers were in more frequent contact with their parents after the separation than before, the key to this type of relationship may be in the grandparents' providing help that does not threaten the instrumental role of the mother and her sense of being in control of the family. Unlike the local grandparents, the helpful grandparents do not become directly involved in the daily management of the family. The financial and emotional support, together with a strong sense of approval of the separation, may aid the divorcing mother in fulfilling her parental responsibilities while providing her with the breathing room she needs.

The directing network consisted of those grandparents who were likely to let their daughters live with them, and from whom the daughters sought, and were given, advice. These grandparents did not provide help in any of the other ways examined and were viewed as being neither helpful nor unhelpful in an overall sense. Because of the apparent dependency upon advice from the grandparents, this network type was labeled "directing." This relationship appeared to center on an emotional enmeshment that was not necessarily associated with frequent contact.

In the detached network, the grandparents offered little help aside from babysitting and had a below-average frequency of interaction both in the last year of the marriage and after the separation. This network pattern was best characterized by a lack of helpfulness on the part of the grandparents.

Having identified these four elementary network patterns, we looked for relationships between them and the adjustment or pathology of the mother and ultimately of her children. In investigating this area, we found an interesting three-generational effect. The four network patterns affected mother and child differently and varied in their helpfulness according to the dimension of adjustment under examination.

Our findings point to the helpful network as the most beneficial to the mother's overall adjustment and to the child's adjustment with regard to behavior problems. The effect on the child tends to be both direct and mediated through the mother's adjustment. These are the grandparents who show a strong acceptance of their adult daughter's separation and a high degree of emotional, financial, and overall helpfulness. This behavior also tends to inhibit regressive possibilities and to enhance the daughter's autonomy.

The child's social adjustment is most benefited by the local network, which is characterized by close residential proximity, frequent babysitting, and an overall high frequency of interaction. The frequency of interaction between the child and the grandparents is beneficial to the development of the child's social skills. The daughters of the local grandparents may feel that they see too much of them, but this type of network has neither a good nor a bad effect on the daughters' adjustment. The directing and detached grandparents were neutral in their effect on both the mother's and the child's adjustment.

Thus the pattern of the parental support network of a divorced mother may influence her child's adjustment through direct influences and also indirectly through her own adjustment. The mother's network can even be a catalyst for change in the child without changing the mother.

The only network pattern that persisted through the third year was the local one. This is not surprising, since this type is closely related to neighborhood structure, a sociological fact that is not necessarily linked to divorce. The other three seem to be more specific responses to divorce; they are interpersonal structures that are fashioned to deal with a transient situation. The transience of most network patterns supports our view that issues of network reorganization usually reflect short-term reactions to the stress of the separation. They display ways that the family mobilizes to deal with the divorcing daughter, which become unnecessary after certain adjustments are completed. In the third year, the type of network does not predict pathology or health for mother or child.

There was one network pattern from the first year, however, whose effects, although not immediate, were manifested in the third. Those children in the detached network group in the first year were less socially competent two years later than were children who had been in the other network configurations.

Our findings show that there are differences in the ways in which grandparents are involved in the separation. Clinicians should therefore consider these differences when deciding which members of the larger network should be included in clinical intervention. In some cases it may be indicated to involve the grandparents and perhaps other members of the extended family, whereas in other cases it may be unnecessary or even counter productive.

Tracking the Changing Family: Utilizing Projective Techniques

The findings we have reported thus far were drawn from our research on 103 families interviewed in the first and third years of separation. We have discussed general trends in adjustment as well as the couple's relationship, visitation arrangements, and the grandparent network. Our data comprised standardized measures of adjustment as well as material derived from an in-depth interview schedule.

While standardized measures reveal overall patterns of adjustment, we also were interested in how the divorce experience alters the child's understanding of the family structure—that is, what happens to the child's conception of the family itself, of who is in the family? We felt that the best way to get at such material was through the utilization of projective techniques, particularly with younger children who might not be equipped to communicate their ideas and feelings adequately to an interviewer. Furthermore, our interest in the divorcing process led us to investigate in this respect changes that might be occurring over just a one-year period from the year of the separation. For this part of our study we collected and analyzed data from a subset of our population—children from the ages of five to eleven in the first year of their parents' separation.[9]

The means we chose for measuring change was the Draw-A-Family Test. Children's drawings of the family are particularly informative for tracking the process of divorce. Drawings make explicit the structural and systemic issues in children's adaptation to divorce, giving us an idea of how the youngsters position the parents in the hierarchy and how they see themselves positioned in relation to the separation. They tell us who the child perceives to be part of the family. By having the child draw the unit at different points in time, we can document how the child's perception of the family changes with the fluctuating relationships brought on by separation and divorce.

When asked to draw the family, the children whose parents have separated are confronted with the anxiety-provoking question, "Who is in my

9. M. B. Isaacs and I. R. Levin, "Who's in My Family? A Longitudinal Study of Drawings of Children of Divorce," *Journal of Divorce* 7(Summer 1984):1–21.

family?" If the father has moved out, can he be included in the drawing? Does moving out of the house mean moving out of the family? We wondered whether the child's perception of the family would reflect the change immediately, or whether it would remain steady in the early separation period and change only after a year or two. We also wondered in which ways actual changes might be reflected in the child's family drawings. When parents have first separated, it is unlikely that the child has consolidated the view of who is in fact still in the family. Well into the second year, however, this consolidation is more likely to have taken place. As even more time elapses from the separation, additional changes may come about in the separated family that would not be occurring in an intact family. A parent may have a new partner living in the home. Remarriage might have taken place, which might usher in not only a stepparent but stepbrothers and stepsisters as well. We were interested in seeing at what point children integrate these newcomers into their perceptions of the family.

The dimensions reported here are family composition—specifically, missing parents and added figures—and power and hierarchy in the family, which we look at through the positioning and comparative size of each parent. We also examined changes in the quality of the drawings over time, particularly changes in creativity and constriction over time as possible differentiators of types of adjustment.

THE FATHER'S DIMINISHED SIZE AND OTHER SIGNS
OF HIS PERIPHERALITY

Our interest in the relative size of the parents was related to what we believe to be the child's conception of who is powerful in the family—that is, the child's sense of family hierarchy. What is striking in our research is the shift that takes place over time. In the first year of parental separation, the children tended to draw their fathers either larger than or equal in size to their mothers. One year later, however, the children in the sample tended to draw their fathers smaller than or equal in size to their mothers, if indeed they included their fathers at all. These results suggest a movement in the child's mind to a perception of the family as a single-parent one, in which the mother is perceived as powerful and in charge and the father's power and influence are considerably diminished.

Children conceived of a number of ways of expressing the father's peripheral status. Some drew him on a different plane from the rest of the family, often positioning him below the rest of the family (see figures 3b and 6b) or in a corner, or they drew only partial figures. One ten-year-old

FIGURE 1

This drawing reveals the creative coping of a child who has figured out a way to include her father as well as keep within the bounds of reality as she knew it.

girl, whose father was hospitalized for depression at the time, commented: "I drew only half of my father. That's how he is." Another child, whose father had moved two hours away yet maintained a relationship with her, solved the problem of his being both in and out of the family by making two drawings and putting herself and her sister in parentheses next to her father (see figure 1). Her sister solved the problem by drawing herself, her sibling, and her mother, and then drawing a jagged line, on the other side of which her father stood alone (see figure 2).

OMITTED FATHERS

An even stronger statement than drawing a very small father is to draw no father at all, and this tendency increases with time. No children omitted their fathers from drawings until they had been separated for at least eight months. This suggests that it probably takes several months for children to begin revising their concept of the family.

Interestingly, in the second year there was a significant correlation between the father's inclusion in the drawings and lack of arguments around visitation. When the fathers were omitted, the mothers tended to report that visits were a source of some arguments, whereas when the child included the father, there were usually no reported arguments around visi-

FIGURE 2

Her sister used a jagged line to separate her father from the rest of the family.

tation. This finding suggests that by the second year of separation, the mother's good will toward the father is a factor in allowing the child to continue to conceive of the family as including this member who is no longer in residence. We see as well the child's own capacity for coalition-making. The child can aggressively banish the offending parent, particularly when he is viewed as the mother's enemy. If visitation, which is the main source of contact between spouses in the second-year postseparation, is free from arguments, the mothers will feel better about their spouses than when disagreement prevails. This is not necessarily true in the first year of separation, when there is greater transition and flux and when disagreements around visitation are expected, since the family is working out that arrangement for the first time. The children then may not yet see themselves firmly in one camp or the other. By the second year, the custodial parent has had plenty of time to recruit the child to his or her side.

Would children who omitted their fathers tend to replace them with someone else? We found that children were more likely to add a figure when they omitted their father. In the first year of separation, in 50 percent of the drawings that omitted the father, another figure—usually a maternal grandmother or aunt—was added. When the father was included in the drawing, only 11 percent of the children added someone. This same trend continued in the second year of separation, perhaps representing an effort on the part of the child to compensate for the missing father by filling his space.

It was striking that the mother was in no instance, in either time period, omitted from the family drawing. It could be that with a separation and divorce, the stability of the family unit is so fundamentally threatened that the child cannot conceive of omitting the custodial parent.

LONGITUDINAL SHIFTS IN CONSTRICTION AND CREATIVITY

Drawings from both time periods were compared for each child, in order to determine if there was a measurable change from one time period to the other. We were not interested in any absolute measure of creativity or constriction, but rather in the shift. Thus, a child who had a constricted drawing in the first time period and produced an equally constricted drawing in the second time period did not get a rating of constricted according to our criteria.

Twenty-four percent of the children showed a drop in creativity and a rise in constriction from the first to the second time period. Figures 3 through 6 illustrate these shifts. It is worth noting that the majority of the children who showed a drop in creativity came from families who did not request or receive our divorce therapy, while the children who received the intervention tended not to show this drop. Furthermore, five children in the sample showed a shift over time in the direction of a rise in creativity. Four of the five had received divorce therapy. It is notable that those children who omitted the father while simultaneously adding someone else did not have drawings that became more constricted with time. This corroborates the idea that other family members indeed step in and compensate for the child's loss by filling the empty space left by the father. Further research is needed to study this natural process of system repair and the pace at which it operates, since it seems to have unusual preventive import. In 63 percent of the sample, we saw no measurable shift in either direction. This is despite the fact that the children were all one year older in the second time period, which would lead us to expect an improvement in their drawings in terms of articulation and detail as a result of development alone.

These findings suggest that a well-timed intervention, even for a nonclinical population, may be beneficial to the child, at least into the second year of parental separation. It also suggests that while the parental separation may not necessarily result in gross maladjustment, it nonetheless takes a toll on the child's vitality and expressive capacity, dimensions not conventionally thought of as centrally involved in the child's adjustment and not necessarily picked up by standardized measures. While our standardized measures reflected improvements in gross pathology that substantiate our notion of divorce as a time-bound stressor, they are not sensitive enough to detect other, more subtle reactions. Future research can best serve by choosing measures that are more sensitive to a greater range of clinically relevant individual markers.

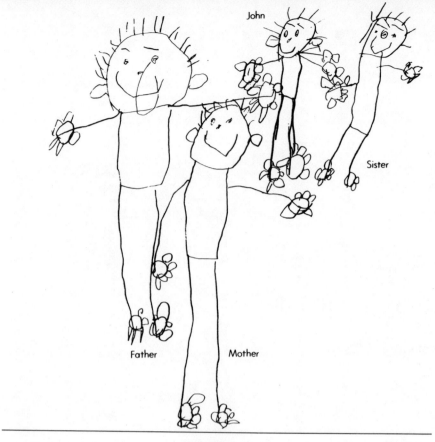

FIGURE 3a

First year: John, age five, eleven months after separation. Note the detail of the fingers and toes.

FIGURE 3b

Second year: One year later, the figures are stereotyped and identical, with no differentiation and no life. Notice that the father, though included, is drawn on a plane beneath the rest of the family. Marcia, added to the drawing, is the mother's live-in lesbian lover. The fingers and the toes are left out, as is the hair, leaving none of the protective layers or tools to handle life.

FIGURE 4a

First year: Tina, age ten, eleven months after separation. She draws her family in great detail. The father is smoking a pipe, and even the smoke reveals activity and vitality. The figures are well differentiated and fairly animated. Even the mother, who is posing, looks actively posing compared with the skeletal figures drawn one year later.

FIGURE 4b

Second year: The figures are uniform, stereotyped, and lacking in animation beyond the happy, pasted-on smiles. All of the richness is gone.

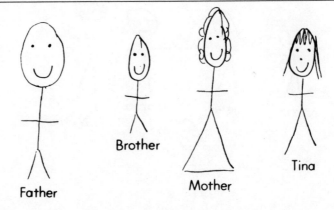

FIGURE 5a

First year: Hector, age eight, six months after separation. Though the figures look angry and distressed, a sense of current affect leaps out at the viewer. The drawing is replete with detail, down to shoelaces, flies on the pants, and teeth. The figures are posed with activity, and the arms are about to jump out at the viewer.

FIGURE 5b

Second year: One year later, the figures have diminished in size and appear calm and sanitized. This seems to be the price of peace—there is virtually no activity and very little detail. The five fingers on each hand drawn in the first year have diminished to two or three per hand, except for the father's, and the joints at the elbows are no longer apparent.

FIGURE 6a

First year: Kim, age eight, one month after separation. Notice the sense of mobility of the body parts, particularly the arms. The figures are clothed, and there is some sex-role differentiation in that the added figure, Aunt Bonny, is wearing a dress.

FIGURE 6b

Second year: There is a loss of all articulation, and mobility of the body parts has ceased, with the arms now all in the same position. There is no detail, and the figures look flattened, as if run over by a steam roller. Notice also the loss of the father's position in the hierarchy.

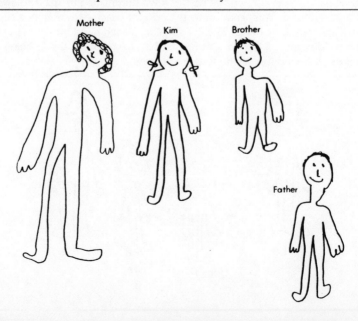

A Look to the Future

The critical issues that have emerged in working with divorcing families have emphasized the deadlocks of couples and their nonending warring, the abdication of parental responsibility, and the impact of the larger network of relatives, friends, and lawyers. For didactic purposes, we have presented these phenomena as relatively compartmentalized and discrete. For example, within the research we have talked about entities of helpful and nonhelpful grandparent networks, and similarly about the couple's relationship after the separation. However, the reality is that divorce involves the rearrangement of a large social system that interacts in complex ways.

This multilevel interactional system is often not immediately apparent either in therapy, where parsimony and economy is often a standard, or research, where methodology demands a degree of reductionism. But both our research and our clinical experience with families reveal a rich, multileveled, noncompartmentalized system capable of extraordinary adaptations. To keep looking for those adaptations systematically will remain our goal when we turn to examine families five years after the separation.

Bibliography of the Families
of Divorce Project

Abelsohn, D. "Dealing with the Abdication Dynamic in the Post Divorce Family: A Context for Adolescent Crisis." *Family Process* 22 (September 1983):359–83.
Eno, M. M. "Four Families of Divorce: Case Studies of Sibling and Peer Relationships." Ph.D. diss., University of Pennsylvania, 1983.
———. "Sibling Relationships in Families of Divorce." *Journal of Psychotherapy and the Family* 1 (Fall 1985):139–56.
Isaacs, M. B. "Needs vs. Rights." *The Shingle* 42 (Winter 1979):19.
———. "Treatment for Families of Divorce: A Systems Model of Prevention." In *Children of Separation and Divorce: Management and Treatment*, ed. I. Stuart and L. Abt. New York: Van Nostrand Reinhold, 1981.
———. "Facilitating Restructuring and Relinkage: Issues in Divorce Therapy." In *Therapy with Remarriage Families*, ed. L. Messinger. The Family Therapy Collections. An Aspen Publication. Rockville, Md., and London, 1982.
———. "Helping Mom Fail: A Case of a Stalemated Divorcing Process." *Family Process* 21(June 1982):225–34.
———. "Dysfunctional Arrangements in Divorcing Families." In *Clinical Issues in Single Parent Families*, ed. M. Lindblad-Goldberg. The Family Therapy Collections. An Aspen Publication. Rockville, Md. Forthcoming.
———. "The Visitation Schedule and Child Adjustment: A Three-Year Study." Manuscript, 1986.
Isaacs, M. B., and Leon, G. H. "Child Outcome and the Relationship between Separated Spouses: A Three-Year Study." Manuscript, 1986.
———. "Mother and Child Adjustment after Parental Separation: A Three-Year Study." Manuscript, 1986.
———. "Social Networks, Divorce and Adjustment: A Tale of Three Generations." *Journal of Divorce* 9(Fall 1986).
———. "Remarriage and Its Alternatives following Divorce: Mother and Child Adjustment." Manuscript, 1986.
Isaacs, M. B., and Levin, I. R. "Who's in My Family?: A Longitudinal Study of Drawings of Children of Divorce." *Journal of Divorce* 7(Summer 1984):1–21.
Isaacs, M. B., Leon, G. H., and Donohue, A. M. "Who Are the 'Normal' Children of Divorce? On the Need to Specify Populations." *Journal of Divorce* (Forthcoming).
Isaacs, M. B., Leon, G. H., and Kline, M. "When Is a Parent Out of the Picture?: Different Custody, Different Perceptions." *Family Process* (Forthcoming).
Leon, G. H., and Isaacs, M. B. "Social Networks and Marital Dissolution: Parental Provision for Divorcing Daughters." Manuscript, 1986.
Montalvo, B. "Interpersonal Arrangements in Disrupted Families." In *Normal Family Processes*, ed. F. Walsh. New York: Guilford Press, 1981.

Index

abdication: acknowledgment of, 216; and cross-generational coalition, 182; as dysfunction, 182; of executive responsibility, 201; levels of, 182

abdication dynamics: arresting, 181–219

abortion, 184, 215–16

abuse: spousal, 226–28

acceptance: attitude of, 89–90

access: parents' right of, 245

accommodation: as needed for healthy blending, 251

accuracy: as basic parental function, 202

acting out: adolescent, 181–82; as dynamic for change, 198–200; as learning experience, 200

adjustment: criteria for adequate, 49; general trends in, 266–70; levels of, 269–70; measuring postseparation, 269

adolescent-parent relationship: challenge as normal in, 176, 178, 195

adolescents: and feedback to parents, 145; fostering dialogue with parents, 203; and parental executive system, 192–202; and postseparation concerns, 181–82

advocate: child, 228–29; father's, 242–43; mother's, 243; therapist as, 81–82; see also child advocate

age: and behavior problems, 270; and improvement in social competence, 270

aggression: aspects of, 127; demonstration of as therapeutic tool, 176

agreement: pretherapy, 17

agreements: skepticism toward, 73–74

alertness: therapist's need for, 129

Allen family, 16, 17–49

alliance: therapeutic, 189

anger: child-parent, 237; fluctuation in levels of, 246–47; relation of, to frustration, 105; silence as evidence of, 171–72; as theme of transition, 180; as therapeutic tool, 163–69, 197–98; therapeutic use of, 209; therapist as butt of, 82; unharnessed, 130

anticipation: creation of parental, 151

anxiety: and career shift, 238

appeals: advocate's recommendation against, 244; danger of, to family, 239

approach: a do-not-blend, 250–55

assessment: request for, 228–29

attack: parental, 185; in vulnerable areas, 127

attorneys: as go-betweens in hostile situation, 234; see also lawyers

authority: appeal to higher, 63; assumption of parental, 198; loss of parental, 192–93; refusal to accept adult, 174

autonomy: increasing of, for older adolescents, 157

balance: organizing toward a productive, 130–32; recognizing the extremely precarious, 132; therapist's role in maintaining, 130